SIR
FRANCIS
WALSINGHAM

Also by Derek Wilson

Out of The Storm: The Life and Legacy of Martin Luther (2007)

Hans Holbein: Portrait of an Unknown Man (2006)

Charlemagne: The Great Adventure (2005)

Uncrowned Kings of England: The Black Legend of the Dudleys (2005)

All The King's Women: Love, Sex and Politics in the Reign of Charles II (2003)

A Brief History of the Circumnavigators (2003)

In The Lion's Court: Power, Ambition and Sudden Death in the
Reign of Henry VIII (2002)

The King and the Gentleman: Charles Stuart and Oliver Cromwell 1599–1649
(2000)

The World Encompassed: Drake's Great Voyage 1577–1580 (2000)

Dark and Light: The Guinness Story (1998)

The Tower of London: A Thousand Years (1998)

Sweet Robin: Robert Dudley, Earl of Leicester (1997)

SIR
FRANCIS
WALSINGHAM

A Courtier in an Age of Terror

DEREK WILSON

CONSTABLE • LONDON

Constable & Robinson Ltd
3 The Lanchesters
162 Fulham Palace Road
London W6 9ER
www.constablerobinson.com

First published in the UK by Constable,
an imprint of Constable & Robinson Ltd, 2007

A copy of the British Library Cataloguing in
Publication Data is available from the British Library.

ISBN: 978-1-84529-138-9

Printed and bound in the EU

1 3 5 7 9 10 8 6 4 2

CONTENTS

List of Illustrations   vii
Preface   ix

Introduction: August 1572, Death in Paris   1
1 Background and Beginnings, 1532–53   3
2 Travel and Travail, 1553–8   19
3 'The Malice of This Present Time', 1558–69   33
4 'In Truth a Very Wise Person', 1569–73   61
5 'To Govern that Noble Ship', England, 1574–80   85
6 'God Open Her Majesty's Eyes': Foreign Affairs, 1578–80   115
7 'She Seemeth to be Very Earnestly
     Bent to Proceed', 1581–4   147
8 'Be You All Stout and Resolute', 1584–8   179
9 No Tomb, 1587–90   223

Notes   253
Bibliography   259
Index   265

LIST OF ILLUSTRATIONS

[1] Sir Francis Walsingham *c.*1585, attributed to John de Critz the Elder. National Portrait Gallery, London. 1807.

[2] *The Rainbow Portrait* by Isaac Oliver. Courtesy of the Marquess of Salisbury.

[3] Hans Holbein made this engraving satirizing the pope's presumption in receiving homage from the emperor. Courtesy of the author.

[4] Racking of Catholic priests by Sebastiano Martellini. By permission of the British Library. 4705.a.8.

[5] *Queen Elizabeth with Burghley and Walsingham* by William Fairthorne, 1655. National Portrait Gallery, London. D21165.

[6] Francis duc d'Anjou. Courtesy of the author.

[7] St. Bartholomew's Day Massacre, 24th August 1572 (oil on panel) by Dubois, Francois (1529–1584) © Musee Cantonal des Beaux-Arts de Lausanne, Switzerland/ Photo © Held Collection/ The Bridgeman Art Library.

[8] The assassination of William the Silent, 1584. Mary Evans Picture Library. 10157890.

[9] The burning of Thomas Cranmer as illustrated in John Foxe's *Actes and Monuments*. By permission of the British Library. C.37.h.2.

[10] William Allen (1532–94), from 'Lodge's British Portraits', 1823 (engraving) by English School, (19th century) © Private Collection/ Ken Welsh/ The Bridgeman Art Library.

[11] The funeral cortege of Sir Philip Sidney (1554–1586) on its way to St. Paul's Cathedral, 1587, engraved by Theodor de Bry (1528–1598) (engraving) by English School, (16th century) © Private Collection/ The Stapleton Collection/ The Bridgeman Art Library.

[12] The Trial of Mary Queen of Scots. By permission of the British Library. Add. 48027.

[13] Bernardino de Escalante's plan for the invasion of England, 1586. Biblioteca Nacional, Madrid. Ms.5785/168.

PREFACE

State-sponsored terrorism, hit men paid to eliminate heads of state, mobs fired up by hate-shrieking 'holy' men, fanatics ready to espouse martyrdom in the hope of heavenly reward, asylum-seekers, internment camps, the clash of totally irreconcilable ideologies. The list is familiar to us but as well as highlighting some of the problems of twenty-first-century Britain, it also offers an accurate picture of England 1570–90. The middle years of Elizabeth I's reign were years of crisis, uncertainty and anxiety. A cultural rift had sundered Europe. In the eyes of the major continental powers – France, Spain, the Empire and the Papacy – Henry VIII had committed the unforgivable sin of rending the seamless robe of medieval Christendom. What had emerged (certainly not what Henry had intended) was the first major independent Protestant state. For decades Catholic Europe, in disarray until the conclusion of the Council of Trent in 1563, was unable to address the problem of the dissident nation but thereafter the forces of Counter-Reformation returned to the offensive, determined to recover lost territories. Top of their agenda was the conquest of heretic England. In 1570, Pope Pius V solemnly declared Elizabeth deposed and her subjects released from their allegiance. France came under the domination of the fanatical leaders of the Guise family, who were determined to avenge the treatment of their kinswoman, Mary Queen of Scots. Philip II of Spain, no less committed to the Catholic cause, commanded the awesome power and wealth of a great trans-oceanic empire and spent years maturing what he referred to as the 'Enterprise of England'.

If we fail to appreciate the tensions and fears of those years it is because historical hindsight plays us false. We see the failure of Philip II's Armada, the exploits of Francis Drake and other pioneer mariners, the Elizabethan renaissance of drama and verse and the era assumes a roseate hue. We are ready to take at face value the idealized image created by Elizabeth's PR machine in the last decade of the reign: the legend of the Virgin Queen, Astraea, Gloriana.

Even supposedly serious historians colluded in the myth-making. William Camden, Elizabeth's first biographer (his *History of the most renowned and victorious Princess Elizabeth, late Queen of England* first appeared in complete form in 1630), was quite open about the amount of veneration he mingled with objectivity.

> That Licenciousness accompanied with Malignity and Backbiting, which is cloaked under the counterfeit Shew of Freedom, and is every-where entertained with a plausible Acceptance, I do from my Heart detest. Things manifest and evident I have not concealed; Things doubtfull I have interpreted favourably; Things secret and abstruse I have not pried into. 'The hidden Meanings of Princes (saith that great Master of History [Polybius]) and what they secretly design to search out, it is unlawfull, it is doubtfull and dangerous: pursue not therefore the Search thereof.'[1]

By the time the Civil War had intervened Elizabeth's reign had assumed the glow of a golden age.

> A Tudor! A Tudor! We've had Stuarts enough.
> None ever ruled like Old Bess in the ruff.[2]

So enthused Andrew Marvell in the 1670s.

His great-grandsire would not have endorsed such a eulogy. There was widespread discontent in late-Tudor England. Queen Elizabeth herself was in part responsible for the insecurity her people suffered. Despite urgent and repeated pleas from courtiers, councillors, parliamentarians and diplomats, she staunchly refused to fulfil what most people regarded as her first obligation: she would not provide the nation with an heir. She rejected the role of wife and mother and she declined to nominate a successor. Worse than that, she tolerated within the borders of her realm a claimant to the crown in the person of Mary Stuart. For more than twenty years the ex-queen of Scotland lived as a virtual prisoner in England and became the focus for plots against the Tudor regime. Mary was the great hope of Catholics at home and abroad. If she could be placed on the throne by a native rising of people loyal to the old faith and aided by a foreign army, the clock could be turned back. England could be restored to that blissful age before Henry VIII had waged war on the pope – or so Catholic romantics fondly believed.

In English government circles perceptions of the international situation varied. Some believed in the existence of a Catholic conspiracy choreographed in Rome. Others remained convinced that the traditional policy of playing Habsburg and Valois interests off against each other was the best way of ensuring England's security. Elizabeth, insofar as she can be credited with a consistent policy, adhered to the latter opinion. Francis Walsingham, her 'foreign minister', was convinced that the upholders of Protestant truth were locked in a cosmic struggle with the dark powers of papal Antichrist. The relationship between monarch and minister flavoured English politics throughout these crucial years. An understanding of Walsingham is, therefore, of first importance for an understanding of the dynamic of Elizabethan politics.

Francis Walsingham is a man about whom we know too little and too much. Copious official correspondence survives in the State papers and other deposits but these only relate to the last eighteen years of his life when he was ambassador to France and principal secretary of state. They tell us little about the forty years leading up to his achievement of high office, nor of his private life. Conyers Read's monumental three-volume biography, written over eighty years ago, helps us very little in this regard, as its title suggests: *Mr Secretary Walsingham and the Policy of Queen Elizabeth*. In recent years Walsingham's activities as head of the Elizabethan 'secret service' (a somewhat anachronistic expression) have fascinated several writers but his role as 'spymaster' covered an even shorter span of time (c.1580–90).

There was, of course, much more to the man that that. He was, for example, an enthusiastic backer of overseas exploration and merchant venturing. He was a cultured scholar so generous with his patronage that Edmund Spenser called him 'the great Maecenas of this age'. But

his most powerful motivation came from his religion – that Protestantism that he had absorbed in family and Edwardian court circles
and which further developed in his years of exile during Mary Tudor's
reign. Some biographers, disinclined to explore Walsingham's beliefs
or considering the evidence too scanty, have been content to apply to
him the catch-all name 'Puritan'. The term does him a disservice,
suggesting as it does to modern minds a joyless, bigoted sobersides.
Add to that his role as Elizabeth's spymaster and the identification of
Walsingham is complete as a sinister, narrow-minded, Machiavellian
power behind the throne.

If, as I have suggested, the war on terror creates similarities between
Elizabeth's England and our own, there remains, of course, one
fundamental difference between the two ages. Religion was central to
all aspects of national and international life four and a half centuries
ago. Political debate was shot through with it. Walsingham and the
queen were both conviction politicians. Both believed that the
security of the nation lay in making right religious choices. They
simply could not agree what those choices should be. To Walsingham
it was axiomatic that England should stand shoulder-to-shoulder with
its persecuted brethren in France and the Netherlands and oppose the
insidious spread of Catholicism with a programme of sound Protestant
preaching and teaching. He was supported in this view by a sizeable
portion of the political nation. Elizabeth was hesitant about encouraging foreign nationals to rebel against their divinely appointed rulers
and was highly nervous of religious radicalism in all its forms. Her
understanding of national stability was of all her subjects supporting
her church, the Church of England, neither Catholic nor Puritan.

This fundamental clash of opinions created intense frustration and
tension between the queen and her secretary of state. She found his plain
speaking at time offensive and he was frequently driven to distraction by
her moral squirming. It is surprising that they could work together at all.
Yet work together they did through this time of national testing.
Therefore exploring their extraordinary relationship illuminates for
us what was at stake in these years. Generations of biographers and
historians have sought to explain what made Elizabeth tick. It is high
time we explored the motivation of Francis Walsingham.

INTRODUCTION

AUGUST 1572, DEATH IN PARIS

They cut down Mathurin Lussault on his own doorstep. The house-holder answered an insistent knocking and when he opened the door a neighbour, screaming obscenities, ran him through. His son rushed downstairs to see what the fracas was about. He was grabbed and stabbed several times. He staggered into the street, where he died. Mathurin's wife, Françoise, threw herself from an upstairs window in a bid to escape the assassins. She broke both her legs in the fall. Friends tried to hide her but, by now, the mob's blood was up. They were forcing their way into homes in their search for more victims. Finding Françoise, they dragged her through the streets by her hair. They cut off her hands in order to get her gold bracelets. What was left of the poor woman was impaled on a spit and paraded through the streets of Paris as a gory trophy, before being dumped in the Seine which was already streaked with red.

On the streets panic reigned. Church bells were ringing. Shots were being fired. As the carnage intensified the air filled with more human sounds – shouts of triumph, religious slogans, screams of fear. The English ambassador to the court of Charles IX threw open his casement in the usually quiet Faubourg St Germain to see what the commotion was about. He was not left long in doubt. Terrified men and women came battering on his door begging for asylum. When the servants let them in they babbled out their tales of barbarism and inhumanity. Tales the like of which the forty-year-old Francis Walsingham had never heard before. As the day wore on more and more fugitives packed into the house. Then soldiers arrived –

royal soldiers – demanding that the enemies of the state be handed over. Francis, though fearful for the life of himself and his family, stood firm. He was able to save the foreign nationals sheltering beneath his roof but the few French Protestants who had sought shelter there he was forced to surrender. They joined the toll of more than 2,000 men, women and children massacred in Paris on St Bartholomew's Day – not far short of the number who perished there during the Terror of 1793–4.

This traumatic experience had a formative impact on Queen Elizabeth's ambassador. He was disgusted by the behaviour of the mob, indignant at the implication of the king and his mother in the atrocity and appalled at his own powerlessness to help the afflicted. These tragic events undergirded his political convictions thereafter and the advice he gave his sovereign. But they did not change his fundamental beliefs that Rome was the whore of Babylon and Catholics the very limbs of Satan. One thing he knew with an unshakable certainty: the religion responsible for such ghastly atrocities must never ever, under any circumstances whatsoever, be allowed to re-establish itself in England.

Chapter 1

BACKGROUND AND BEGINNINGS

1532–53

There is a sense that tombs and graves bring us close to the departed. It is understandable that people should think of memorials as material conduits to their deceased loved ones. It is perhaps less intelligible for historians to seek contact with their subjects by visiting their final resting places. Fortunately, no such temptation besets the biographer of Sir Francis Walsingham. In 1590 his remains were quietly and honourably interred in St Paul's Cathedral. His memorial, along with scores of others, vanished without trace in the fire of 1666 and the subsequent building of Sir Christopher Wren's basilica. Interestingly, a similar fate befell the tombs of Francis' parents. William and Joyce Walsingham were members of the congregation of St Mary Aldermanbury, close by the Guildhall, and were, presumably, interred there. Like the cathedral, St Mary's suffered in the Great Fire of London. Also like St Paul's it was rebuilt in Wren's neoclassical style. Sadly, its afflictions were not over. The Blitz of 1940–1 destroyed the new church. After the war it *was* rebuilt – but not *in situ*. A strange fate awaited it. Its stones were meticulously numbered and shipped across the Atlantic to Fulton, Missouri, where they were reassembled on the campus of Westminster College as a memorial to Sir Winston Churchill.

So we can make no physical contact with Elizabeth's minister or his immediate antecedents. In a way it is fitting that this should be so. It adds something to the mystique of a man who was self-effacing in his lifetime and who has remained something of an enigma ever since. Walsingham was that rarity among members of the Tudor establishment – a man who reached the political heights not by greasing palms, elbowing aside rivals and flattering his sovereign and her close attendants, but by talent, industry and the honest application of his principles. It is largely for this reason that a gauze screen of vagueness obscures his early career. There is no trail of correspondence with the rich and powerful such as an ambitious man might leave. There are few references in his later writings to his parentage and the self-conscious steps by which he reached the summit of Elizabeth's government. Diligent search among local archives has disclosed all that is known and probably all that ever will be known about Sir Francis' origins.

However, there is a line of approach which enables us to augment the bare catalogue of land transactions and wills. Walsingham was a man of his time. Indeed, his life is incomprehensible without a consideration of the momentous events which occurred throughout six decades of religious, political and social revolution. This was an age in which prominent men had to take sides, to declare themselves for the old faith (Catholicism) or the new (Protestantism or, more accurately, evangelicalism). The motives for such a declaration might be religious conviction, self-advancement or a combination of the two and there were always those who skilfully mastered a Vicar of Bray-style flexibility. Nevertheless, we can deduce much about mid-Tudor men and women by the company they kept and the familial alliances they made. The Walsingham genealogical tree is, therefore, informative.

The Walsinghams of the fifteenth century (which is as far back as we need to go) were in trade but already upwardly mobile. Francis' great-great-grandfather was a shoemaker and his great-grandfather a vintner. Both were honoured men in their professions, prominent members of their respective guilds and well known in London society. They had accumulated property in the capital and – a mark of true gentility – owned a modest country place in Kent (Scadbury Manor, Chislehurst). From this solid base the next generation took a further significant step up the social ladder. James Walsingham was put to the law and, by the time Henry Tudor, Earl of Richmond, grabbed the Crown in 1485, he was well established in the London

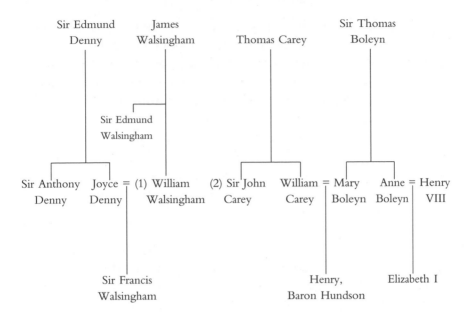

courts. It could not have been a more propitious time for following a legal career.

The English had (and still have) an ambivalent attitude towards lawyers. They were seen as men who could manipulate ancient statutes to their own advantage, who favoured the rich against the poor and were not averse to taking bribes. At the same time, anyone seeking justice had to employ the experts and by 1500 more than 3,000 new suits per annum were being presented in the courts of the capital alone. The law was a hard trade to master but a lucrative one to follow. More importantly, it was becoming a stepping-stone to that place where *real* fortunes were to be made – the royal court. For half a century the fate of rival royal dynasties had been decided by baronial armies. The new king decided that the weight of his regime would be borne not by steel blades but by paper statutes. He would employ the nation's best legal brains to strengthen his position and secure the succession for his heirs. Over the ensuing decades the balance of the royal Council changed; the barons and senior ecclesiastics who had assumed that they were indispensable to the government of the country had to make room for new men, versed in the law and loyal only to the Crown.

James Walsingham, Francis' grandfather, never made it to the very top of the tree – membership of the royal Council – but he was one of the leaders of royal society: a justice of the peace, member of various royal commissions and Sheriff of Kent in 1486–7. He consolidated his position in the county and acquired a grant of arms from the College of Heralds. And he ensured that his two sons would be drawn to the attention of the king. When he died, full of years, in 1540 he had cause for satisfaction that his family had received significant marks of royal favour. He could not, however, have foreseen that his youngest grandson, Francis, was destined to become one of the nation's leaders. His greater expectations were focused on the career of his son and heir, Edmund.

The young extrovert prince who came to the throne in 1509 as Henry VIII sought his companions among macho, athletic, patriotic Englishmen like himself. It was no coincidence, therefore, that Edmund received a martial training. In 1513 he gathered some retainers about him and joined the 20,000-strong force being hur-riedly assembled on the northern border by the Earl of Surrey to ward off a Scottish invasion. The ensuing victory at Flodden was one of the most bloody and decisive ever achieved in the long history of Anglo-Scottish warfare. Several captains were afterwards knighted by Surrey – among them Edmund Walsingham. The young man's exploits were brought to the attention of the king and Edmund's place among the young blades of the court was secured. He appeared frequently in the tiltyard as an accomplished horseman and exponent of sixteenth-century martial arts. In 1520 he was chosen as one of the knights to accompany the king to France for the sumptuous diplomatic display which has gone down in history as the Field of Cloth of Gold. It was a signal sign of Henry's confidence in Edmund that, in 1521, he gave him charge of England's major fortress-prison, the Tower of London. The man responsible for the Tower was the Constable and, for most of this period, that was Sir William Kingston, but it was the Lieutenant who actually resided there and was responsible for day-to-day administration.

Sir Edmund Walsingham was destined to be Lieutenant of the Tower during its most bloody and controversial years. Henry VIII ruthlessly used the grim stronghold for cowing opposition to his policies, disposing of possible Yorkist rivals and for applying the 'final solution' to some of his marital entanglements. Among the notable prisoners incarcerated there and executed within the walls or on the adjacent hillside were Thomas More, Bishop John Fisher, Queen Anne Boleyn, Queen Catherine Howard, the Marquess of Exeter, the Countess of Salisbury, Thomas Cromwell, Earl of Essex and Henry Howard, Earl of Surrey. There were many more smaller fry who faced torture, deprivation and the axe in Henry's police state.

Edmund Walsingham proved himself to be the ideal jailer and guardian of the Tower's grisly secrets. He carried out his duties without flinching and was ever determined to demonstrate his unreserved loyalty. In reality, he could do no other. The men and women entrusted to his care had incurred the royal displeasure. To show sympathy for them would be to run the risk of arousing Henry's mercurial ire. He might – and did – lament to Sir Thomas More that he was unable to make his quarters more comfortable but, as he explained, 'Orders is orders'. We can gauge something of Sir Edmund's temperament from the case of John Bawde. Bawde was one of the lieutenant's own servants. He fell under the spell of Alice Tankerville, a prisoner in Coldharbour within the Tower of London. So besotted was he that he tried to help her to escape. The bid failed and his complicity was revealed. Sir Edmund's rage (doubtless fuelled by fear for his own position) was boundless. He had Bawde thrown into Little Ease, the Tower's most notoriously vile cell. The prisoner was subsequently racked, condemned in a speedy trial and hanged in chains.

While Sir Edmund was leading an eventful life at the centre of power, his younger brother, William, was being groomed to take over the family responsibilities in Kent. He followed his father's profession, held senior positions in London's legal establishment and was prominent in the affairs of his shire. He steadily added other lands to the family's holdings and, by 1530, was well established as a substantial gentleman with court connections. But William's fortunes were mixed and his aspirations far from being smoothly accomplished. He married, sometime in the early 1520s, Joyce Denny, daughter of

Sir Edmund Denny, a minor courtier on the staff of the Exchequer. Perhaps the introduction to a court colleague was effected by William's brother. The union, moderately important at the time, was to prove extremely influential in the later years of Henry's reign. Joyce's brother, Anthony, was another of that small army of hopefuls seeking preferment at court. He was fortunate in finding a short cut to royal favour. There were scores of men who held posts in the innermost chambers of the court but few of them could count themselves as the king's friends. One of the privileged band of intimates was Sir Francis Bryan, soldier, diplomat and tiltyard companion of the king. Bryan was a gentleman of the privy chamber and trusted by Henry with delicate diplomatic missions, including an embassy to Rome in connection with his intended divorce from Catherine of Aragon. Anthony Denny, William Walsingham's brother-in-law, was a member of Bryan's entourage and his patron ensured his steady, but unspectacular, promotion. By the mid–1530s Denny was a groom of the chamber, one of those who attended the king most intimately. He was an educated, cultured man of pleasing disposition and Henry increasingly warmed to him.

William, therefore, built up a corps of valuable contacts in the Tudor establishment but fate sometimes clouded her face from him. His well-connected wife had a succession of five successful pregnancies but they all resulted in girls. Not until 1532 did she present her husband with an heir, who was christened Francis. Two years later, just when everything was going well for him, William Walsingham died. His widow was still in her twenties and had been left well provided for. Despite having five daughters to dower, she was quite a good catch and it was probably not difficult for her family to find another suitable husband for her. Unsurprisingly, the chosen groom was a Hertfordshire neighbour of the Dennys who was also well established at court. John Carey was connected to Anne Boleyn, his brother, William (now deceased), having married Anne's sister, Mary.

We can now begin to see a picture of the circle in which the young Francis grew up. The social focus of the royal court from the mid–1520s was the Boleyn family. Sir Thomas Boleyn had long been a courtier and diplomat but when the king became involved with his daughters – first Mary and then Anne – titles, lands and favours were poured out on the Boleyn clan. In 1529 Sir Thomas became Earl of Wiltshire and Ormonde. Ambitious courtiers now clamoured for his friendship and patronage. This, in turn, meant that they had to support King Henry's campaign to dump his wife and make Anne his queen. The Walsinghams and the Dennys were on the outer rim of the Boleyn circle. Sir Francis Bryan, Anthony Denny's patron, was a cousin of the Boleyn girls and dedicated to their advancement. Denny seems to have been groomed by Bryan to succeed him in office, for he became a member of the privy chamber staff in about 1533 and took Bryan's place as second chief gentleman in 1539. He will certainly have been instrumental in securing Boleyn kinship for his sister by her marriage to Sir John Carey.

But much more was involved in all this than a few ambitious families jostling for power, influence and promotion. The 'King's Great Matter' (the divorce crisis) coincided with the arrival in England of the radical religious ideas of Martin Luther. In 1517 this German monk had challenged the power of the pope to absolve the departed from the pains of purgatory. In 1521 he had defied pope and emperor at the Diet of Worms and been condemned as a heretic but, protected by his prince, he had embarked upon a mammoth programme of books, pamphlets and sermons calling for a root-and-branch reform of the church. This evangelical revival was the cause célèbre of the age. The new ideas touched so many chords of indignation and dissatisfaction among the thinking classes of Europe that they spread with astonishing rapidity. In England students at the universities and the inns of court, merchants, tradespeople and courtiers were eagerly reading banned books smuggled into the country. From 1525 the English New Testament, translated and printed by William Tyndale from the safety of Germany, was being studied with as much clandestine zeal as the bishops were expending in tracking down the subversive volumes and making bonfires of them. The clamour for ecclesiastical reform and spiritual revival coincided with Henry VIII's personal disagreement with Rome and, though it did not provide justification for the king's action (Luther actually opposed the divorce), it did provide theological support for resisting papal authority. It is not surprising that the Boleyns and their friends favoured the new movement (though we should not dismiss this as mere cynical opportunism) and gave cautious support to radical preachers.

Henry VIII failed to appreciate the full implications of the emerging Reformation. He could see that it might be useful to him but he had no desire to be tarred with the brush of heresy. For that reason court evangelicals had to tread warily. One man who saw more clearly than most the revolution in English church and state which might be accomplished was Thomas Cromwell, whose rapid rise to the position of chief minister between 1529 and 1531 took all observers by surprise. Cromwell, a convinced evangelical and 'a layman of protean talents',[1] convinced the king, not only that he could solve the matrimonial problem, but that he could free the Crown entirely from papal authority and vastly increase its wealth to boot. Cromwell made common cause with the Boleyn faction and embarked on a series of measures that would make the 1530s the most momentous decade in English history.

Francis Walsingham was born, probably, in 1532 and his early years were shaped by the religious fervour and social upheaval of the Reformation. Within months of his birth Henry VIII had married Anne Boleyn and disembarrassed himself of Queen Catherine. Sir Thomas More, the leading opponent of the king's Great Matter, had resigned as Lord Chancellor and would soon find himself in the Tower. Cromwell had embarked on a series of parliamentary measures which would, one-by-one, sever the cords binding the English church to Rome. Thomas Cranmer, a committed reformer, had been made Archbishop of Canterbury. And, on 7 September 1533, Queen Anne was delivered of a daughter, christened Elizabeth.

Of Francis' childhood we know nothing but it is reasonable to assume that he spent most of it on his stepfather's estate at Plashy, Hertfordshire. It is not beyond the bounds of possibility that he met Princess Elizabeth during these years, for, in 1540, John Carey was appointed bailiff of the nearby royal manor of Hunsdon which was one of the homes where she lived under the guardianship of Margaret, Baroness Bryan, mother of the king's favourite. It is tempting from what we know of his later life to envisage the young Walsingham as a quiet, serious and studious boy and this may not be far off the mark. Apart from older sisters, his only regular companions were the two half-brothers his mother bore her second husband. Studious Francis certainly was, for he later showed himself to be cultured, widely read and a master of languages.

As he grew towards manhood in the closing years of Henry VIII's reign his knowledge of the monumental events convulsing the country steadily grew. He saw abandoned monasteries and the carts trundling along country lanes loaded with stone, lead and the furnishings that had once adorned the houses of monks and nuns. In church he listened to the fiery evangelical preachers appointed by his relatives. He would have been too young to appreciate the threat of civil war in 1536–7 when opponents of religious and social change launched a rebellion in Yorkshire and Lincolnshire. He heard his elders discussing the tense situation at court. The aftermath of Anne Boleyn's fall in 1536 was an anxious time for her supporters and protégés. King Henry, for reasons that may never be clear, had turned violently against his second wife and had her conveyed to the Tower on trumped-up charges of adultery. Francis' Uncle Edmund was among the small audience who witnessed her execution. Anne received no succour from her family. All her relatives distanced themselves as far as possible from their patroness.

Those at court who favoured evangelical religion feared a backlash but there was no such reversal of their fortunes. The royal household was divided into factions with distinctly religious hues. The see-saw of royal favour raised and lowered first one group, then the other. There were occasional purges of highly placed 'heretics'. The last one occurred as late as 1546 when the Catholic faction tried to destroy Henry's sixth queen, Catherine Parr, and, by association, all leaders of the evangelical group. These were anxious days for Anthony Denny, whose wife was one of the queen's closest friends. However, the overall trend in these years favoured the reformers. Cromwell's parliamentary campaign progressed steadily. The king replaced the pope as head of the church in England and, in 1539, an officially approved translation of the Bible was set up in every parish church. Even the sudden fall of Cromwell in 1540 proved to be only a temporary setback. A younger generation of pro-reform men rose to prominence at court – men like Edward and Thomas Seymour and John Dudley. The redistribution of monastic land in effect made all ambitious nobles and gentlemen complicit in the Reformation. Everyone wanted to benefit from the biggest land grab in the nation's history.

The Walsinghams and their kin were determined not to miss out in this once-in-a-lifetime opportunity. Sir Edmund added to the family estate in Kent, acquired houses in London and speculated in parcels of land in various counties. He was a member of the House of Commons in Henry's last parliament. But the man who emerged as leader of the family's fortunes was Anthony Denny. He was one of the few attendants who managed to enjoy the king's friendship and confidence through thick and thin. (Others were Thomas Cranmer and William Butts, the royal physician – both convinced evangelicals.) He was knighted in 1544 and, two years later, achieved the highest privy chamber office of groom of the stool. He was entrusted with the privy purse out of which he made large disbursements on the king's behalf. Even more importantly, he and his brother-in-law, John Gates, were licensed to apply the sign manual to all royal documents. Henry, bloated and increasingly incapacitated by pain from his ulcerated legs, was often unable to attend to business and so a dye stamp of his signature was made which could be imposed on letters and official papers and later inked-in by a clerk. It was this that, from September 1545, was entrusted to Denny and Gates. It signifies the enormous trust Henry reposed in these two intimates and, of course, it gave them considerable power. Denny became expert in caring for his irascible employer and using his influence to help the cause of reform. He was, for example, able to save fellow evangelicals denounced by their Catholic enemies. He secured the post of tutor to Princess Elizabeth for his old friend and fellow member of St John's College, Cambridge, Roger Ascham. Tangible proofs of royal favour were showered upon Denny. By the end of the reign his estates in Hertfordshire alone covered 20,000 acres.

Now Francis' family enjoyed that prominence which showed itself in favourable marriage alliances for his sisters. Mary married Sir Walter

Mildmay, the youngest son of Cromwell's principal agent in the dissolution of the monasteries. No one was better placed to profit from the sale of lands and Mildmay senior built an extremely impressive mansion at Moulsham, near Chelmsford, in the heart of his new estates. Walter trained in the law and joined his father in the Court of Augmentations, the body set up to administer confiscated church property. He was well on the way to a prosperous career. Elizabeth married Geoffrey Gates, brother of Anthony Denny's friend and colleague, Sir John Gates, and, on his death, Peter Wentworth, heir to considerable estates in Buckinghamshire, Oxfordshire, North-amptonshire, Essex and Surrey. Peter and his brother became pro-minent (and vociferous) parliamentarians in Elizabeth's reign. It is highly significant that all the leading members of this familial network were prominent religious radicals. They represented that constituency of home counties' squires with influence at court and in the City upon which Tudor government largely relied. Eleanor Walsingham was married to William Sharington, member of the privy chamber and a protégé of Sir Francis Bryan. The two remaining girls, Barbara and Christiana, also married into substantial families with court connec-tions.

There can be no doubt about the origins of Francis Walsingham's evangelical beliefs. He grew up in an atmosphere of radical religion and loyalty to the house of Tudor. His convictions can only have been strengthened when he left home to continue his education. In the year following Henry VIII's death (1547) he matriculated at King's College, Cambridge. Now he found himself in the company of volatile students who brashly argued their opinions on all matters political and religious.

Walsingham was at King's College from 1548 to 1550. The timing for an eager and impressionable student could scarcely have been more crucial. With the accession of the nine-year-old Edward VI the brakes which had been sporadically applied to the Reformation were now released. The leaders of the government – Edward Seymour, Duke of Somerset, and (from the autumn of 1549) John Dudley, Earl of Warwick (and later Duke of Northumberland) – were Anthony Denny's friends and fellow evangelicals. At the beginning of the new reign Denny was appointed to the royal Council and served there till his death in September 1549. Archbishop Cranmer had their support in bringing radical religious change to every parish in the land. The Latin mass was swept away and a new Prayer Book in English was appointed to be used in all churches. To drive home the radical change in the religion of England the reformers were determined to purify church interiors and rearrange the furniture. Altars were replaced by plain tables, often brought out into the chancel or nave. New pulpits and lecterns were installed to emphasize that the ministry of the word was more important than the celebration of the sacrament. Before the new reign was many months old an injunction went out in the king's name ordering clergy to 'take down, or cause to be taken down and destroy' all images which had become objects of veneration or foci of pilgrimage.

In several of the Cambridge colleges radicals went at their task with a will. Builders, plasterers, painters and labourers were everywhere carrying out demolition work and making good the damage. At Christ's workmen spent two days 'helping down with images and mending the pavement under Christ's image'. In Jesus university dignitaries supervised the removal of six altars. Scaffolding was erected in Queens' so that painters could whitewash offending tableaux. At newly founded Trinity College the bursar sold off £140 worth of mass vestments and altar plate. And at King's Francis Walsingham arrived in time to witness the dismantling of the high altar.[2]

Most senior academics needed little urging to oversee the sweeping away of objects of superstition. Cambridge was the intellectual home of the English Reformation. It was here a generation earlier that Thomas Cranmer had encountered the works of Luther. His close colleague, Nicholas Ridley, had progressed from Master of Pembroke to Bishop of Rochester. Hugh Latimer, fellow of Clare and since 1535 Bishop of Worcester, was the most celebrated preacher of the age. Roger Ascham of St John's, the foremost scholar of the age, as well as being tutor to Princess Elizabeth, held the post of University Orator. Twenty-five Cambridge men had perished as martyrs for the reformed faith between 1531 and 1538.

The university of the fens continued to lead the intellectual crusade for reform. In the year that Francis went up to King's, Cranmer secured one of the major international Protestant celebrities for the vacant post of Professor of Divinity. Martin Bucer was a veteran reformer who had been at the centre of religious change in Europe since the early 1530s. A Catholic backlash had ousted him from Strasbourg and he now arrived in Cambridge as an honoured refugee. Francis was among the undergraduates who eagerly sat at the great man's feet. A contemporary described the experience thus: 'Dr Bucer cries incessantly, now in daily lectures, now in frequent sermons, that we should practice penitence, discard the depraved customs of hypocritical religion, correct the abuses of fasts, be more frequent in hearing and having sermons, and constrain ourselves by some sort of discipline.'[3] Simplicity of life, self-discipline, regular religious devotion, rejection of empty externals – if we would know how Francis Walsingham acquired these lifetime habits we need look no further.

Another new appointment in 1548 was that of John Cheke as Provost of King's. Cheke, one of the most prominent humanist scholars, was already Professor of Greek in the university but was often absent from Cambridge on royal business. He was tutor to the king and a member of the privy chamber. He was related by marriage to another ex-Cambridge student who, as secretary to the Duke of Somerset, was just beginning a remarkable political career. His name was William Cecil. As a fellow commoner Francis enjoyed, among other privileges, the right to sit at table with the fellows and to be a party to their conversation. When Cheke was in residence, therefore, the student would have listened to the wisdom coming from the lips of a man whom Ridley called, 'one of Christ's special advocates and one of his principal proctors'.

The reformers did not have everything their own way. Quite rightly in such a prominent seat of learning teachers and students were free to debate controversial theological issues. The reactionary faction had formidable champions, foremost among whom was Stephen Gardiner, Master of Trinity Hall and Bishop of Winchester. As well as demanding outward conformity to the reformed religion, the authorities were intent on winning minds. In May and June 1549

Nicholas Ridley arrived to preside over a series of disputations on the doctrine of the mass. The university church was packed to hear some of the best brains of the day locked in argument, citing Scripture and the Fathers in support of their competing opinions. It would be surprising if Walsingham had missed such an opportunity. Ridley, perhaps inevitably, proclaimed that the evangelical disputants had won the debate. Gardiner was not persuaded by this intellectual exercise but he had little opportunity to protest: within days he was a prisoner in the Tower of London.

At Michaelmas (29 September) 1550 Francis Walsingham left Cambridge without taking a degree, as was quite common among the student sons of noble and gentry families who were not bent on an academic career. It was his intention to continue his education at the inns of court and there can be little doubt that his ambition was directed towards a career at the royal court. Sir John Fortescue, the great fifteenth-century legist eulogized the kind of rounded education a young man received at these 'finishing schools':

> [T]here is in these greater inns, yea and in the lesser too, beside the study of the laws, as it were a university or school of all commendable qualities requisite for noblemen. There they learn to sing, and to exercise themselves in all kind of harmony. There also they practise dancing, and other noblemen's pastimes, as they use to do which are brought up in the king's house. On the work days the most part of them apply themselves to the study of the law. And on the holy days to the study of the holy scripture: and out of the time of divine service to the reading of chronicles. For there indeed are virtues studied, and all vices exiled. So that for the endowment of virtue, and abandoning of vice knights and barons, with other states and noblemen of the realm place their children in those inns, though they desire not to have them learned in the laws, nor to live by the practice thereof.[4]

Mastering the varied accomplishments fostered at Gray's Inn, young Francis could be assured of a secure place in the establishment. With a legal training, friends and relatives in high places and an impeccable evangelical faith he could be reasonably confident of promotion within the Edwardian regime. To add to his CV he decided to spend some months in foreign travel. Knowledge of European customs and languages would equip him well for diplomatic service. But there were other attractions on the continent for this eager young Protestant.

We do not know his itinerary during this 'gap year' but it seems more than likely that he was drawn to one or more of the leading Reformation centres such as Geneva, Basel or Zurich. Geneva was the strongest magnet for evangelicals at this time for it was here that John Calvin reigned supreme. Walsingham will have known of his teaching from *Institution of the Christian Religion*, a monumental, systematic manual of reformed doctrine which went through several editions and eventually extended to four books and eighty chapters. But Calvin was not content with theory. He wanted his city to be a shining example to the world of what a Christian commonwealth could be and organized its civic life, under the joint control of magistrates and ministers, in a way that would encourage the citizens to personal and corporate holiness. Ardent evangelicals flocked to Geneva from all over Europe to hear Calvin preach and learn how a truly godly political system could be established. Life in the Protestant cantons certainly made a lasting impression on Walsingham. In later years, amid the stresses and strains of government work, he sighed that he was 'weary of the place I serve in and . . . wish myself among the true-hearted Swiss'.[5] Even at this stage of his life young Francis was developing earnest and sober character traits similar to those which came to be associated with the hardworking Swiss.

The prevailing regime in England had much in common with ruling establishments in the cantons. There were frequent exchanges between church leaders and scholars and theological opinion in England was moving steadily from Lutheranism to the more radical opinions which held sway in the Helvetian republics. The fact that Protestant states were in a minority in mainland Europe strengthened the bonds between them and the Tudor state. In 1552, when Walsingham returned to take up his studies at Gray's Inn, Protestantism seemed more secure against the forces of Counter-Reformation

in the land which Shakespeare later described as being guarded by a
'moat defensive' than it was in some of the German and Swiss states.

There was much to encourage a young evangelical. The Reformation was proceeding apace and he was well placed to play his part in
creating a godly commonwealth in his own country. But everything
hung upon a very slender thread – the life of a teenage king.

Chapter 2

TRAVEL AND TRAVAIL

1553–8

The shock of Edward VI's death, in July 1553, was profound to those who had believed that the Reformation in England was safe under the leadership of their young Josiah (the boy king who had revitalized the religious and national life of ancient Israel). The immediate aftermath was dramatic and confusing. Walsingham, in the legal community between Westminster and the City, was aware of the rumours about the king's health. Edward had not been seen in public for several weeks. It was 8 July before the news broke that the boy king had died and that his cousin, Lady Jane Grey, had been proclaimed queen. Bemused crowds turned out to watch the young woman, her husband and leading courtiers who made their way by river and road to the Tower, where monarchs traditionally went to prepare for their coronation. Everything seemed set for an uncontested transfer of the crown. Edward's half-sisters were nowhere to be seen. Elizabeth did not move from Hatfield and Mary was at the royal manor of Hunsdon – or so it was thought. Walsingham may have been among the first in the capital to hear from friends in the country that the elder princess had fled into East Anglia and was sending messages to urge the people to come to her aid.

Walsingham may have heard from his contacts at court that the nation's leaders were divided. Some supported the late king's wishes that his Catholic sister should be permanently disbarred from the succession, while others agreed with Sir Nicholas Throckmorton:

And, though I liked not the religion
Which all her life Queen Mary had professed,
Yet in my mind that wicked notion
Right heirs for to displace I did detest.[1]

Throckmorton probably spoke for the majority. In his manoeuvring to maintain the impetus of the Reformation the Duke of Northumberland had lost the moral high ground. People were suspicious of him and the young woman perceived to be his puppet and there was widespread sympathy for the 'wronged' Princess Mary. Those, like Walsingham, who feared what Catholic Mary might do if she came to the throne found themselves in the uncomfortable position of having to rely on the government's show of naked force. On 14 July Northumberland set out with a mounted posse to apprehend the princess and bring her back to London. Days of confusion followed in the capital. Contradictory rumours flew around. Rival preachers ranted. Then the news spread from the Tower that Northumberland's erstwhile supporters had changed sides. Two days later (20 July) information came from Cambridge that the duke had capitulated in the face of overwhelming military odds. The sudden change of fortune took everyone by surprise. 'Not a soul imagined the possibility of such a thing . . . When the proclamation was first cried out the people started off, running in all directions and crying out, "the Lady Mary is proclaimed Queen!".'[2] On 3 August Mary rode into her capital among scenes of general rejoicing.

General but far from universal. Convinced Protestants and people who had been closely connected with the previous regime had good cause for anxiety. That constituency certainly included Francis Walsingham. He continued quietly with his studies but kept a wary eye on the course of events. In order to quiet her confessionally divided nation Mary declared that she had no intention of forcing men's consciences but those who knew her and her closest advisers were in no doubt that they were bent on a full restoration of the Catholic faith. For men like Stephen Gardiner, now appointed Lord Chancellor, Mary's accession was just the latest phase in a struggle between true faith and heresy that had been going on for a quarter of a century.

A reluctant parliament was dragooned into repealing the ecclesiastical legislation of the previous reign. Cranmer, Ridley and other architects of religious change were imprisoned. Throughout the country churches were instructed to return to unreformed liturgy. Hard-pressed churchwardens, who had but recently paid for objects of superstition to be removed now had to pay for them to be put back again. The bulk of the queen's subjects accepted all this with either relief or irritation. It was when Mary announced her intention to marry her Spanish first cousin once removed that she pushed her people too far.

England's politicians and diplomats were extremely wary of the Habsburg Empire, a superpower the like of which had not been seen in Europe for seven centuries. Charles V ruled an empire that embraced Spain, the Netherlands, southern Italy and central Europe from Burgundy to the troubled Hungarian border region where Christian West faced Ottoman Muslim East. (The German lands acknowledged the overlordship of an *elected* Holy Roman Emperor but the Habsburgs had effectively annexed this title and position.) Added to this were Spain's New World possessions, widely believed to be supporting Habsburg pretension with untold stores of gold and silver. Charles V, for political reasons, was eager for his son and heir Philip, soon to be invested with the crown of Spain, to marry Mary Tudor. To many Englishmen the thought of their country being absorbed by the monolithic Habsburg state was anathema.

But there was also a clash of ideologies. Charles saw himself as God's appointed vicegerent, the latest in a line of Christian emperors whose prime duty it was to ensure the triumph of militant Catholicism. He was imbued with the spirit of the *reconquista*, which had seen the last Moors expelled from Spain. He vigorously defended his eastern boundary against the Turk. This crusading zeal extended to internal affairs. Ever since Innocent III, in the thirteenth century, had called on temporal rulers to launch the Albigensian Crusade against the Cathars of southern France, emperors had assumed the responsibility of extirpating heresy from their dominions – by force if necessary. Throughout most of his reign Charles fought – and finally lost – a war against the spread of Lutheranism in Germany, and his

Netherlands territories were so affected by the Reformation that the execution of over 2,000 martyrs failed to rid the region of heresy. The attraction of the English match for Charles was that it would guarantee his ships safe passage through the Narrow Seas, enabling him more effectively to defend the commercially important Low Countries from French expansionism and religious innovation.

Philip had been well trained in the duties of a Christian monarch. Lacking his father's political acumen, he fell back on rigid dogma and narrow-minded obstinacy. For him heresy and treason were not just two sides of the same coin; they *were* the coin – completely mingled like metals to form the alloy of heinous offence to God and man. Referring to his problems in the Netherlands, Philip wrote:

> Before suffering the slightest damage to religion and the service of God, I would lose all my estates, and a hundred lives if I had them, because I do not propose, nor do I desire to be the ruler of heretics. If it can be, I will try to settle the matter of religion without taking up arms, because I fear that to do so would lead to their total ruin. But if I cannot settle matters as I wish, without force, I am determined to go in person and take charge of everything, and neither the danger nor the destruction of those provinces, nor of all the rest I possess, can deter me from this end.[3]

The Spanish Inquisition has achieved a well-deserved notoriety. Its teeth and claws were sharpened on Muslim and Jewish citizens during the *reconquista* and it had recently begun to turn its attention to rooting out Lutheran cells. Under Philip II the Holy Office became an instrument of the Spanish state for enforcing religious and political conformity. Torture, informers and all the methods of the police state were employed, even against leading churchmen. By the end of the 1550s hundreds of Spaniards had faced autos da fé in the principal cities of the realm and hundreds more had fled. Foreign nationals were not immune from investigation by the inquisitors and stories were soon spreading in England of merchants and travellers who had suffered imprisonment, trial and other indignities.

It is not surprising that throughout England a marriage alliance with

Spain was regarded with indignation and horror. Many of Mary's subjects, whatever their religious convictions, had reason to be hostile to the Habsburg match which took place in July 1554. Within months the popular mood had changed. People who had lit bonfires and cheered Mary through the streets of her capital now threw mud at members of Philip's entourage and daubed walls with anti-Catholic graffiti. The new reign was not six months old before a widespread plot came to life. In the event, Sir Thomas Wyatt was the only one of the conspirators to take action but his march on London with a band of Kentish supporters was enough to cause serious alarm. Treasons, real and imagined, continued to trouble the regime and early in 1556 an elaborate plot led by Sir Henry Dudley, involving French troops and the support of men close to the court, came near to success.

By this time the queen's subjects had other reasons for bitter discontent. England was dragged into the Habsburgs' latest war with France. The crops failed. An influenza epidemic claimed tens of thousands of victims – and Mary had introduced her version of the Inquisition. She never intended to be a persecutrix and her councillors were at one with Philip in urging a softly softly approach to the religious question. But Mary was shocked to discover that she could not put the clock back. Landowners were not prepared to restore monastic property to the church. Parliament would not relinquish the authority in religious issues it had gained in the 1530s. Bold evangelical preachers could not be easily silenced. Illicit presses poured out anti-government pamphlets. Worst of all from Mary's point of view, her subjects did not flock back with thankful hearts to the restored mass. Protestantism was driven underground, not exterminated. To the queen's frustration over the failure of her religious ambitions was added her genuine alarm at rebellion and her growing unpopularity. To assert her authority and that of her bishops she took an increasingly hard line on heresy. Protestant asylum-seekers were expelled. Thousands of men and women were examined about their beliefs. Hundreds were imprisoned. At least 287 were burned at the stake. Over 800 convinced evangelicals fled abroad. Since these were largely well-to-do, educated Protestants who could afford to leave home and settle in a foreign land the loss to the nation was not inconsiderable.

Moreover they did not abandon the hope of reconverting England. Some of the exiles became ardent propagandists who flooded their homeland with partisan pamphlets. Others were directly involved in plots against the regime.

Francis Walsingham did not hurry to join the flood of religious emigrants, even though London was rapidly becoming an uncongenial and even a dangerous place. Forced attendance at the popish mass distressed him and he may well have become a focus of government attention. The first victims of the new regime were those most closely associated with its predecessor. Several of Walsingham's friends and acquaintances found themselves taken in for interrogation. The government had no widespread extermination policy but as trails were discovered leading to secret presses, unauthorized religious gatherings and the hatchers of plots, they had no alternative but to follow them up. Sooner or later the bishop's men would come knocking at Walsingham's door. He knew people who were involved in Wyatt's rebellion. He was, at the very least, acquainted with John Day, the publisher of subversive literature who had withdrawn to Stamford, from where, financed by William Cooke, Cecil's brother-in-law, he continued his business. With this and other information in his possession Francis was vulnerable.

Walsingham had good reasons for quitting England and family matters provided him with the opportunity to do so. At what point Walsingham decided to leave for more congenial and safer climes is not known. We only have tantalizing glimpses of his movements over the next few years. The cities of Basel and Padua feature prominently in the sparse account of his peregrinations but this may be due to the random survival of records and may not indicate the real significance of his sojourn in these places. Right at the beginning of Mary's reign he could claim a good reason for applying for a passport.

In 1553 his aunt, Lady Denny, died, leaving a young family of four daughters and three sons as orphans. Jane Denny's close relatives took charge of the girls and Francis accepted responsibility for their brothers. The boys, all under the age of fourteen, cannot have been in any danger but presumably the family was determined to have them brought up in a good Protestant environment. By the autumn of 1554 the Dennys were at Padua in the charge of John Tamworth (soon to be Walsingham's brother-in-law). It seems likely that Francis was with them. About this time he enrolled in the university. A year later we find the party in Basel where the Dennys were left in the care of Walsingham's friends. He then hastened back across the Alps to resume his studies.

The fact that our knowledge of Francis' itinerary is so sketchy should not deceive us into dismissing the exile years as unimportant. On the contrary, they were formative. He emerged from this life of scholarly vagabondage with beliefs strengthened, opinions defined, friendships established, understanding of continental religion and politics clarified and character developed. The policies he later pursued in government stemmed directly from his experiences between 1553 and 1558. The 500 or so men of substance and conviction (most of them young) who spent all or part of Mary's reign in the Protestant hot spots of Europe constituted a kind of evangelical university. They sat at the feet of the leading scholars of the Reformation – John Calvin at Geneva, Peter Martyr Vermigli at Strasbourg (and, later, Zurich), Heinrich Bullinger at Zurich. The exiled community also produced its own notables. Walsingham's old teacher, John Cheke, went to Padua, as he said, 'to learn not only the Italian tongue but also philosophically to course over the civil laws'. He devoted part of his time there to lecturing on Demosthenes to his fellow countrymen. John Jewel was a talented Oxford lecturer who had fallen under the spell of Peter Martyr when the latter, attracted to the university by Cranmer, taught there between 1547 and 1553. He followed his hero to the continent and acted as Peter Martyr's assistant. Richard Cox, formerly Chancellor of Oxford University, turned up at Strasbourg and became famously locked in theological dispute with another exile, the fiery Scot, John Knox. Two bishops, John Bale of Ossory and John Posset of Winchester, used the safety of their European havens to launch anti-papal polemics across the Channel. Posset died at Strasbourg in 1556 but the others went on to be members of the Elizabethan establishment.

But the two men who would make the biggest impact in the next

reign were William Whittingham and John Foxe. It was they who
gave England the two books which changed it for all time. Whittingham who, though a layman, became minister to the English community at Geneva, supervised the production of a new translation of
the Bible. Its Calvinistic tone shaped the theological thinking of two
generations of English Christians and it was not superseded until the
appearance of the Authorized Version in 1611. Foxe gave his fellow
countrymen a bestseller which set in aspic their perception of the
Church of Rome – the *Acts and Monuments of the Christian Religion*,
better known as the *Book of Martyrs*.

This enormous and immensely influential work, which went
through four editions (each larger than the one before) during the
author's lifetime, covered the entire history of the Christian church
and, in particular, those members of it who had died for their faith.
Foxe continued the work of fellow exiles, notably John Bale and
another religious refugee Edmund Grindal (later to be Archbishop of
Canterbury), and their writings were not mere academic exercises
produced by men with time on their hands. They sprang form the
anguished need of the 1550s émigrés to find answers to such questions
as 'Why was God permitting the slaughter of his English saints?',
'How had the Catholic church fallen into such grave error?', 'What
role was England destined to play in the establishment of the true
faith?' and 'How did all this fit in with the divine eternal scheme of
things?' These were certainly questions which were exercising Walsingham and we shall not understand his later career if we do not
address the deep concerns that he and his fellow asylum-seekers felt or
the theological and philosophical mindset they developed to deal with
those concerns.

Bale and Foxe, like their fellow evangelicals at Basel, had no doubt
that England was marked by providence for a special destiny. Their
writings combined Biblicism and nationalism. Bale's *Scriptorum Illustrium Maioris Britanniae Catalogus* traced the history of England from
such illustrious semi-mythical figures as Brutus, Joseph of Arimathea
and King Arthur down to the mid-sixteenth century. In parallel it
chronicled the development of the papacy, represented in the early
centuries by faithful and devout pastors but, from the time of Boniface

VIII (1294–1303), by agents of Antichrist, who tried to usurp the temporal authority of kings and emperors. But human history was not just played out on the temporal plain. Bale's prayer was the same as Milton's, a century later:

> what in me is dark
> Illumine, what is low raise and support;
> That in the height of this great argument
> I many assert eternal Providence,
> And justify the ways of God to men.[4]

Everything that happened was predestined by God and foretold in his word, particularly in the Book of Revelation. St John's vision was the key to:

all the chronicles and most notable histories which hath been written since Christ's ascension, opening the true natures of their ages, times and seasons. He that hath store of them and shall diligently search them over, conferring the one with the other, time with time, and age with age, shall perceive most wonderful causes. For in the text [of Revelation] are they [the causes] only proposed in effect, and promised to follow in their seasons, and so ratified with other scriptures, but in the chronicles they are evidently seen by all ages fulfilled.[5]

Bale, followed by Foxe, asserted that the story of the Christian centuries centred on the struggle between the 'true' church, the elect of God, and the agents of Antichrist working both inside and outside the institutions of religion. As far as England was concerned this theme was intertwined with the independence of the state from foreign subversion. Henry VIII had expelled the pope and instituted reform of doctrine and liturgy. Inevitably, the beast of Revelation was fighting back, hence the dreadful persecution currently raging, but his days were numbered and the endtime was near. This was the theological foundation upon which Walsingham and the returning exiles built all their thinking about English politics:

the effect of the propaganda initiated by the Marian exiles would be felt in all phases of public life in the reign of Elizabeth. Government would more and more have to be carried on to the accompaniment of discussion by men with the confidence in their own opinions bred by such a faith, an increasingly passionate interest in the affairs of the realm, and a familiar apparatus of images and ideas for speculation, expression and communication. Nothing like this on any such scale had ever happened in England before.[6]

However, it was far from true that all the refugees returned home with a uniform politico-religious programme to advance. Factions within the Protestant camp centred around the issue of whether or not the Reformation had gone far enough. Conflict flared up at Frankfurt over the form of worship to be used in the English church there. Richard Cox argued for the use of Cranmer's 1552 Prayer Book. But John Knox rejected it as a half-papist 'mingle-mangle'. Soon other exile communities were divided between those who looked for a continuation of the Edwardian tradition and those who wanted to purify doctrine and liturgy – which meant adopting thoroughly Calvinist patterns. The use of the word 'Puritan' to designate this party seems to have originated in Basel.

There can be no doubt that Francis Walsingham's sympathies lay with this more austere section of the Protestant community. His precise legal mind easily sifted truth from semi-truth and falsehood. He discerned principles clearly and, perhaps too readily, saw complex issues in stark black and white. At the same time he was very aware of political realities. Calvinist polity involved the creation of a godly commonwealth governed by a twofold system of secular rulers and ministers of religion. Those who held the power of the sword under God were to submit to spiritual councillors in all matters of morality and church discipline. This was difficult enough to achieve in a city state such as Geneva. The problems attendant on converting to such a regime the ancient monarchy of England with its long-established governmental and judicial systems were daunting to contemplate. Furthermore, the sermons and writings of Calvin and other Reformed ministers were scarcely flattering in their references to contemporary monarchies.

The courts of princes . . . were represented by Calvin as nests of ambition, hypocrisy, flattery and servility. He singled out particularly the corruption of judges and the venality of judicial office, as well as the advancement of the unworthy, as being the order of the day there. Advancement, if it is achieved, is no more than 'fetters of gold', and the sensible man is content with a private station, for 'there will be, I say, more liberty in many a poor man's house, than in those great pits, the courts of princes'. He noted also a 'theology of the court', which prostitutes itself to the service of the powerful. And . . . he identified 'flatterers of princes' as one of the main threats to the *sinceritas fidei* in his time.[7]

Henry VIII had been invested by parliament with the supreme headship of the English church. His fiat ran in all aspects of the nation's life – spiritual as well as temporal. Under Edward VI and Mary, the authority of the Crown in matters spiritual had been wielded to swing official policy violently in different directions. Walsingham was astute enough to realize that under a new Protestant regime, which would presumably be led by Elizabeth, Henry VIII's only remaining reformers would have to rely on the unassailable power of the monarch to carry their policies but, at the same time, that monarch would have to be persuaded to yield to devout, theologically educated spiritual advisers. At best, movement towards a truly 'purified' state church might be achieved but only by the skilful application of tact and subtlety.

There was nothing remotely tactful or subtle about a book published in Geneva by John Knox in the spring of 1558. *The First Blast of the Trumpet Against the Monstrous Regiment of Women* attacked the female rulers of England, Scotland and France (Mary Tudor, Mary of Guise and Catherine de Medici) but it went much further than the indictment of individuals: 'To promote a woman to bear rule, superiority, dominion or empire above any realm, nation or city is repugnant to nature, contumely to God, a thing most contrarious to his revealed will and approved ordinance and finally it is the sub-version of good order, of all equity and justice.'[8]

The timing of this diatribe could scarcely have been worse. It

enraged Princess Elizabeth months before her accession and reinforced her dislike of Protestant radicals. Calvin and other leaders
hastened to dissociate themselves from Knox's language. Their
problem – and it was one Walsingham shared – was that they agreed
with his premise. In the biblical hierarchy of creation women *were*
inferior to men, and the sorry state of England seemed to support the
scriptural principle. Mary Tudor's regime was fragile specifically
because she was a woman in a man's world. In matters of policy
she deferred to her husband and to forthright councillors like Stephen
Gardiner and her own archbishop, Reginald Pole. In dynastic affairs
her sole responsibility was to give birth to a healthy heir. Her failure in
this regard was a personal and, in Catholic eyes, a national and
religious tragedy. How the fact of female dependence on men could
be squared with the *fait accompli* of a Protestant queen became the
subject of much, sometimes sophistical, debate and, in terms of
practical everyday government, the problem would colour the
relationship between Elizabeth and her Council.

This, of course, was all in the future as Walsingham continued his
continental peregrinations – a mixture of educational programme,
cultural grand tour and evangelical pilgrimage. He spent a considerable part of these years not in one or other of the Protestant shrines
but in Catholic Padua, pursuing his legal studies. Padua was a
dependency of Venice and it was said of citizens of the Serene
Republic that they considered themselves Venetians first and Christians second. The Queen of the Adriatic was intensely independent,
particularly in its relationship with Rome. In Venetian territory papal
authority was kept at arm's length, senior ecclesiastics were barred
from the Great Council, the powers of the Inquisition were circum-
scribed and clergy enjoyed few special privileges. Venice welcomed
strangers of all religious persuasions who could contribute to the
commercial or cultural life of the state. If Protestant visitors con-
gregated together for their own type of worship, the authorities did
not pry too closely into their activities. Scores of prominent Englishmen enjoyed liberal Venetian hospitality, including Francis Russell,
Earl of Bedford, the doyen of English Protestants, and Edward
Courtenay, Earl of Devon.

Padua's chief claim to fame was its ancient university, already more than 300 years old when Walsingham arrived. He enrolled in its great law school and increased his knowledge by studying with the finest European experts in the *corpus juris civilis*. It is now that we obtain our first glimpse of Walsingham's character. He obviously impressed both his confrères and his seniors, for, in December 1555, he was elected to the office of Consularius of the English Nation in the law faculty. This meant that he represented and exercised authority over his fellow countrymen. The student body was divided into twelve 'nations' according to their place of origin. The chosen representative of each nation looked after his colleagues' interests and even had a say in the running of the faculty. In return the authorities looked to him to ensure the good behaviour of his compatriots. It was an office requiring tact, firmness and diplomacy: students were no less boisterous in the sixteenth century than they are today. The twenty-three-year-old Walsingham must have possessed a gravitas which commended him to students and teachers alike.

With French, Italian, German, Swiss, Spanish, English and other national contingents all living cheek by jowl in the narrow confines of the medieval city it cannot have been easy to keep the peace but to national rivalries were added religious differences. For the English exiles these were only intensified by news from home. As the Marian persecution grew in intensity Walsingham and all his colleagues had friends and family caught up in the Protestant witch-hunts. Those known to Walsingham included Nicholas Ridley, burned at Oxford, and John Cheke whose capture and forced recantation were a propaganda coup for the new regime. Cheke was kidnapped by government agents near Antwerp, bound and blindfolded and thrown into a ship. Within days he was in the Tower of London, where fear of the stake drove him to recant. Although freed, he went into a rapid decline and died overwhelmed with grief and shame for his betrayal of the truth. Lesser fry also suffered. Walsingham's contemporary at King's, John Hullier, was one of the few men to be burned in Cambridge. On a blustery Maundy Thursday he suffered long and terribly as the wind blew the flames away from his body, denying him a quick death. Almost more shocking were the final

indignities heaped upon the gentle Martin Bucer whose sermons and
lectures had moved Walsingham and his friends. With great ceremony his remains were dug up after almost six years and burned in the
market place.

All the news which reached the exiles was not unwelcome. There
were stories of frequent anti-government riots and demonstrations.
Public reaction to the burnings was not what Mary and her bishops
had hoped. In London, where most of the martyrdoms occurred,
citizens resented religious zealots prying into their affairs and the arrest
of neighbours. By now many held the queen in ridicule and contempt. The one event that could have saved the situation for Mary
was the birth of a male heir. Ironically, it was the queen's failure to
conceive the desired prince which created for her the same dilemma
that had faced her father and begun the whole Reformation and
Counter-Reformation crisis. In the autumn of 1557 Mary had
convinced herself that she was pregnant. Catholic hopes were raised
only to be cruelly dashed when after eleven months, the humiliated
queen admitted that she had been deceived.

According to rumours emanating from sources close to the throne
the queen was constantly on the alert for assassins and was afraid to
show herself in public. Pious Protestants had no doubt that all this was
God's judgement on (in the words of John Knox) 'the wicked Jezebel,
who for our sins, contrary to nature and the manifest word of God, is
suffered to reign over us in God's fury'.[9] Many were the debates
Walsingham must have participated in with his friends about the
unique problems which beset a state when its head was a woman. The
political attitudes he developed during his years of exile formed the
basis of all his thoughts and actions when he became a principal
adviser to a female ruler.

Chapter 3

'THE MALICE OF THIS PRESENT TIME'

1558–69

No one, including the new queen, knew what to expect of the reign which began on 17 November 1558. When the news of Mary's death arrived in the English evangelical brotherhoods abroad bells were rung, bonfires lit and flags waved. Services of thanksgiving were held in the churches of the exiled communities. Several men, hoping for positions of influence in church and state, packed their bags in readiness for a speedy return. A great deal of wishful thinking went on. Edwin Sandys (soon to be Bishop of Worcester) reported excitedly to Heinrich Bullinger: 'The queen has changed almost all her councillors and has taken good Christians into her service in the room of papists and there is great hope of her promoting the gospel and advancing the kingdom of Christ to the utmost of her power.'[1] Bullinger, who was well versed in the toings and froings of church politics, urged caution and wariness in letters to his English friends. Sir Anthony Cooke (William Cecil's father-in-law and one-time tutor to Edward VI) acknowledged receipt of such advice and particularly that the advocates of reform should leave their squabbling behind in Geneva, Zurich and Strasbourg. 'There is great hope,' Cooke insisted, 'that the spirits of the papists are entirely cast down and that they will not offer to attack us, unless our own discord should afford them an opportunity.'[2] But if Cooke hoped that the returning exiles would agree to sing from the same hymn sheet he was whistling in the wind.

Elizabeth desired a church that was united and Protestant. United, because, as events over the last quarter of a century had demonstrated, religious division was a political nuisance and potentially expensive.

Protestant, because Catholicism meant putting her people (and herself) under the authority of the pope and she was not prepared to surrender the total power achieved by her father. If she was under any illusion at all about how difficult it would be to settle the realm after the changes and chances of the previous three reigns she was very speedily disabused. In London Protestant extremists expressed their new freedom by pulling down altars and abusing priests. Catholics were no less forthright. The Bishop of Winchester, preaching at Mary's funeral, had demanded that returning Protestant exiles should be hunted down and put to death. On the first Sunday after her accession Elizabeth had her chaplain, Dr William Bill, preach the public sermon at St Paul's Cross. The following week the Bishop of Chichester mounted the same pulpit and denounced everything Bill had said. 'Believe not this new doctrine,' he ranted, 'it is not the gospel, but a new invention of new men and heretics.'[3] For this contumely the queen sent Bishop Christopherson to prison, where, soon afterwards, he died. Elizabeth replaced him with the zealous returned exile, William Barlow. Other problems were not resolved so easily. The vast majority of bishops and senior ecclesiastics were Marian appointees, ready to resist change doggedly. They could not be summarily sacked without cause.

The same was not true of the royal Council. Elizabeth removed most of her half-sister's advisers from office and replaced them with men of her own choosing. The criteria on which she based her selection (advised by her right-hand man, William Cecil) were Protestant conviction and 'steadiness'. By that word I mean men who were not fanatical in the expression of their opinions. Elizabeth had no intention of replacing Mary's dogmatic Catholic councillors with doctrinaire evangelical ones. Though she admitted two or three returning exiles to her intimate body of advisers, she preferred men who had either made their peace with Mary or lived quietly during her reign.

One of Elizabeth's chosen confidants was Francis Russell, Earl of Bedford. After his sojourn in Geneva and Venice he had returned to England in 1557 and was received by Queen Mary, probably at the urging of Philip II, who needed the help of England's nobility in his war with France. Russell was one of the captains who took part in the siege of St Quentin in that year. In the early days of the new reign it was Russell who became the main hope of the returning exiles. Rudolph Gualter, minister in Zurich, wrote fulsomely to the earl:

in your journey into Italy last year by way of Zurich you made such diligent inquiry into all things which make for the cause of the church and of religion, that it was easy to be perceived that this cause was far more dear to you than all other things whatever . . . I now rejoice the more both for yourself and for England, as I understand that you are advanced by the queen's majesty to the highest dignity.[4]

Russell had, indeed, been raised to the highest dignity. He was appointed Lord Lieutenant of Dorset, Devon, Cornwall and the city of Exeter and Lord Warden of the Stannaries. This made him the most powerful man in the west of England and he saw it as his responsibility to accept leadership of what rapidly became an evangelical 'party'. 'I can truly promise,' he reported to Gualter in January 1560, 'that this our religion, wounded and laid low as it were with a whirlwind by the tyranny of the time, and now, by God's blessing, again beginning in some measure to revive, will strike its roots yet deeper and deeper . . . As far as I can, I am exerting myself in this matter to the utmost of my poor abilities.'[5]

Russell instituted several 'sound' preachers to vacant benefices. But, in the early months of the reign, the strategic priority was to ensure a strong Protestant representation in parliament. The establishment of the official national religion was the first task to be undertaken by Elizabeth's first parliament. It was vital for the reformers to win the debate and they knew they had a fight on their hands. The upper house was dominated by bishops and Catholic peers. Therefore, it was vital to engineer a Protestant majority in the Commons. Russell, aided by Cecil and other friends, ensured that the West Country (still one of the more conservative areas of England) returned some good evangelicals. Thus it was that Francis Walsingham became MP for Bossiney (Tintagel), Cornwall.

Since the writs for the new parliament went out in December and the assembly convened on 23 January, it is clear that Walsingham lost no time in returning home. Letters must have passed to and fro as soon as the news of Elizabeth's accession reached the continent. He was offered the Cornish seat and promptly accepted. The mayor and half a dozen or so burgesses (the only people eligible to vote) duly did their duty by his lordship and Walsingham, after what can only have been a brief visit to his home, was on his way to Westminster.

His first experience of national politics proved to be very trying. William Cecil, now secretary to the Council and Elizabeth's fixer, prepared draft legislation which he hoped would lay the essential foundation for a religious settlement without provoking concerted opposition. There was an embargo on all preaching until parliament had delivered its verdict. The immediate objective was to reinstate the royal supremacy and the Edwardian Prayer Book of 1552. The upper house, with its Catholic majority, was always going to be a problem but trouble immediately flared up in the Commons. Opposition to the Cranmerian liturgy came not just from Catholic members but also from radical evangelicals. The squabbles that had troubled the foreign communities quickly manifested themselves at home, 'some declaring for Geneva and some for Frankfort' as John Jewel reported.[6] Day after day there were furious debates in the parliament chamber. Anthony Cook complained: 'We are now busy in parliament about expelling the tyranny of the pope and restoring the royal authority and re-establishing true religion. But we are moving far too slowly . . . The zeal of the queen is very great, the activity of the nobility and the people is also great; but still the work is hitherto too much at a stand.'[7]

Knowing how vital it was to set the tone for the new reign, partisans argued at length and with fervour. Some did not hesitate to call upon powerful friends abroad to intervene in the debate. Thus it was that Rudolph Gualter in Zurich wrote to warn the queen herself against her own more moderate advisers:

There are not a few persons, who, though they perceive that popery can neither honestly be defended, nor conveniently retained, are endeavouring by and bye to obtrude upon the churches a form of religion which is an unhappy compound of popery and the gospel, and from which there may at length be an easy passage to the ancient superstition.

Gualter urged Elizabeth not to be swayed by pragmatism ('reasonings of the flesh' as he called it):

Your majesty is aware of that saying of Christ, who declares that the *new piece* of evangelical doctrine will not suit the *old garments* of superstitions. And he also solemnly warns us not to put the fermenting and wholesome *new wine* of the gospel into *old leathern bottles,* unless we would have not only these to perish, but that to be spilled at the same time. From the experience of not a few instances in our Germany, we assuredly know it to be impossible ever to consult the peace of the churches, or the purity of religion, as long as any relics of superstition are retained.[8]

This was not the best way to approach Elizabeth Tudor. It is small wonder that she developed an antipathy towards those who were pejoratively labelled 'Puritans'.

Cecil had hoped to have the parliamentary business finished by Easter but when the Commons did eventually cobble together a bill to be sent to the 'other place' the Lords rejected it. The session ended in disarray with nothing resolved. Queen and Council, therefore, ordered parliament to reconvene in April. Even then, it was only by some very adroit (not to say shady) manoeuvring that they got through both houses a uniformity bill and a supremacy bill (naming the queen as 'Supreme Governor' rather than 'Supreme Head' of the English church). The latter made history by being the first piece of religious legislation for which not a single bishop voted. Inevitably, there had been compromises and, inevitably, those compromises pleased very few people. There was much muttering among the members who returned to their homes after 8 May. The religious debate was far from over.

What part did Francis Walsingham play in all these events? Infuriatingly, we do not know. There are no extant records of the debates in either house. The government campaign was led by Cecil and Francis Knollys, vice chamberlain of the royal household (one of the few former exiles to be on close terms with the queen), but what they said and who supported them remains a total mystery. However, since Walsingham enjoyed the patronage of Bedford, Cecil and Knollys we can infer two things. The first is that he was a firm supporter of government policy. The second is that he was regarded as a safe pair of hands. No firebrand he! The man who had exercised tact and diplomacy when dealing with teachers and taught in Padua could be relied on to approach the tricky and emotive problems of the emerging Elizabethan state with a level head. It was not much later that he gave this advice to an impatient Puritan friend: 'We have great cause to thank God for that we presently enjoy, having God's word sincerely preached and the sacraments truly administered. The rest we lack we are to beg by prayer and attend with patience.'[9] The twenty-eight-year-old Francis Walsingham had reached a maturity which enabled him to balance ideological commitment and circumspection. He was quite clear and steadfast in his beliefs but he knew there were better ways of achieving his ends than trumpeting his faith defiantly in the ears of friend and foe alike.

And, in any case, he had personal concerns to attend to. Within months of his return his mother died and Francis took over the running of the family estates in Kent. The time had come to settle down and to give thought to his dynastic responsibilities. Thus, in 1562, he married into the 'nobility' of the City. His bride was Anne Carleill, widow of a leading vintner and daughter of a former lord mayor. This union gives us our first glimpse of another of Walsingham's interests – merchant venturing. Anne's family was closely involved in the recent founding of the Muscovy Company, set up to exploit trade with Russia and the Baltic. It would not be long before Walsingham invested in the company's voyages. Anne brought with her a sizeable fortune and a young family. Walsingham now had the means to acquire a more substantial country seat in the county he knew and loved best. He took a lease on the manor of Parkebury in Hertfordshire, close by the Carey and Hunsdon estates where he had been brought up – and where, incidentally, William Cecil was a near neighbour.

Sometime in 1562 (probably November) Cecil made a memorandum for himself: 'Mr Walsingham to be of the house'. He was
forming his plans for Elizabeth's second parliament and, in his quest
for sound men, Walsingham's name stood high on the list. When it
came to the election Francis was selected by both Banbury, at the
instigation of Francis Knollys, and Lyme Regis, which was in Bedford's pocket. He decided, perhaps out of loyalty to his old patron, to
sit for the Dorset constituency. Once again, he appears to have made
no mark on the subsequent proceedings. This led P.W. Hasler, the
historian of parliament, to deduce, 'it is clear that the Houses of
Commons held little appeal for him'.[10] In fact, there is no contradiction between his earlier lack of political activity and his later
prominence. The House of Commons was far from being an obvious
ladder for the ambitious public figure to climb. For one thing,
parliament met irregularly and only when summoned by the sovereign. It was only in session for five per cent of Elizabeth's entire reign.
She and Cecil both hoped to keep the 1563 session short. If it were
not for the fact that taxes could only be levied when granted by peers
of the realm and the representation of the mercantile and gentry
classes, they would not have called it at all. When it did meet it was
often at loggerheads with the regime. These were the years in which
the House of Commons was learning how to flex its muscles, to
challenge government policy, to ask awkward questions and to
demand answers. There were three areas of policy in particular which
concerned MPs: religion, foreign affairs and the succession (i.e. the
queen's marriage). Since Elizabeth regarded all these as prerogative
matters, potential conflict was in the air every time the members filed
into the old St Stephen's Chapel. All in all it is not surprising that
Walsingham should regard attendance in parliament as a duty to be
performed rather than an opportunity to further his career. Add to this
the fact that he later showed himself to be a man who preferred the
corridors of power to its public platform and his absence from the
records in the 1560s is adequately explained.

He was prospering materially and accumulating property during
this decade. Anne Walsingham died after only two years of marriage,
leaving a handsome bequest to her husband and, after a decent period

of mourning, he paid earnest court to Ursula Worsley, another widow who was mistress of substantial lands. Her late husband, Richard Worsley, had been Captain of the Isle of Wight, lessee of the lands of Carisbrooke Priory and owner of Appuldurcombe and Woolverton manors, as well as estates in Dorset and Wiltshire. Walsingham's eager pursuit of this prize began within months of Richard's death for we find him writing, in October 1565, to Sir William More, the Worsley executor, asking him to persuade the lady from 'her resolution of sole life'.[11] That process apparently took some time, for it was another eighteen months before Francis and Ursula were wed. Almost immediately Walsingham gave up his Hertfordshire residence and settled with his enlarged family (Ursula had two sons) in the substantial Worsley house at Appuldurcombe. His application for the lease of Carisbrooke Priory indicated his determination fully to occupy Worsley's shoes.

Walsingham's decision to move his base to a place far distant from the court and from his own home turf was not made on solely financial grounds. In fact we can detect in this move early evidence for his involvement in that Protestant expansionist circle which revolved around Robert Dudley. The Isle of Wight was a crucial bastion in England's defence system. It guarded the approaches to Portsmouth and Southampton and from there watch could be kept on traffic passing up and down the Channel. Its coves and inlets were useful places where clandestine visitors from France could be landed. In addition Carisbrooke Castle was a secure prison within whose stout walls men could be 'persuaded' to yield up any information they might have concerning potential threats to the realm. It was, therefore, vitally important to the government that the Isle of Wight should be in safe hands.

At the end of 1565 the captaincy of Carisbrooke Castle was entrusted to the soldier-diplomat, Edward Horsey. Horsey was a bluff, bold, unscrupulous patriot – and a died-in-the-wool Protestant. During Mary's reign he had not only gone into exile, he had also been a prime mover in the Dudley plot. In the early days of the new reign he attached himself to Robert Dudley and through him gained the somewhat reluctant favour of Elizabeth. Very soon he had ships scouring the Channel for enemy vessels and for easy prey whose cargoes he could appropriate. He was, therefore, one of the first Elizabethan sea dogs, those adventurer-pirates of whom the queen officially disapproved and unofficially found very useful. Before the reign was more than a few years old Horsey served the queen in various military and diplomatic situations. He was a patron of Calvinist clergy and, in 1562, secured the appointment of William Whittingham, erstwhile colleague and supporter of John Knox, as chaplain to an army sent over into France. Horsey was committed to the policy of England's making a common front with the Huguenots against the Catholic Guise faction which dominated the French court. Someone else who advocated the same policy was Elizabeth's first ambassador to France, Nicholas Throckmorton, who managed to enjoy Elizabeth's favour despite his firm and firmly expressed Puritan opinions. These men were well known to Walsingham (Throckmorton had held the Lyme Regis parliamentary seat in the 1559 parliament) and, by 1565, they were already part of a political grouping which would become more confident and vociferous over the years. They were all concerned for the security of the realm and well understood the military and naval importance of the Isle of Wight. Walsingham had influential support in his suit for Ursula Worsley's hand.

By no means did he spend all his time in the country. In the spring of 1568 he exchanged the old family house in St Mary Aldermanbury parish for a more commodious town residence beyond the city walls, close to the church of St Giles Cripplegate. Here, a short walk from the open country of Moor Fields and Finsbury Fields, he was away from the foetid airs of the close-packed metropolis yet near enough to the court when his advice was sought or when he was called upon to execute some commission for Cecil. It was only a few months later that he wrote a letter to the secretary which has often been referred to as the beginning of Walsingham's public career. In fact, the contents make it quite clear that Walsingham was by now a well-established confidant of Cecil, specializing in foreign affairs. He wrote the letter at the behest of Throckmorton, who was too ill to attend to the matter in person. That, in itself, tells us that Francis was a trusted intermediary likely to be listened to seriously by Cecil. A messenger, Robert Stewart, had arrived from the French Huguenot leaders with vital information but Elizabeth had refused to receive him. Stewart was known as a plain, outspoken Calvinist who could not trouble himself to master court etiquette. What he regarded as earnestly pleading God's cause (ie the Huguenot cause) Elizabeth interpreted as presumptuous preaching. Moreover Stewart's message was one Elizabeth had not wanted to hear. She was not prepared to intervene in France on the Huguenots' behalf. Thus it was that Throckmorton pleaded on the messenger's behalf. Walsingham, passing on his friend's appeal, apologized for Stewart's unsophisticated behaviour but insisted that queen and Council could not afford to neglect the information he brought across the Channel.

In December Walsingham wrote again to Cecil, this time on his own behalf, to pass on intelligence which had come direct to him. He explained that he could not vouch for the accuracy of the information but:

Weighing [the informant's] earnest protestation of the credit of the party it came from, the nature of the matter as of the greatest importance, the malice of this present time, the allegiance and particular goodwill I owe to her majesty and the danger that might come to me by the concealing thereof if any such thing (which God defend) thereafter should happen, I saw in duty I could not forbear to write . . . I beseech your honour that I may without offence conclude that in this division that reigneth among us, there is less danger in fearing too much than too little and that there is nothing more dangerous than security.[12]

'Malice of this present time?' 'Division that reigneth among us?' 'Nothing more dangerous than security?' These are alarming – and, perhaps, alarmist – words. What exactly was Francis concerned about and how realistic were his fears? To unravel the answers to those questions we must backtrack to the beginning of the reign. By 1558 the glory days when Henry VIII had contended fiercely for a place at the top table alongside Charles V and Francis I were long past. It was:

in those years since Henry VIII's death that the new Queen, and most of the men who for the next three decades were chiefly to counsel her, had come of age or served their political apprenticeships. It was their experience of England's plight under Edward VI and Mary that shaped their approach and conditioned their thinking about their country's foreign relations under Elizabeth. That chastening experience had given them a more realistic appreciation, than had been possible in the years of affluence, of England's small stature alongside the Leviathans of the continent. They now knew that they had neither the men nor the money to compete on land with Habsburg and Valois in the way that Henry VIII and Wolsey had tried to compete. Their means would not stretch to conquer Scotland, let alone to conquer France. The loss of Calais, and their inability even to attempt its recovery, dramatically emphasized the lesson that the days of continental adventure were over. They had learned, too, that they must not look to foreign alliances to make good their own weakness. Henry VIII had discovered how little foreign allies were prepared to do for England's benefit. Northumberland and Mary had shown how easily the friendly embraces of either of the great continental monarchies could develop into bear-hugs almost as dangerous to England's independence as their hostile assaults.[13]

The lesson Elizabeth drew from this was that her best course was splendid isolation. Her inclination was to keep out of continental squabbles, using such diplomatic influence as she had (principally the bait of a marriage treaty) to encourage foreign princes to seek her support. She was a past mistress at prevarication, keeping her brother monarchs and their envoys dangling.

Unfortunately for such a cost-saving policy, detachment was hard to achieve and would ultimately become impossible. During her first ten years the queen was overtaken by events which progressively restricted her freedom of manoeuvre. We must now survey those years. The narrative may be told as a tale of three cities – Rome, Paris and Edinburgh.

We begin with Rome because it was the nerve centre from which impulses spread throughout every nation of Europe, producing political results which became more and more extreme. After more than four decades of ineffectual response to the spread of Protestantism the papacy had finally got its act together. Pope Pius IV summoned the Council of Trent to reconvene in 1562. This council had been on and off since 1547, bedevilled by internal disputes and the limited support of the major Catholic powers. Europe's rulers were concerned about two things – the power of the papacy and the internal peace of their own dominions. How they chose to deal with the spread of heresy affected both. The failure to eradicate by torture, fire and military might the beliefs of Lutherans, Zwinglians, Calvinists and fringe sectaries had led governments to hope that some theological accommodation could be made but successive popes had set their faces against compromise and when the final session of Trent ended in December 1563 every major tenet of Protestant belief had been vehemently rejected. To cheers and applause from the assembled bishops and cardinals (most of them from Italy and Spain) the pope closed the final session with the ringing cry, 'Anathema to all heretics! Anathema! Anathema!' There was to be no truce, no peace treaty. Nothing was contemplated but ultimate victory; the restoration of religious unity and uniformity. It was a declaration of total war. In pursuing it, loyal sons and daughters of mother church were urged to set aside all political, diplomatic and even moral considerations.

The principal focus of Rome's ire was England. In recent decades Habsburg and Valois monarchs had limited the power of the papacy in their lands and drawn into their own hands many of the ecclesiastical powers wielded within their borders. But the King of England had gone much further. He had expelled the pope, severed all links with Rome, appropriated church property and presumed to proclaim himself head of a breakaway heretic church. The failure of Mary Tudor's counter-reformation only served to rub salt into the wound. Now this renegade nation was under the rule of Henry Tudor's bastard daughter. Rudolph Gualter accurately identified the Roman strategy which had become absolutely clear to England's political leaders and their friends abroad:

[I]t is sufficiently evident that the Roman antichrist is employing all his power and exertions towards this object, namely, that the carrying into effect the council of Trent may at length produce its intended result. Your neighbours [France and Spain] make no secret of this; and though they are restrained by ancient treaties . . . and the terms of a general peace, in which provision is made that no one shall give any trouble to another on account of diversity of religion, yet they are making many attempts, by which it plainly appears that they are seeking an occasion of disturbance.[14]

Had the papacy, after Trent, fallen back into the decadent, worldly, luxury-loving habits of the Borgia and Medici popes, who were more concerned about Italian politics than the purity of the faith, the campaign of the 'Antichrist' would not have been pursued so vigorously but, in the person of the new Pontiff, Pius V (1566–1572), the Tridentine church found a champion of an awesome personal piety and chilling reforming zeal. Born Antonio Ghislieri, this puritanical cleric was for many years the Grand Inquisitor and was dedicated to purging the church of impropriety, corruption and error. As pope he enjoyed unlimited authority to intensify his regime of purging the church and extending the war against heresy. It was not only libertines and publishers of un-authorized books who lived in fear of Pius's informers, agents and enforcers. There was no limit to this zealot's range of activity. It extended from the expelling of prostitutes from Rome and the forbidding of bull-fighting to anathematizing princes who showed leniency to Protestants and the funding of religion-inspired rebel-lion. On 23 February 1570, this Roman ayatollah issued the papal bull *Regnans in excelsis* against Queen Elizabeth:

We declare the aforesaid Elizabeth to be a heretic and abettor of heretics and we declare her and her supporters to have incurred the sentence of excommunication . . . we declare her to be deprived of her pretended claim to the aforesaid kingdom and of all lordship, dignity and privilege whatsoever. Also, we declare that the lords, subjects and peoples of the said kingdom and all others who have sworn allegiance to her are perpetually absolved from any oath of fidelity and obedience. Consequently, we absolve them and we deprive the same Elizabeth of her pretended claim to the kingdom . . . And we command and forbid her lords, subjects and peoples to obey her . . . we shall bind those who do the contrary with a similar sentence of excommunication.

In Paris papal directives received mixed responses. It was all very well for the head of the church to order unyielding opposition to Protestants but attempts to take a firm line destabilized the nation and, in fact, plunged it into civil war. Partly as a result of Calvinist missionary activity, the number of Protestants in France had, over the decade 1552–62, grown from almost zero to around two million. In over a thousand locations men and women deserted the mass to engage in vernacular worship and express their belief in the singing of metrical psalms. Moreover, the new faith had attracted adherents from all sections of society, so that little Huguenot congregations enjoyed the protection of city corporations and powerful aristocrats. Supporters of the Reformed faith could be found in the parlement of Paris and, more importantly, among the intimate advisers of the king. Since other prominent courtiers were devoted to the Catholic cause the potential existed for religious rivalry at the highest level of French life. Within months of Elizabeth's accession France, too, experienced a change of ruler. King Henry II was killed in a tournament accident and was succeeded by his fifteen-year-old son Francis II. Within eighteen months Francis was also dead from an ear infection. The crown now passed to a younger brother who, at the age of eleven, became Charles IX of France. Real power lay in the hands of the boy's mother, Catherine de Medici. But the rule of a minor inevitably encouraged faction-feuding at court and Catherine found herself having to perform a balancing act between the Catholic Guise party and the house of Bourbon, the champions of the Huguenots.

Catherine's recipe for keeping the peace was to allow limited toleration to the Protestant minority. By the Edict of Saint-Germain Huguenots were not allowed to worship in towns but might assemble in the open countryside during the hours of daylight. Catherine's attitude was extremely liberal by the standards of the time. For example, English Catholics did not enjoy the same freedom. However, such pragmatism could not satisfy religious partisans of either colour. As one Catholic spokesman stated:

> religion is the primary and principal foundation of all order, and the bourgeois and citizens are more bound together and united by it than by their trade in merchandise, the communication of laws, or anything else in a civil society . . . there is never more trouble or a greater tempest in a commonwealth than where there is some schism or dissension concerning the issue of religion.[15]

Ironically, it was a sentiment with which Walsingham and his friends would have heartily agreed. It seemed self-evident to sixteenth-century Europeans that political and social cohesion and stability were dependent on religious unity – one king, one law, one faith. It followed that anyone exercising or promoting a religion other than the one sanctioned by the government was guilty of sedition. Toleration implies that internal peace is more important than truth, for if opposing theologies are allowed to co-exist then neither can be the sole repository of truth. Such a view was unacceptable to all Catholic and Protestant activists.

Confrontation turned into civil war in the spring of 1562. Fighting broke out all over France. The Huguenots, led by the Bourbon Prince de Condé, commanded several towns and proved difficult or impossible to dislodge. More importantly, this confessional slugging match became the focus for the international Reformation struggle. The pope sent 2,500 troops and Philip of Spain provided the Guises with limited financial backing. Four thousand cavalry arrived from Germany to support the Huguenot cause. And, in England, the queen responded reluctantly to appeals for aid.

In the early years of her reign Elizabeth was uncertain about how to respond to events on the continent. She had inherited a war with France but differences had been settled in April 1559 by the Treaty of Cateau-Cambrésis. In response to later developments Throckmorton in Paris strenuously urged his royal mistress to set aside the agreement

in order to succour Condé's forces. His despatches pointed out that
what was happening in France was only part of a mounting campaign
aimed at all Protestant rulers, including Elizabeth herself. If the
Huguenots were crushed the Guises would not hesitate to make
common cause with their allies in Scotland to strike at England. The
apparent attractions of appeasement – peace and avoidance of expense
– were illusory. Elizabeth tired of Throckmorton's importuning. She
sent over another diplomat, Sir Thomas Smith, to act as a brake on the
activities of her headstrong ambassador. But Throckmorton was now
supported by Robert Dudley and by a majority on the Council. Men
who had experienced exile and others who were closely associated
with them felt a personal as well as an ideological obligation to their
co-religionists. They were indebted to their friends abroad who had
helped them during Mary's reign. Now it was their turn to respond
charitably to the entreaties of others suffering for the cause of the
Gospel.

Elizabeth saw things from a very different perspective. In her ethical
scheme of things loyalty of subjects to their anointed ruler had pride of
place. Aiding rebels was something she found difficult to square with
her conscience. On the other hand there was Calais. This port,
England's last possession on the European mainland, had been lost
in the recent war. At Cateau-Cambrésis she had agreed a face-saving
formula by which the French promised to return it after eight years
but no one believed that this would actually happen. Calais had
strategic importance as a base from which to keep a check on traffic
through the Narrows. But its prestige significance was greater. Its loss
had been a blow to national pride. Its recovery would be a feather in
Elizabeth's cap. She realized that exploiting the current difficulty of
Catherine de Medici would provide valuable diplomatic leverage.
She agreed to send Condé 170,000 crowns and an English force under
the command of Ambrose Dudley, Robert's brother, recently created
Earl of Warwick, to hold Le Havre (called Newhaven by the English)
and Dieppe until such time as Calais was handed over. The Newhaven Venture turned into a fiasco. Warwick set out in high hope
with several Calvinist captains (including Edward Horsley) and
ministers in his entourage. But the war went badly elsewhere for

the Huguenots (Throckmorton actually managed to get himself captured by the enemy) and within months they were obliged to negotiate a peace. The English garrison was left high and dry. Elizabeth refused to send more money to reinforce the defences and when the port, now also suffering an outbreak of plague, was besieged Warwick was obliged to surrender. Elizabeth did not fail to draw the moral about interfering in the internal affairs of other states.

In France the peace was short-lived. Conflict broke out twice more during the 1560s. Civil war is always the worst kind of war. In our own age, we have witnessed in Africa, the Middle East, the Balkans and elsewhere the bestial behaviour of which frenzied mobs are capable. Calvinist preachers urged congregations to acts of iconoclasm. Jesuit priests stirred their people to blood lust and murder. Charles de Guise, Cardinal of Lorraine, employed death squads. Stories such as this were commonplace: Marguerite de Hurtelon, a Huguenot widow, was slaughtered along with her four children and the family servants. 'Almighty God,' one protester expostulated to the king, how can you allow such crimes to go unpunished: 'these execrable executioners . . . slit the throat of this mother, then shot her five times in her breasts with a pistol and then burned the hands and feet of Faith, her eldest daughter, in order to make her tell them where her mother had hidden some money . . . after the massacre [they led] pigs into the house; in order to make them eat up all those poor dead corpses.'[16]

Stories such as this and a host of equally revolting rumours circulating in England reinforced the popular perception of Catholicism Foxe's *Acts and Monuments* was already fostering. Walsingham and his friends continued to urge English intervention in France not only to support their co-religionists, nor even to raise the Gospel standard in the cosmic warfare against Antichrist, but to erect barriers to protect England from the infiltration of papist agents. By the end of the decade the Bishop of Winchester took it as axiomatic that Pius V was sponsoring desperate men who 'besiege the tender frame of the most noble virgin Elizabeth with almost endless attacks and most studiously endeavour to compass her death both by poison and violence and witchcraft and treason and all other means of that kind which could ever be imagined and which it is horrible even to relate'.[17] Elizabeth's persistence in remaining 'a most noble virgin' made the Protestant Reformation more vulnerable. Until England had a royal heir everything hung upon the slender thread of her life.

By 1570 there was a claimant – a Catholic claimant – to the throne; one who would for years be an albatross round the neck of Elizabeth's government. In August 1561 the eighteen-year-old Mary Stuart arrived in Edinburgh to take up residence in her capital. She was the only child of James V and the great-granddaughter of Henry VII of England. She had, briefly, been Queen of France as wife of Francis II, thus uniting the crowns of the two nations – a situation alarming to the new Queen of England. With the death of Francis that particular threat disappeared but she remained a dynastic inconvenience. In Catholic eyes Elizabeth was a bastard and, therefore, Mary should by right occupy the English throne as well as the Scottish. Moreover, Mary was a Guise on her mother's side. Accordingly, she figured prominently in the scheming of her uncle, the Cardinal of Lorraine. This fact rendered her continued presence in France inconvenient to her mother-in-law, who objected to the Guise faction pursuing their own dynastic diplomacy. Catherine was, therefore, very pleased to see the back of Mary in August 1561.

Elizabeth did not share this satisfaction, partly because in the complex relations which ensued between the two neighbouring kingdoms she found herself at loggerheads with Cecil and the majority of her Council. In the 1550s Calvinism had spread even more rapidly in Scotland than in France, a state of affairs which surprised and delighted John Knox, who reported gleefully: 'If I had not seen it with my own eyes – my own country, I could not have believed it.' The leaders of the nation resented the French domination of the government during the regime of the regent, Mary of Guise. Left to her own devises Mary would have sought some accommodation on the religious issue. It is ironical that the two events which forced her hand were the accession of Elizabeth Tudor and the return of John Knox. The emergence of a Protestant state in the south strengthened the hand of the Lords of the Congregation as the Calvinist leaders called themselves, and Knox's fiery preaching stirred them to rebellion. They formed a new church or 'kirk'. Elizabeth was pleased to have a Protestant ally north of the border and welcomed the withering of French influence. What she could not stomach was the rising of the people against their divinely appointed sovereign.

Mary faced the same basic problem as her sister sovereign to the south – how to establish acceptable and effective female rule in a situation where the words 'female rule' were regarded as a contradiction in terms. Early in her reign she actually confronted John Knox (now the minister of St Giles' Cathedral, Edinburgh) on the subject of the 'monstrous regiment' and obtained from the bigoted preacher a partial retraction. But Mary was not Elizabeth. She lacked the intellectual stringency and emotional control of the older woman. Elizabeth had had her fling with Robert Dudley in 1559–60 and had then settled (with at least initial reluctance) to a celibate life. That was impossible for Mary. She needed a man to share her throne and her bed. And her choices were abysmal. In 1565 she married her cousin, Henry Stuart, Lord Darnley. Elizabeth was furious because this made Mary's claim to the English Crown even stronger. She wanted to strengthen the ties between the two queendoms – but on her own terms. She had even proposed her beloved Robert as a suitable husband but Mary was not prepared to accept Elizabeth's cast-offs (and Dudley had no stomach for the match either). It took very little time for Mary to realize that Darnley's charm was but a mantle thrown over the character of an arrogant, ambitious and ruthless bully. He initiated plots and intrigues with the sole purpose of reinforcing his own position. Religion was simply a tool to be used for achieving his own ends. News and rumours from north of the border spread rapidly along the international evangelical grapevine:

Within these few days king Philip privately sent thither a certain Italian abbot, with Spanish gold; a craft man, and trained for intrigue . . . The new king [Darnley], who had hitherto abstained from going to mass, and had of his own accord attended the sermons, for the sake of popularity, when he first heard of the ship being expected to arrive on the morrow, became on a sudden more confident, and having taken courage, would no longer play the hypocrite. He went to church, and ordered mass to be said before him as usual. At that very time Knox, who is a preacher in the same town, and in the next church, was declaiming with his accustomed boldness, before a crowded congregation, against the mad idolatries, and the whole pontifical dominion. In the mean time this ship of king Philip, tossed about by the winds and tempests, shattered and broken by the waves, with its mast sprung, its timbers stove in, the pilots lost, bereft of crew and cargo, is driven, a mere wreck, and filled with water, upon the coast of England. I doubt not but that this has happened by divine providence, to teach the infatuated king what a dangerous thing it is to hear mass.[18]

This report from John Jewel, Bishop of Salisbury, is typical of news circulating in the circle of Walsingham and his friends.

Others were not content passively to receive news about affairs in Scotland. Cecil and his conciliar colleagues were disturbed that Catholicism was in the ascendant in Scotland and that the Lords of the Congregation were on the defensive. Anything that destabilized the political situation north of the border was to England's advantage and they did everything in their power to promote discord. So when their Scottish allies informed them of an assassination plot which would cause mayhem at Mary's court they gave it their tacit backing. The result was the brutal murder of David Rizzio, Mary's secretary and, supposedly, her lover and a papal spy, in March 1566. The repercussions of their bloody act were exactly what Cecil had wanted – feuds, plots and counter-plots around the Scottish throne. They culminated, less than a year later, in the assassination of Darnley at Kirk o'Field. The chief conspirator was James Hepburn, Earl of Bothwell, who aimed to step into the murdered king's shoes. Within weeks he had achieved his objective. He was divorced from his wife and married to Mary with what was considered to be, at the very least, indecent haste.

The obvious inference was widely drawn from this sequence of events: Mary and Bothwell had long been lovers and had together planned the death of Darnley. The Lords of the Congregation, many of whom were up to their elbows in the late king's blood, encouraged this false rumour and, in distant London, William Cecil played his part in spreading the calumny in diplomatic quarters. By the autumn suspicion had turned into widely believed fact. The veteran diplomat at Strasbourg could confidently assert to Bullinger:

> The bishop of London, I suppose, has given you an account of the parricide perpetrated by the queen of Scots, and her justly deserved punishment, namely that she has been taken prisoner, and compelled to abdicate the kingdom, after having confessed that her husband had been taken off by her counsel and co-operation; and that her most profligate paramour had taken refuge in some maritime fortress built upon a rock.[19]

The truthful elements in Christopher Mont's letter were that Mary and Bothwell had attempted to face it out with the Lords of the Congregation and been defeated. The one-year-old Prince James had been crowned king and his mother was in captivity. She escaped and, on 16 May 1568, fled into England where, for the next nineteen years, she would be Elizabeth's prisoner.

'The monastery of El Escorial is as majestic and sublime as the religion that brought it into being; as severe and melancholy as its august founder.' So says the official guide book and the best way to gain a quick impression of the character of Philip II of Spain is to visit the monastery-palace complex which he planned as soon as he became king and began to build in 1563. It stands on a shoulder of the Sierra Carpentera, commanding a wide plain. It is massive, gaunt, severe of line and intimidating. It is also a religious statement. It was designed as a replica of Solomon's Temple and fronted by imposing statues of six Old Testament kings. At its heart stood the great Basilica of St Lawrence and the royal apartments were so arranged that Philip could watch the celebration of mass through a squint in the wall of his own chamber. Philip made much the same impression on contemporaries as did the building which deliberately mirrored his life. By the mid-sixteenth century Spain had emerged as the first western superpower and its ruler bestrode the world like a colossus, his rule embracing both East and West Indies, as well as much of Europe.

The mariners of other seagoing nations never accepted the division of the globe made two generations earlier when popes had solemnly 'granted' unexplored regions to the rulers of Spain and Portugal but Iberian globalisation was a *fait accompli*. Philip did not doubt for a moment that he owed his position to God and that his paramount responsibility was the extension and defence of Catholicism.

To dedicated Spanish imperialists the potential for further conquest was limitless. Since God was on Spain's side, victory was guaranteed. Philip's agents were forever urging him to advance by faith, even if it meant overextending Spain's impressive, but nevertheless finite, resources. They begged him to drive all Muslims from the Philippines, to annexe North America and even to conquer China. Philip did not dismiss such pipe dreams out of hand; after all, with God all things are possible. But, inevitably, he was more concerned with events closer to home.

The long feud with France had come to an end in the Treaty of Cateau-Cambrésis and Philip was thereafter free to concentrate on his worldwide mission. This involved succouring his colonies in the Americas and the Indies, pouring ships, men and treasure into the struggle against Islam in the Mediterranean and eastern Europe, and doing everything in his power to combat heresy. Yet much as he wanted to extirpate heresy among his European neighbours, the triangular relations of France, England and Scotland presented baffling diplomatic problems. Philip supported the Guise faction in order to restore France's Catholic unity but also because the Calvinists in his Netherlands province would draw encouragement from Huguenot successes south of the border. The same arguments might have persuaded him to go to the aid of Mary Queen of Scots but to strengthen her position would have meant also strengthening France's Scottish relations and provoking English enmity. Although the pope and his own ambassadors urged him to take a firm line with Elizabeth, Philip preferred, for the time being, to preserve diplomatic niceties and court her friendship. He believed – hoping against hope – that she would eventually 'come to her senses' and reconvert.

His preoccupation – his necessary preoccupation in view of its commercial importance – was with the Low Countries. Ironically, it was when this most pragmatic of bigots decided on an impressive show of strength that he set in motion that train of events which would lead to war with England, the Armada fiasco and the progressive collapse of Spanish rule. In the mid-1560s the Protestant revivalism that had swept France and Scotland hit the Netherlands. Calvinist preachers toured the country and radical groups enjoyed the protection of leading nobles. It was not long before iconoclastic mobs were attacking priests and Catholic churches. The outrages were sporadic and the regent, Margaret of Austria (Philip's half-sister), managed to bring most disaffected areas under control with a mixture of force and diplomacy. However, by then Philip had overreacted. He was appalled that such an affront could have been offered to the Catholic church in his own territories. He told one of his own ministers that the news from the Low Countries weighed heavily on his soul. He vowed that the accursed Protestants would pay heavily for their presumption.

The chosen agent of his wrath was the veteran Fernando Alvarez de Toledo, Duke of Alva, who arrived in 1567 with 10,000 Spanish, Neapolitan and German troops. Alva was a byword for ferocity. Over the next six years he arrested and tried 12,000 people and executed at least 1,000, including leading members of Netherlands society. As the new regent he treated his subjects with utter contempt, taxing them heavily and removing several of their ancient privileges. The inevitable results were the resentment of a population who felt their religion and nationhood were being suppressed; emigration of Protestants to England, Scotland, Germany and Switzerland; the emergence of a resistance movement. Opposition was led by William the Silent, Prince of Orange. His base was in Germany but his more effective means of damaging the Spanish imperial regime was a band of pirates-cum-freedom-fighters known as the Sea Beggars who preyed on Philip's shipping and ports.

Of course, news of Alva's atrocities reached England rapidly.

The duke of Alva is clearly acting the part of Phalaris[20] among our Low-Country neighbours. All persons of wealth, of whatever religion, are living in the greatest danger. For men, the rich especially, are daily dragged to execution, without regard to any form of law . . . Our commerce with the Netherlands has been interrupted on this account. Last winter the Spanish vessels, which through the medium of the Genoese merchants conveyed money to Alva from the pope, were driven by a tempest into our harbours, which are both numerous and safe. The sum, I believe, was 300,000 crowns. This sum, sent as it were from heaven, as all the neighbouring nations are raging with war, our queen, that she might have money ready against every emergency, determined to borrow from the merchants themselves, giving sufficient security for the repayment, at a given time, both of the principal and interest; a plan which has often been adopted by other sovereigns. When Alva heard this, he caused all our merchants now in the Netherlands to be arrested, together with their vessels and their freight. Our government did the same both to the Spaniards and Netherlanders. Our merchants therefore are now compelled to exercise their trade at Hamburg, a place far less convenient, and this to the great detriment of the whole of the Netherlands.[21]

Elizabeth's impounding of the 'heaven-sent' Spanish gold, reported here by Bishop Grindal, marked a dramatic shift in relations between London and Madrid. It was not uncommon for maritime traffic through the Narrows to seek shelter from bad weather or pirates which was why English goodwill was so important to Spain. In November 1568 five ships carrying much-needed coin for Alva put into Plymouth and Southampton. It was an opportunity Elizabeth could, quite literally, not afford to ignore. She resorted to legal technicalities to justify hanging on to the treasure. The truculent Spanish ambassador, Guerau de Spes, protested loudly and also urged Alva to take reprisals against English vessels and merchants in the Netherlands. Alva, in turn, responded with his usual outraged impetuosity, imposing trade sanctions which did more damage to the commerce of his own territory than it did to England's. So far from backing down, Elizabeth imposed reprisals against Spanish goods and merchants. What is important about this argument is not the rights and wrongs of it, but the mutual suspicion and the suppressed hostility which provoked it.

England and Spain were already moving towards a state of cold war; this incident simply precipitated something that was in train anyway. The Spanish government was pledged to the full restoration of papal Catholicism. England was emerging as the major obstacle to the achievement of this objective. The one person at the centre of international affairs who refused to believe (or, perhaps, refused to acknowledge) the inevitability of confrontation was Queen Elizabeth. For her, war with fellow monarchs was both economically disastrous and morally repugnant. It was probably for this reason that, in the early weeks of 1569, William Cecil summarized the state of the realm's affairs for the edification of his royal mistress. He pointed out that the years of peace England had enjoyed were the result of good fortune which could not be expected to last. Spain had been preoccupied with its war against the Turks and its need to subdue rebellion in the Netherlands. France was riven by religious strife. Scotland's rulers were dependent on English goodwill and their ex-queen still carried the stigma of Darnley's murder. But all this was likely to change. Islamic hopes had received a severe blow with the death of Suleyman the Magnificent. Protestant minorities were being suppressed in the Low Countries and France. As long as Mary Stuart lived she was the hope of Catholics both sides of the border and a potential marriage prize for royal families intent on making mischief for England. He urged Elizabeth to accept the reality of the situation and shoulder her responsibilities as a Protestant monarch. She should help to establish a reformed European bloc by allying with Denmark, Sweden and the German Protestant princes, while giving generous aid to persecuted Calvinist minorities and strenuously enforcing the Act of Uniformity at home.

Walsingham, by now a trusted friend and colleague of the secretary, agreed with this assessment. Cecil knew his man. Walsingham was passionate about his faith, a straightforward, no-nonsense advocate of reform. He was an earnest patriot with a touch of the xenophobe about him. He also – and this was more to the point – had extensive connections throughout Europe. We have already seen several examples of the kind of correspondence between members of the European evangelical brotherhood who assiduously passed on whatever information and gossip came their way. We need not doubt that Walsingham was in frequent receipt of such letters. Through the Huguenot churches in London and his agents on the south coast Walsingham kept a close watch on cross-Channel comings and goings. In August 1568 he furnished Cecil with a list of suspicious foreigners who had recently entered the country. By this time Walsingham had become one of the few discreet men the secretary could trust to deal with his own secret agents.

One such as Thomas Franchiotto or François, an Italian Protestant living in France and employed there to ferret out the machinations of the Guises. In 1568 Cecil entrusted to Walsingham the interrogation of Franchiotto. The result was a vague, though nevertheless alarming, warning that Catholic activists were plotting to poison the queen. There was a growing number of such reports from about this time. Many lacked substance but all had to be taken seriously – the eternal problem of officials in charge of national security. With Franchiotto's aid Walsingham worried away at the intelligence from France. Members of the Guise faction were talking about sending aid to their kinswoman, Mary Stuart, and provoking Catholic rebellion in England but it was no more than talk; the French court wanted to maintain friendly diplomatic relations with England. When Franchiotto passed on information about troops being embarked in Marseille for an assault on England he may well have been exaggerating in order to underline his usefulness to his paymasters.

Cecil probably entrusted this espionage project to Walsingham because he was preoccupied with a much more sensitive and difficult foreign policy problem which involved him in almost daily attendance on his royal mistress. The Scottish regent, James, Earl of Moray (Mary's half-brother), had sent to Westminster copies of Mary's correspondence (the so-called Casket Letters) which purported to prove her complicity in Darnley's murder. His objective was to justify Mary's deposition in the eyes of the English queen. The letters were a clever mish-mash of documents from Mary's hand put together with interpolations in such a way as to leave no doubt about Mary's guilt. Moray knew it. Cecil knew it. Elizabeth suspected it. She wanted her sister queen to be exonerated and restored to her throne. Cecil was determined that this should not happen. When a tribunal was set up to examine the evidence he manipulated the proceedings. Elizabeth refused to be manoeuvred. She simply called a halt to the investigation. Mary's guilt or innocence was left undecided. No one was satisfied – except Elizabeth, who was becoming highly adept at the game of not committing herself.

Walsingham had clearly made up his mind on the matter and was anxious to do what he could to help. 'I am willed by [Franchiotto],' he wrote to Cecil, 'to advertise you that if for the discovery of the Queen of Scots' consent to the murder of her husband there lack sufficient proofs, he is able (if it shall please you to use him) to discover certain that should have been employed in the same murder who are here to be produced.'[22] This was not intelligence gathering; it was intelligence manipulation. It would be easy to accuse Walsingham of dishonesty but truer, I believe, to charge him with excessive zeal. Determined to protect queen and country from the blight of Catholicism, he was ready to be persuaded that papist plots were everywhere and that Mary Stuart was an unprincipled woman who was an important part of the international conspiracy. If he saw conspirators under every bush it was a fault he readily acknowledged. 'There is less damage in fearing too much than too little,' he advised Cecil. It may well have been his partisanship that kept him away from court. From the vantage point of his ideological mountaintop Walsingham saw, or thought he saw, the whole political landscape in hard-edged clarity and found Elizabeth's irresolution frustrating. Writing to Robert Dudley, Earl of Leicester, less than three years later he observed:

I conceived great hope by your letter of the 16th of August that her Majesty would have taken profit of the late affairs, but finding in her Majesty's letters lately received not so much as any mention made thereof maketh me utterly to despair thereof . . . I beseech your Lordship, do not give over to do what good you may, for it concerneth as well God's glory as her Majesty's safety.[23]

Cecil may well have concluded that, valuable as Walsingham was, he would scarcely fit in well at court. However, he might be just the man for the vacant embassy in Paris.

Chapter 4

'IN TRUTH A VERY WISE PERSON'

1569–73

Sometime in the early autumn of 1569 a political pamphlet hit the booksellers' stalls. It was entitled *A Discourse touching the pretended Match between the Duke of Norfolk and the Queen of Scots*. Its author chose to remain anonymous. However, on two manuscript copies that have survived, the little diatribe is attributed to Walsingham. Was this really the first of his very few ventures into print? To answer that question we need to understand the crisis that provoked it and decide what it was meant to achieve.

During these crucial and sometimes perilous months the two important centres of activity were the Council chamber and the northern border lands. Cecil's behaviour over the seizure of the Spanish gold had opened up a rift among the queen's advisers. Norfolk and Arundel headed a group incensed by policies which, in their opinion, needlessly provoked the hostility of Spain and they used this diplomatic 'blunder' as a crowbar with which to lever the secretary out of office. They tried to have Cecil arrested at the Council table and hustled off to the Tower but a plot that might have worked in her father's day would be quite alien now, given Elizabeth's attitude towards her ministers. Just as Cecil had gone about policy-making without consulting his colleagues, so this faction began planning their own alternative national strategy. Royal marriages were, as ever, uppermost in councillors' minds and, at some point during their brainstorming, the idea emerged of marrying Mary Stuart to the Duke of Norfolk. The proposed theory was that this would facilitate Mary's restoration, which Elizabeth desired, ensure that

Scotland pursued pro-English policies, pacify the major powers and dampen smouldering Catholic discontent at home. But there were those in the plot whose designs were more sinister. There was little cohesion among the schemers (which largely explains their eventual failure). Variations of the plan were abroad, designed to make it appeal to as many supporters as possible. There were those who saw in the scheme nothing more than the solution to the succession problem. Mary's right of inheritance would be restored but with a husband who was, outwardly, a conformist Protestant, the religious settlement would be safe. Then there were covert or overt Catholics in league with de Spes, the Spanish ambassador, and papal agents who hoped to make Mary and Norfolk the figureheads of a movement to remove Elizabeth (by violence if necessary) and restore the old faith.

In the early stages of the intrigue Norfolk and his colleagues sought to widen support for their plans. They sounded out several members of the old nobility, especially the leaders of the northern (and more conservative) shires such as the Earls of Westmorland (Norfolk's brother-in-law) and Northumberland. In August they secured a majority within the Council for the marriage of Mary to a peer of the realm (as yet unnamed). Cecil, still feeling insecure after the earlier attack and also severely ill with gout, had no alternative but to go along with this outwardly. That did not prevent him working against the scheme in his own subtle ways. One of these may have been commissioning the *Discourse touching the pretended Match*.

The author confined himself strictly to a consideration of the character and motivations of Norfolk and Mary and then went on to discuss whether the ex-queen should be married to an Englishman or to a foreign prince. Needless to say, he was not flattering about either of his subjects. Mary was 'a Papist, which is evil, or else an Atheist, which is worse'. She was in alliance with Catholic forces abroad who were set on overthrowing the Protestant regime in England. As to Thomas Howard's faith, all the writer was prepared to say was that he was not 'settled in Religion'. He painted a picture of a popular young nobleman whose affability was a cloak for ambition and who was so weak-willed that he would soon be in thrall to his Scottish wife.[1]

The *Discourse* must have been written between August and early

October 1569, for, after that, events moved rapidly and none of the changed circumstances are referred to in the pamphlet. It certainly expressed or supplemented arguments Cecil was not able to put forward in Council and seems to have been intended for circulation among those members of the political nation who were being canvassed by the Norfolk party. It has some similarities to a memorandum Cecil had drawn up three years earlier when he was worried about the possibility of Robert Dudley marrying Elizabeth. Then he had set out the pros and cons of the queen's match with Dudley as opposed to a union with Cecil's preferred candidate, the Archduke Charles of Austria.

The pamphlet could have been engineered by Cecil but equally it could have been circulated by some opportunist partisan hoping to curry favour with the secretary. In March 1570 it provoked a counterblast – *Answer to a little book that was published against the marriage of the Duke of Norfolk and the Scottish Queen*. The anonymous author had no doubt that the *Discourse* emanated from one of the London Puritan 'brotherhoods' which he proceeded to paint in lurid colours:

> The grand captains among them will seem to have intelligences, yea sometimes from Councillors, such is their audacity. For this is a general rule amongst them that he hath most commendation of them that can learn most news. It anything happen either abroad or at home otherwise than they would have it then straight, their forge is full trimmed till that they have put abroad in lieu of that three or four lies. Thus they spend their time in brewing of mischief, sometimes by devising such pretty pamphlets as this before, sometimes in sending or throwing of letters without name, wherein they have singular felicity to show their rhetorical indicting, sometimes in setting a preacher at work to rail where they list, and for a change of exercise they will make fair weather where they most hate, to see if they can suck out any poison there to set at work their restless mills.[2]

This is basically an accurate picture of the close Puritan congregations who were energetic in exchanging news with their Calvinist friends at home and abroad and in bringing pressure to bear on the leaders of church and state.

Now Walsingham was certainly a member of just such a congregation as the *Answer* castigated. His church, St Giles Cripplegate, was a hotbed of Puritanism. In 1565 the vicar was Robert Crowley, one of the City's leading firebrand preachers and ringleader of the extremist clergy who objected to wearing the vestments ('popish rags') prescribed by the Prayer Book. His incumbency did not last long. In April 1566 he made a scene at a funeral because the lay clerks were wearing surplices. He was promptly deprived of his living. His place was taken by John Bartlett, the lecturer (ie independent preacher supported by the parish), who was not a whit less outspoken than Crowley. The Bishop of London tried unsuccessfully to silence him also and, when Bartlett insisted that it was his duty to instruct his flock, he was placed under house arrest. This provoked an enormous backlash in the parish. Sixty St Giles' ladies besieged the bishop in his palace and it was several hours before they were persuaded to disperse. Not to be deprived of 'sound' preaching, the people of St Giles now secured the services of a young zealot by the name of John Field who was a close colleague of John Foxe and was helping the historian to edit the latest edition of *Acts and Monuments*. Field rapidly grew to be as effective a leader of radical opinion as his predecessor had been. Not only did he organize like-minded clergy into an anti-espicopal brotherhood, he also co-authored the *Admonition to the Parliament*, a trenchant pamphlet urging further reform and spiced with such invective as the denunciation of Elizabeth's Prayer Book as 'an unperfect book, culled and picked out of that popish dunghill, the mass book, full of abominations'. It is scarcely surprising that Field also fell foul of the ecclesiastical establishment and ended up doing a spell in Newgate jail.

This was the kind of Christian ministry under which the Walsinghams sat Sunday by Sunday and with which we may assume they were, at least broadly, in sympathy. The extremists were much encouraged by the support of top people. Crowley boasted that he had 'friends enough to have set the whole realm together by the ears'.[3] It was largely as a result of supporters in high places that

Crowley was later restored to St Giles Cripplegate – though it is significant that he had by then somewhat modified his views. By the mid-seventies the Dudley brothers – Robert, Earl of Leicester and Ambrose, Earl of Warwick – had clearly emerged as the political leaders of a Puritan party. Francis Walsingham was, by then, identified as one of their party. He formed a link between the worlds of headstrong religious extremism and the court and Council. But this does not mean that he was, himself, an ultra-radical.

When we turn to the *Discourse* what strikes us is that it does *not* exude fanaticism. Despite the assertion of the author of the *Answer*, there is no hint in the *Discourse* of violent Puritan polemic or religious radicalism. The author accepts the ecclesiastical status quo and commends the queen's leniency in not pursuing the enemies and critics of her church. 'God be thanked,' he comments, 'that hath so provided for the continuance of religion as he hath given us a prince that favoureth religion.' The writer does allow himself the observation that lack of sound preaching has encouraged popery on the one hand and atheism on the other but there is no suggestion that he is anything other than a loyal member of the English church. He sticks carefully to his chosen subject and if he is dissatisfied with the Elizabethan religious settlement he keeps quiet about it. He pens a reasoned case that Mr Secretary himself could happily have identified with.

What does emerge from the pamphlet is that its author was informed about foreign and domestic affairs. He seems well acquainted with the Guise family – 'a race that is both enemy to God and the common quiet of Europe'. He knows that Murray, the Scottish regent, is so well disposed to Elizabeth that 'during his government she may assure herself of most perfect union'. His honest analysis of the religious sympathies of the English people is that two-thirds of them are inclined towards Catholicism. Here is an author with his finger on the pulse of current affairs.

So far, the attribution of the *Discourse* to Walsingham seems to hold up. However, in the concluding paragraphs an argument is advanced which it is difficult to imagine Walsingham assenting to. The author recommends marrying off Mary to a Spanish or French prince on the grounds that this would sow discord between the two leading Catholic powers. Although Walsingham was among the few political figures in England who embraced a conspiracy theory based on a Rome-Paris-Madrid axis, he would not have advocated such a risky policy of placing in the hands of Valois or Habsburg aspirants a valid claim to the Crown of England. In fact the *Discourse* was the work not of Walsingham but of his close contemporary and fellow lawyer, Thomas Norton.

Norton was one of the up-and-coming politicians of the day and a vigorous, if moderate, Puritan reformer. He married the daughter of Thomas Cranmer, the Archbishop of Canterbury who had been burned by Mary. Norton threw himself zealously into everything he undertook. As well as pursuing his legal profession, he wrote political pamphlets and poetry. With Thomas Sackville he created the early English tragedy *Gorboduc*, a play heavy with contemporary political comment. He entered the Commons in the first parliament of Elizabeth's reign and became one of its most active members, particularly interesting himself in the cause of church reform. He worked in committee with John Foxe and the Puritan publisher, John Day, to produce a modified version of the Prayer Book which, they hoped, would create a consensus on such vexed questions as vestments. Alas, nothing ever came of the this eirenical initiative. It has long been known that, in later years, Walsingham was Norton's patron and that he found the pamphleteer a useful mouthpiece for his own policies. We can now see that the connection between the two men was so close from the earliest days of Elizabeth's reign that Walsingham could be identified by some contemporaries as the author of the *Discourse*.

In the real world of politics the situation rapidly developed beyond the point of academic debate about the Howard-Stuart marriage. In mid-September Elizabeth confronted Norfolk and his nerve broke. He took himself off to his estate at Kenninghall without royal permission. The queen angrily summoned him to return but when he did set out for Windsor (Elizabeth had been sufficiently alarmed to take up residence in her most secure palace) he got no farther than the Chilterns. He was met on the road by armed guards who conveyed

him to Burnham, Buckinghamshire, and the house of Paul Wentworth, Walsingham's brother-in-law. Here the duke was detained in
strict isolation until a military escort arrived on 4 October to convey
him to the Tower. Howard's allies were thrown into confusion. Most
followed their political instinct and hastened to distance themselves
from the unfortunate earl. But in the north, Westmorland and
Northumberland panicked. Ordered to present themselves to the
Council to be examined for their part in the conspiracy, they raised
the standard of revolt. With about 5,500 men they overwhelmed
Durham and marched on southwards, intent on reaching Tetbury
Castle in the Derbyshire Peaks, where Mary Stuart was lodged. For
many of the little army who marched behind banners displaying the
five wounds of Christ this was a Catholic crusade reminiscent of the
Pilgrimage of Grace a generation earlier. An appalled merchant
reported the news that soon reached London:

> While the aforesaid persons were in arms prosecuting their impious
> attempt, they not only threw down the communion tables, tore in
> pieces the holy bible and godly books, and trod under foot the printed
> homilies, but also again set up the blasphemous mass as a sacrifice for
> the living and the dead. And as a farther cloak to their pretended piety,
> they caused some crosses and some banners of certain saints, whom
> they either believed to be their patrons and defenders, or pretended
> they would be, to be carried in procession among their arms.[4]

Ordinary countrymen welcomed the earls' initiative and a mass in
Durham Cathedral was attended by a crowd of worshippers. Their
betters were more circumspect. No men of substance joined the
march. Mary was moved to a fresh place of confinement (her sixth
change of address in a single year) but even had she not been her
rescuers would have found Tetbury a bridge too far. North of York
the rebels faltered and were soon in retreat. By the end of the year the
Northern Rebellion was all over and Elizabeth's generals were
attending to the grisly business of hanging scores of traitors (though
not the 700 victims Elizabeth had demanded). Two years later
Northumberland was handed over by the Scots and executed at

York, where his head was raised on a pole above Micklegate Bar. His co-conspirator eked out a long and dreary life as a pensioner of Spain in the Netherlands.

Meanwhile Cecil's intelligence machine had been hard at work exploring the international ramifications of the plot. Preliminary examination of Howard and his servants at Burnham had thrown up the name of Roberto Ridolfi. Ridolfi, a Florentine banker, was already known to the secretary, because he had volunteered his services as intermediary between Elizabeth and the Duke of Alva with a view to ending the trade war. This was no more than a ploy to worm his way into Cecil's confidence. This shadowy figure has been called a double agent but the term with its overtones of modern spy stories, both fact and fiction, may be too specific. Ridolfi seems to have been one of those people who desire to be among the world's movers and shakers, employ a vivid imagination to conceive grandiose schemes and are plausible enough to take in even experienced statesmen. Like a sinuous snake Ridolfi slithered through Europe's tangled ideological and political jungle, wholly indifferent to the consequences of his intrigues. He was already using his financial activities as a cover to smuggle money from the pope to Mary and her English sympathizers. He was in the Norfolk marriage plot at an early stage and, by the spring of 1569, was working with the arch intriguer Guerau de Spes on a much more far-reaching scheme. With typical panache Ridolfi called it the 'Enterprise of England'. The details of this grand design were changed over ensuing months because they were never more than ill-conceived opportunist ideas tailored to fit the objectives of whomever Ridolfi was negotiating with at the time. The more extreme plans involved the assassination of Elizabeth and her replacement with Mary, married either to Norfolk or Don John of Austria (Philip's half-brother). Constant themes were a popular Catholic rising in England, aided by Spanish gold and troops from the Netherlands. The government urgently needed to make some sense out of the swirling rumours. Clearly Ridolfi had to be interrogated. The man entrusted with the task was Francis Walsingham. On 7 October he received a message from Cecil co-signed by Leicester, who had now thrown his weight behind the Secretary: 'The Queen's

Majesty hath commanded us to write to the Lord Mayor of London for the apprehension of Roberto Ridolfi, whom her Majesty would have remain in your house without conference until he may be examined of certain matters which touch her Majesty very nearly.'[5]

The question that springs immediately to mind is why the softly-softly approach? If it was solely a matter of extracting information, the quickest and most effective treatment for Ridolfi would have been to march him straight to the Tower and give him a sight of the rack. There are various possible answers. It may be that the government, ever short of money, did not want to be heavy-handed with a member of the international banking community. Possibly Elizabeth ordered any inquiries about the sensitive marriage issue to be conducted discreetly. But there could be a deeper motivation: Cecil might have entertained hope of 'turning' Ridolfi and having a mole in the conspirators' councils. Or Ridolfi may have exuded such an air of innocence that the Council hesitated to proceed too vigorously. Our basic problem with the Ridolfi plot is that we do not know for certain who was fooling whom.

If Walsingham was instructed to conduct a thorough, probing investigation, it must be admitted that he made a pretty poor fist of it. Ridolfi remained in his house for six weeks, during which time he was examined at least twice and had his lodgings searched. All he admitted was that he had known about the Mary and Norfolk marriage plan (which, anyway, was the subject of common gossip) and that he had conveyed money to the prisoner-queen. When, on 11 November, Leicester and Cecil wrote to order Ridolfi's release on recognisances there was more than a hint in their letter of dissatisfaction with Walsingham's handling of the situation. The queen, they said, was aware that the Florentine had revealed what he knew 'in part' and that 'if she were disposed to be severe [she] might force him to confess more'.[6]

By January 1570 Ridolfi's bond had been returned to him and, despite the Northern Rebellion and the issuing of *Regnans in excelsis*, he enjoyed complete freedom of movement in England. He employed his time and energies in distributing the papal bull and refining a Catholic plot through communication with Rome, de Spes and

Mary's representative, the Bishop of Ross. Ridolfi was not alone in furthering schemes for a Catholic comeback. The air was alive with plots and Cecil was on the alert to sniff them out. The Spanish ambassador was up to his ears in intrigue. He discussed plans with some Lancashire gentlemen to spirit Mary away to the Isle of Man and confidently reported to his master that, when the trumpet sounded 10,000 good Catholics would spring to arms. In December 1570 he and his associates were examined by the Council – and merely dismissed with a severe reprimand. By this time Norfolk had been restored to liberty and Ridolfi had resumed his secret communication with the duke. The leniency with which the Council handled all these potential traitors and subversives would have been sheer criminal incompetence if there were no reason for it. It is probably correct, therefore, to conclude that the plotters were being deliberately kept in circulation – and under surveillance. Does this provide us with a clue for understanding a tantalizing reference which Walsingham entered into his journal on 24 December: 'I went to the court and had conference with my Lord of Leicester and Mr Secretary about a matter of great importance?'[7]

Cecil never wavered in his conviction that Mary Stuart was a very limb of Satan and that the realm could not be safe until she was disposed of. In this he was completely at odds with Elizabeth and many of his conciliar colleagues. But he was not the sort of man to abandon his principles or prejudices simply because he was in a minority. Few politicians were more subtle or unscrupulous than William Cecil. He meant to prove his point and one way to do it was to allow the conspirators sufficient rope to hang themselves. Through 1570 he watched the comings and goings between the Spanish and French embassies and Mary's household. For some months Walsingham continued to be his go-between with Ridolfi. But Walsingham was not fully in his master's confidence as far as the Florentine was concerned. In October 1570 he could commend Ridolfi to Cecil as a man 'who standeth on terms of honesty and reputation'.[8] Walsingham was not yet the crafty spymaster of legend. Nor, it seems, was Cecil grooming him as an intelligence officer, for in February 1570 he ordered him away from the national centre of intrigue to go on a diplomatic mission to France. In August and September Walsingham attended the French court as special ambassador. Then, at the end of the year, he took up residence as permanent ambassador.

We will return shortly to his relations with the French court but first we must pursue the Ridolfi business through to its conclusion. In March 1571 the banker crossed the Channel and went straight to Alva to refine the Enterprise of England. It was only a few weeks later that, by 'happy chance', his messenger, Charles Bailly, was apprehended at Dover carrying incriminating letters for the Bishop of Ross. Under torture Bailly revealed all he knew about Spanish plans and the machinations of certain English noblemen abroad. Cecil was still having to cope with the aristocratic faction in the Council who resented the influence of a mere commoner. In February Elizabeth had strengthened his hand and confirmed her confidence by raising him to the peerage as Baron Burghley but friends of Howard were agitating for the duke's full restitution to favour and hinting what would happen to Cecil when the 'proper' balance of government forces had been restored. Then, lo and behold, other 'accidental' discoveries were made which gave the international conspiracy almost the appearance of a farce.

One of Philip II's councillors leaked information of his master's plans to a merchant friend, not realizing that he was in Walsingham's pay. What this man revealed was that Ridolfi had gone to Spain and had had audiences with the king. Philip had agreed a plan which hinged upon Elizabeth's assassination during her summer progress. After that Norfolk would mobilize Catholic support at home while Alva assembled an invasion force in Zeeland. This would be transported across the Channel by an Anglo-Spanish fleet. The admiral of the English contingent was to be, of all people, John Hawkins, the notorious privateer and the predator on Spain's transatlantic trade. At Cecil's prompting this master mariner had managed to persuade de Spes that he was resentful of his treatment by Elizabeth and ready to turn his coat. The ambassador and his royal master believed what they wanted to believe because they were engaged in a Catholic jihad. Philip told Alva: 'I hold my charge from God to do this to be so explicit, that I am extremely determined and resolved to proceed . . .

doing on my side everything possible in this world to promote and assist it.'[9] Of all the conspirators the only one who kept a cool head was Alva. He was sceptical of Ridolfi's ambitious plan and unwilling to commit himself until a Catholic rebellion had actually taken place. Perhaps he was also suspicious about the apparent failure of the English government to discover what was going on. Burghley, of course, did know what was going on. The latest intelligence reached him on 5 September. He passed on an embellished version to Elizabeth and was gratified by her angry reaction. Before nightfall he had penned a letter to the Earl of Shrewsbury, Mary's jailer, warning him of a plot to snatch the ex-queen. Across the outside he splashed his directions to the messenger: 'haste, post haste, haste, haste, for life, life, life, life.' Other information had 'chanced' to come his way concerning money, secret codes and fresh correspondence between Norfolk and Mary. It was, he concluded, enough.

Intelligence officers now, as then, feasted on 'abjects, orts and imitations', ever striving to make scraps into a coherent meal. Their political masters frequently go a step further and put their own spin on intelligence to make it say what they want it to say. Cecil did this. Taken as a whole the written and oral evidence he accumulated did not add up to a substantial threat to the state. But in a war of ideologies anything that can conjure up the fear of *potential* horror is valuable. Mr Secretary had more than enough proof to have de Spes sent packing back to Spain, to return Norfolk to the Tower and to steer a state trial to the proper verdict. The news that Elizabethan justice did not stay its hand from plucking down the nation's premier peer would, Burghley hoped, be sufficient to discourage any Catholic fanatics who might put faith above country. It would also demonstrate that Elizabeth's trusted ministers were in control of the situation.

Walsingham meanwhile entered the diplomatic service in Paris very reluctantly. He felt inadequate for the task – and not without reason. He had no experience in the tactful handling of princes and great officers of state. Personal ostentation was quite alien to Walsingham's nature, and to his faith. Extravagance of dress, keeping up with fashion and learning the latest dances smacked of pride and vanity – and they were sins. Flattery and dissimulation proceeded from the father of lies and were, therefore, anathema to him. Although taciturn and tight-lipped in his general demeanour, Walsingham tended to be outspoken and even belligerent in matters that affected his faith. More immediately to the point, he did not have a deep purse. Ambassadors were expected to maintain a large staff, entertain lavishly as a means of enhancing their nation's prestige and to spend whatever was necessary to bribe officials, purchase information and sustain a corps of their own agents. They had to be ready to meet expenses out of their own resources, and rulers were often very sluggish about reimbursing their representatives.

To understand Walsingham's appointment and what it was the government expected of him we need to look closely into diplomatic relations between the major powers. To describe them as tense would be an understatement. We have already seen how Guerau de Spes interpreted his mission. He used underhand methods in the aggressive pursuit of Spanish and Catholic interests and his style was frequently confrontational. Eventually he was adjudged to have overstepped the mark by involvement in the Ridolfi plot and Elizabeth requested his recall. The ambassador had left in a fury of denunciations of the 'heretical' Cecil who, he asserted, was so worried about a resurgence of Catholicism that he had sent the bulk of his fortune to Germany in readiness for a hurried departure.

But the diplomatic waters had been well and truly muddied a couple of years earlier. As her envoy to Spain Elizabeth had nominated John Man, Warden of Merton College, Oxford. It was hardly a sensitive decision. Man was an abrasive religious enthusiast with a talent for rubbing people up the wrong way. During Mary's reign he had been deprived of his university appointments. His arrival at Merton in 1562 had been the signal for unseemly quarrels among the fellows, some of whom resigned rather than submit to the rule of this ardent Calvinist. Man enjoyed the patronage of Archbishop Parker and dedicated to him his translation of Wolfgang Musculus' *Commonplaces of Christian Religion*, 'a body of sound divinity, purged from the errors of popery'.[10] In London Man was associated with the group to which John Foxe and John Field belonged. On the face of it, therefore, he does not seem to have been the most obvious choice as the only Protestant senior diplomat at the Spanish court. The Earl of Arundel was probably not alone among the councillors as being surprised by the appointment of 'a man of low position and small merits'. Man was very soon at the centre of a diplomatic row and the only thing that is surprising about his career in Spain is that it lasted a little over two years. An envoy who engaged in theological argument with his Catholic hosts, distributed Protestant pamphlets and referred to the pope as 'a canting little monk' was never going to win friends and influence people. However, he certainly had right on his side when he demanded – unsuccessfully – that he and his staff should be allowed freedom of worship within the embassy. And, for all his bigoted troublemaking, he did not engage in plots against the monarch, as de Spes did. However, he did infuriate Philip who told Elizabeth that her representative richly deserved to be burned at the stake and demanded Man's recall. The disgraced ambassador, broken in health, made his weary way home in the summer of 1568. He was not replaced. Furthermore, whenever Cecil had occasion to take a tough line with Spain he often dragged up the 'appalling' treatment of Elizabeth's representative.

Men such as de Spes, Man and Walsingham were clearly chosen not so much to smoothe over possible causes of discord as to assert firmly – forcibly when necessary – their government's religious position. But what do we understand the word 'government' to mean? In the case of Spain government meant King Philip, a workaholic bureaucratic monarch who tried to keep his hands on every aspect of foreign and domestic policy. Philip was, as we have seen, a devout son of holy church with a divine mission to extirpate heresy wherever it reared its hydra heads. It is hardly surprising, therefore, to find his representatives maintaining a staunchly Catholic stance.

Elizabeth, on the other hand, was no committed partisan. The main plank of her foreign policy was to keep England out of harm's way by encouraging traditional Franco-Spanish mistrust. It was Cecil and his supporters who wanted her to assume the more positive role of Protestant champion. On the Man incident, the queen claimed ignorance of her envoy's extreme opinions. The fact that he had not fled to foreign Calvinist and Zwinglian havens during Mary's reign persuaded her that her ambassador was a moderate. Her secretary encouraged her in this delusion and Cecil also probably represented Walsingham as a man discreet in matters of religion.

Cecil, now working closely with Leicester, was anxious to replace Sir Henry Norris as ambassador to France. Norris, as well as being a religious moderate, also had a hot line to Elizabeth via his wife, who had been for several years one of the queen's favourite attendants. By contrast Walsingham was Cecil's man and one whose Calvinist convictions were clear cut. The 'forward' party in the Council had an armoury of techniques for 'managing' the queen and steering policy in the required direction. One was forcing the pace in foreign courts through England's ambassadors.

During the twenty-eight months of his residence at the French court Walsingham was charged with two major responsibilities: to support the political aspirations of the Huguenots and to achieve an Anglo-French treaty as a means of containing Spanish ambitions. There were two ways of formalizing cross-Channel friendly relations. The most secure would be a marriage alliance. Failing that, the next best option was a defensive treaty. Since Elizabeth was the only surviving member of her immediate family any political union based on marriage would involve her taking a husband from among the French princes. There were two available among Catherine de Medici's remaining sons; Henry, duc d'Anjou (born in 1551) and Francis, duc d'Alençon (born in 1555). Elizabeth was old enough to be their mother but this did not prevent sporadic negotiations from being carried on with varying degrees of seriousness.

Walsingham's gut feeling was against yoking his queen together with a Catholic consort. In such a situation who would exercise the greater influence? Anjou was not just of the Roman persuasion: he was an ardent Catholic young man under the sway of the Guises. On the other hand, England needed a secure Protestant dynasty in order to survive the international Catholic conspiracy. Elizabeth had to have an heir. This was a real dilemma and Walsingham explained to Burghley how he had struggled with it:

> I was very much perplexed what course to take . . . But when I beheld
> her Majesty first, how she in her own judgement did think it expedient
> for her to marry; secondarily that if her Majesty did mean to marry
> abroad this was the only gentleman fit for her to marry; thirdly the
> discontentment of her subjects for not marrying: fourthly, how
> presently she is beset with a number of foreign practices, the execution
> whereof only stayed upon the event of this natal; I then resolved that it
> was most fit for me to forget myself and to think only of her Majesty
> and her safety.[11]

Dutifully, he threw himself into the negotiations which dragged on
for over a year. They failed finally upon the religious issue: Elizabeth
was not prepared to grant her prospective husband full and unfettered
practice of his faith. That, at least, was the official diplomatic sticking
point. The deeper reality was that, when it came to the crunch,
Elizabeth could not face sacrificing herself on the altar of matrimony.

This left a relieved Walsingham able to concentrate on the more
congenial task of bringing into being a union of states to counteract
the forces of the Counter-Reformation. Walsingham believed that
war with Spain was inevitable. He knew from his various contacts and
paid agents that, though the Enterprise of England might be forced
down Philip's agenda by more pressing items such as war in the
Mediterranean and the Netherlands, it would never be abandoned.
The Ridolfi plot and current events in the Low Countries bore
sufficient evidence of the utter ruthlessness of Catholic reactionaries.
For fanatics the pope's blessing sanctified any and every kind of evil –
treason, murder, massacre, invasion. The Roman juggernaut was a
fearful thing and it would need a stout barrier to halt its progress.
Walsingham, therefore, favoured the creation of a defensive Anglo-
French treaty which might later be extended to embrace the German
Protestant states. In strongly advocating this change of policy he was
moving beyond the role of ambassador and becoming more a
councillor *in absentia*. His frustration arose from the difficulty of
persuading his superiors to share his assessment of the international
situation. From his location at the very hub of European diplomacy he
had a clear view of the movement of events but often his was a voice

crying in the wilderness. Rather like Winston Churchill in the 1930s, Walsingham prophesied impending disaster unless precautions were taken in advance. But Elizabeth was not convinced about Spanish hostility and the French government was seized by political paralysis.

Catherine and Charles formed no consistent programme because they were at the mercy of Catholic and Huguenot factions. In England Reformation had either advanced or retreated because the Crown had given a clear lead and been ready to crush all dissidents. The country was still bitterly divided but the Elizabethan settlement held because Catholic aristocrats had been neutered by shows of force and outmanoeuvred by government intervention in regional politics. In France things were very different. The aristocratic parties headed by the Guises and Coligny had considerable backing throughout the country and did not hesitate to appeal over the king's head to potential supporters in foreign courts. Religious rivalry even intruded itself into the royal family. The duc d'Anjou regarded himself as a Catholic champion and this made his brother, the king, look favourably on Coligny and his friends. Catherine had two major concerns: not to be shouldered aside by any of the faction leaders and to prevent a further outbreak of civil war. But she was almost powerless against the scheming of the politicians, the mental weakness of the king and the fervid religious passions of the populace stirred up by priests, preachers and pamphleteers.

The invidious position of the Crown is well illustrated by an event all Paris was talking about in December 1571. Under cover of darkness a group of workmen armed with picks and crowbars made their way to the rue St Denis accompanied by a troop of the royal guard. They arrived at a gap in the street of modest houses, a place where until two years earlier a dwelling had stood. It had been the home of the de Gastines family who had been arrested and two of whom had been hanged for holding Protestant meetings and worship. Spurred on by power-crazed clergy, their neighbours had then torn the house down to purge the district of all taint of heresy, erecting in its place a crucifix to mark the triumph of the 'true' faith. It was this memorial of persecution that the king ordered to be removed. A self-confident monarch would have made a show of the event, leaving no doubt to the Parisians just who was in charge. Instead, the work was carried out in nocturnal secrecy and under armed guard for fear of a Catholic backlash.

If it is difficult for a modern secular society to understand the intense mutual hatred which possessed Catholic and Protestant combatants in sixteenth-century France, it is only necessary to consider the murderous violence with which rival Sunni and Shia Muslims confront each other in today's Islamic world. The parallel is very close: the legitimizing of violence in a 'holy' cause, the inter-lacing of religion and politics; the fiery oratory of mullahs; the cult of martyrdom; above all the conviction that actions in this world carry eternal consequences of blessing or damnation in the world to come. Events in the early months of 1572 confirmed the international character of the threat facing the Protestant states of Europe. In January Burghley wrote to describe an assassination attempt he had recently escaped. Two young Catholic hotheads had been set up by Borghese, de Spes' steward, to shoot the secretary. The would-be assassins were executed on Tower Hill with maximum publicity and Borghese spent an uncomfortable month in prison before being sent packing after his master.

In May the Catholic church celebrated the election of a new pope. The elevation of Ugo Boncompagni as Gregory XIII was ominous news for England. Gregory was known as an energetic reformer who might be expected to expend enormous energy in the fight against heresy. He was, moreover, a close friend of Philip II. Walsingham was under no illusion about the difficulty of the task facing him. Together with representatives of William of Orange, the German Protestant princes and the Huguenot leaders he laboured to bring about the desired alliance. His principal in this endeavour was the veteran Protestant scholar and councillor, Sir Thomas Smith, sent over by Elizabeth as her special envoy. Negotiations dragged on and on. Catherine and Charles were reluctant to indicate their abandonment of Mary Stuart's cause and even more hesitant about agreeing to support England in the event of attack by a Catholic power. However, on 19 April 1572, Smith and Walsingham at last were able to sign the draft Treaty of Blois.

The new agreement was a remarkable achievement which marked a change of foreign policy direction for both nations. England and France threw in their lot together against the might of Spain. There was the distinct prospect that neighbouring states might join the alliance. Furthermore Charles and Catherine effectively stopped supporting Mary Stuart. Blois might have, for a few years at least, preserved the European balance of power and obliged Philip to reassess his policy towards England and the Netherlands. But such an optimistic outlook failed to take account of the sheer malign energy of the Guises and their religious fanaticism. In the third week of August 1572, the leaders of the Catholic faction made a bid to annihilate their enemies. Coligny and his friends were at the summit of their influence. They had come to Paris to celebrate the marriage of Margaret de Valois, the king's sister, to the Huguenot Henry of Navarre. What was designed as part of the programme of reconciliation was denounced by preachers on the Guise payroll as a 'perverse, Godless union'. On the morning of 22 August a hired assassin took a shot at Coligny as he returned from the Louvre where he had been in conference with the king. According to legend at the vital moment the admiral knelt to adjust his overshoes and took the force of the arquebus blast on his right arm and not in his chest. While the would-be murderer made his planned getaway on horseback Coligny was led away bleeding profusely. But his wound was not mortal. All it achieved was to stir up the Huguenot hornets' nest.

That was good enough for the Guises. Indeed, it may have been precisely what they intended. At a hurried meeting with the king and the queen mother the decision was taken to exterminate the Huguenot leadership (so conveniently gathered in Paris) and to put out the story that Coligny and his associates were planning a coup, which made a pre-emptive strike both urgent and necessary. In the small hours of Sunday 24 August the duc de Guise set out with a troop of a hundred personal and royal guards to tour the lodgings of a score or more Protestant activists and slaughter them in their beds. Thus began the St Bartholomew's Massacre. As news of the atrocity and the king's support for it spread, lynch mobs rampaged through the city in an orgy of bloodletting. Where the Catholics of Paris led, their counterparts in the provinces followed. No precise figures for the carnage can be given but 3,000 deaths in the capital and 10,000 more nationwide are generally accepted to be a modest estimate. France experienced no tragedy on this scale until the Terror of 1793–4.

Number-crunching is irrelevant. What matters is the impact of the massacre on those who had to find their way through the diplomatic debris it had scattered far and wide across Europe. The massacre underlined in blood 'the polarization of rival religious creeds after the closing session of the Council of Trent' and 'meant that politicians increasingly saw themselves as combatants engaged in a cosmic confrontation between right and wrong'.[12] Gregory XIII ordered a celebratory *Te Deum* and issued a medal depicting an angel brandishing a sword and the triumphalist legend 'Huguenots slaughtered'. In Rome the French purge was hailed as the greatest triumph of truth over error since the eradication of the Cathars, three centuries earlier. In the Low Countries the Duke of Alva broke into an uncharacteristically devout paean of praise: 'The events in Paris and France are wonderful, and truly show that God has been pleased to change and rearrange matters in the way that He knows will favour the conservation of the true church and advance His holy service and His glory.'[13] Burghley wrote in a more subdued tone to Walsingham but he, too, invoked Providence: 'I see the Devil is suffered by the Almighty God for our sins to be strong in following the persecution of Christ's members.'[14]

Sadly, we do not have any record of Walsingham's immediate reaction. Possibly his outrage was too fierce to be expressed in writing. The messenger he sent to London with his report of the massacre was doubtless entrusted with a full verbal account of the ambassador's distressing experiences during the days of chaos. We have to rely on later references by Walsingham and others. 'Many of my countrymen, partly of acquaintance and partly of the noble houses of this realm . . . had all tasted of the rage of that furious tragedy, had not your honour shrouded them.'[15] So reminisced Timothy Bright who, as a young medical student, was caught up in the mêlée and for whom the terrifying memory was still vivid seventeen years later.

Francis and his wife were woken early by the sounds of church bells

and distant gunfire. They came from across the river to the ambassadorial residence on the Faubourg St Germain. Walsingham sent to
know what was happening. When his servants returned with dis-
jointed but alarming news Walsingham knew that he had two
responsibilities – to protect his own household and to succour any
of Queen Elizabeth's subjects who might be in danger. He had all
doors and windows barred and bolted and he sent to the king to
demand protection. Later in the morning a troop of royal guards
arrived to keep the mob away from the house. If the Spanish
ambassador is to be believed, the action came too late to save two
of the ambassador's servants who had been dragged out and butchered
by a gang of Catholic thugs. Already men and women fleeing for their
lives were besieging the embassy. Walsingham welcomed them in –
Englishmen, Germans, Netherlanders and a few French Huguenots –
and certainly saved several lives. The refugees exchanged tales of the
horrors they had witnessed in the clamorous, foetid, high-summer
streets. One of the victims of lawlessness was a young Englishman
who had arrived only the day before the troubles to take up the post
of tutor to the sons of a resident English nobleman. When accosted by
the rabble he was given no chance to explain his presence. He was a
foreigner! He was a Protestant! That was enough for him to be cut
down where he stood. Days later Walsingham complained to the king
that three of his countrymen had been murdered. Several more had
been subjected to dreadful indignities. Three of them had been
'treated' to a horse ride through the capital so that they might see
for themselves the piles of corpses in the streets and the bodies floating
in the Seine.

As soon as a measure of calm had been restored Walsingham sent
his wife and daughter back to England and sought an audience with
Charles. It must have been hard for him to preserve the niceties of
diplomatic protocol and he had, understandably, reached the conclusion that neither the king nor his mother could be trusted. His own
inclination was to quit France at the earliest opportunity but for that
he had to await instructions from home. His superiors were urgently
considering their position against a background of popular outrage.
Huguenot refugees were pouring into the country begging asylum –

with all the difficulties that always provokes. Preachers harangued their congregations, pointing out that those – like Alva and Charles IX – who professed papal religion were sworn enemies of the Gospel of peace and reconciliation. Angry pamphleteers demanded reprisals, particularly the immediate trial and execution of Mary Stuart and the tearing up of the Treaty of Blois. For the government matters were not that simple. Recent policy had been based on forging friendly links with France in order to forestall Spanish aggression. Elizabeth could not afford to be at odds with *both* leading Catholic states. Moreover, despite the St Bartholomew horrors, Catherine de Medici was once more urging an Anglo-French marriage alliance – this time between Elizabeth and the youngest French prince, the duc d'Alençon. When Walsingham was summoned to the queen mother's presence he found her trying to unshackle herself from the results of the August events. Like Elizabeth, she was manoeuvring for a position that would allow her maximum freedom of movement. Having obtained his queen's permission, Walsingham begged leave to quit the French court. The king refused, assuring the ambassador that he desired the continuance of good relations with England.

Walsingham was totally unconvinced. As well as the shock he had received on 24 August and the days following, he felt personally betrayed. He had laboured tirelessly in the cause of Anglo-French amity. He had overcome his own initial reservations. He had convinced himself and his superiors that Charles and Catherine's protestations of friendship were genuine. Now he had to report to the Council that he had been wrong. A month after the bloodbath he reported:

Your Honours, by the King and his mother's answers, may see great protestations of amity. I am sorry that I cannot yield that assurance thereof that heretofore I have done, where I may seem to have dealt overconfidently, but I know that your Honours do consider that my error in that behalf was common with a great many wiser than myself, and therefore I hope you do hold me excused.

Seeing now there is here neither regard had to either word, writing or edict, be it never so solemnly published, nor to any protestation made heretofore to foreign princes for the performance of the same;

Seeing the King persecuteth that religion with all extremity that her Majesty professeth . . .

Seeing that they that now possess his ear are sworn enemies unto her Majesty . . . seeing that the King's own conscience . . . maketh him to repute all those of the religion, as well at home as abroad, his enemies . . .

I leave it to your Honours now to judge what account you may make of the amity of this crown. If I may without presumption or offence say my opinion, considering how things presently stand, I think less peril to live with them as enemies than as friends.[16]

In November, writing to Burghley about Charles IX, he stated bluntly: 'I never knew so deep a dissembler.'[17]

Walsingham had to endure his residence in France for a further six months. It was an uncomfortable experience. He was obliged to further policies he did not believe in and negotiate with people he did not trust. At court there were gaps in the personnel which had once been filled by friends now slain. On every day spent in the capital he had to pass houses still bearing the white crosses daubed there by Catholic persecutors to mark the dwellings of doomed Huguenots. The winter of 1572–3, spent separated from his family in what he could only consider an alien land, was long and bitter for him. To make matters worse, by February he had run out of money and was obliged to remain in Paris when the court moved to Moret.

Relief came at last in mid-March. Walsingham received news that the queen had appointed a successor who would be taking up his appointment within weeks. To be fair to the queen and the Council, they had not been unsympathetic to Walsingham's pleas for recall. The problem had been finding someone of Walsingham's calibre to replace him. At least one distinguished courtier who had received the black spot had wriggled out of the honour being offered him. On 19 April he took his leave of the king. Charles expressed his complete satisfaction for everything he had done in the service of Anglo-French amity. Walsingham was, Charles declared, 'in truth a very wise person'. It was not an accolade the Englishman can have found reassuring or flattering.

More gratifying was the message recently received from the Earl of Leicester. 'You know what opinion is here of you and to what place all men would have you unto, even for her Majesty's sake . . . the place you already hold is a councillor's place and more . . . for ofttimes, councillors are not made partakers of such matters as you are acquainted withal.'[18] During his embassy and perhaps for some time before, Walsingham had enjoyed the confidence of Leicester and Burghley. They had shared with their protégé some of their own opinions, anxieties and aspirations – matters they could not open up to conciliar colleagues. Walsingham was the queen's appointee but he understood well the dynamics that operated within the power triangle at the centre of English politics. 'I conceived great hope by your letter of the 16th of August, that her Majesty would have taken profit of the late affairs,' he wrote to Leicester in 1571. 'But finding in her Majesty's letters lately received not so much as any mention made thereof maketh me utterly to despair thereof . . . I beseech your Lordship, do not give over to do what you may, for it concerneth as well God's glory as her Majesty's safety.'[19]

Dudley and Cecil knew their man. They knew what place they would 'have him unto'. The French embassy had been a testing ground and Walsingham had come through with flying colours. He had married firmness and tact. He had shrewdly judged the subtly changing international situation. He had kept himself and his superiors well supplied with valuable intelligence. The basis for his evaluation of men and events was his evangelical commitment and, if he sometimes was over-eager about airing his religious principles, he was learning that there was 'a time to speak and a time to be silent'. Elizabeth was still cautious in her appraisal of Walsingham but she could not deny being satisfied with his performance in France. His mentors were hopeful of seeing him advanced to higher office.

Chapter 5

'TO GOVERN THAT NOBLE SHIP',
ENGLAND
1574–80

Historical perspective inevitably involves foreshortening. Time be-comes concertinaed. Major happenings dominate the narrative. The 'uneventful' periods between them attract only brief notice. As a result we miss the tension and drama which were very real to contemporaries. We are also in danger of underestimating the sig-nificance of events which have not hit the historical headlines. That is certainly true of the years we are about to explore. In the apparent trough between the shock of the St Bartholomew's Massacre and the failure of the Spanish Armada England enjoyed a time of technical peace. But any suggestion of tranquillity and sharp contrast with its war-torn neighbour states is an illusion. This was a period of intense *sturm und drang*. As Walsingham established his place in the govern-ment he and his colleagues were beset by mounting anxieties. Events on the continent, to which they had to adjust, were tumultuous and bewilderingly complex. Meanwhile at home the problem of Mary Stuart had not gone away and England became the target of a massive Counter-Reformation offensive which embraced infiltration by spe-cially trained priests and murderous plots against the queen and her ministers. Yet, in the midst of all these problems the one which preoccupied councillors on a daily basis was their conflict with a politically inept sovereign.

The popular imagination has been dazzled with the Gloriana myth and the accomplishments of Drake, Raleigh and the late-Renaissance dramatists. Under Elizabeth's rule England enjoyed almost thirty years of peace and when it did take on the might of Philip II's Spain it emerged victorious. The basis of maritime and mercantile expansion was well and truly laid in this half-century. Constitutional discord rumbled underground but never broke the surface. Small wonder that, long before the Stuart regime had run its course, men were already looking back wistfully to the golden age of 'Good Queen Bess'. In fact, the Gloriana myth was a construct of the post-1588 era and the more durable results of late-sixteenth-century English history emerged either from politico-economic forces which would have existed whoever was on the throne or the appearance of remarkably talented individuals – or both. If England's garden blossomed in these years it was because it was tended by a group of green-fingered political gardeners who interpreted the wishes of their imperious employer, occasionally ignored them and always brought their own ideas and inspiration to bear. It was the queen's ministers who had personal experiences of life beyond the borders of the realm and who were closer to the realities of life in the English shires. Elizabeth, throughout her entire life, never ventured abroad. In fact she never travelled more than a hundred miles from her own capital. One fact which irritated the queen's ministers when their advice was ignored or overruled was that they really did understand the workings of national and international politics better than she did. In their correspondence among themselves Walsingham and his colleagues grumbled that the queen's decisions, 'groweth out of her majesty's own disposition, whom I do find daily more and more unapt to embrace any matter of weight'.[1] But all they could do was face out the queen's tantrums, endure with patience her procrastination and double-mindedness, shoulder the blame when things went wrong, watch the queen take all the credit for success and, generally, make the best of a bad job.

They certainly did not do what some later commentators have done – confuse style and substance. Elizabeth was a past-mistress at PR. She was a consummate actress. Sometimes Walsingham had to play a supporting role in her amateur theatricals. In March 1576 he was present at an audience the queen gave to the Sieur de Champagny, an envoy from the Governor of the Spanish Netherlands. She wanted to impress the diplomat with her friendly intentions towards

Spain and insinuate that any impression to the contrary had been given by her ministers. Walsingham was scripted as the fall guy. According to Champagny's report, 'The Queen spoke very bitterly to Walsingham, and was so provoked that she struck one or two of her women.'[2] She was, of course, famous for her gracious public speeches, all written and practised for maximum effect, but one gets the impression that even her 'spontaneous' outbursts to her councillors were well rehearsed. Elizabeth's most famous role was that of the Virgin Queen, wedded to her people, but it was just that, a role.

Elizabeth Tudor's primary motivation (one might suspect that it was, at times, her only motivation) was self-preservation. Given the dangers, humiliations and discomforts of her early years it is not surprising that this should be so. Once in power she wrapped herself in a specifically feminine version of monarchical mystique which was reinforced at court by a constant round of plays, masques, pageants, poems and songs, apostrophizing her semi-divine attributes. The queen lived in a stage set of flattering allegory only emerging from it to parade before her people sprinkled with magic dust. Elizabeth had star quality and it was this which impressed diplomats, courtiers, the elite of the shires and those of her humbler subjects privileged to get a glimpse of her. But just as her world was light years away from theirs, so was her heart. She did not love her people.

Had she done so she would have sacrificed herself on the altar of matrimony or, at least, have nominated a successor. For whatever psychological and policy reasons, she rejected the married state for herself and could be very bitter when members of her entourage chose connubiality. (She even had an aversion to married clergy.) Like her father, she feared potential challenge from those who stood in the line of succession. Henry VIII had exterminated all the Yorkist claimants on whom he could lay hands. Elizabeth used other methods to neutralize possible rivals. She tried to prevent Mary Stuart's marriage to Darnley and made the somewhat desperate suggestion that she be united with the Earl of Leicester. The only other close contender was the unfortunate Catherine Grey. She married without the queen's consent and then had the additional effrontery to fall pregnant. Elizabeth was incandescent with rage and sent Catherine to the Tower. The miscreant was released after two years but only to be placed under house arrest with a succession of minders. She was still in her twenties when she died in 1568. Henry Hastings, Earl of Huntingdon, who could trace his descent in the female line from Edward IV's brother, George Duke of Clarence, was long denied office and complained that he and his wife suffered the queen's displeasure through no fault of their own.

'I do not think anything is more enjoyable to this queen than treating of marriage . . . She is vain and would like all the world to be running after her, but it will probably end in her remaining as she is.'[3] The new Spanish ambassador, Guzman de Silva, could express himself frankly in his reports and his assessment of Elizabeth's character accurately depicts one side of her personality. She *was* vain – and jealous and possessive and vindictive and petulant. Her principal courtiers, no less than genuine suitors, had to play elaborate love games and she relished the power that this gave her over them. She flirted outrageously with the leading men in her life and if they happened to be married she banned their wives from court because she could not tolerate rivalry for their affections.

To this luxuriant demi-monde of extravagant make-believe Francis Walsingham was a complete stranger. Though the role of secretary involved almost daily attendance on the queen and residence in the court wherever it happened to be, he was in this world but not of it. He could never have brought himself to play the beribboned fop or the macho champion of the tennis court or the tiltyard. Elizabeth was never comfortable with his dour and earnest evangelicalism. But she was wise enough to know that she needed his detailed knowledge of the political scene and his down-to-earth advice. For his part, Walsingham saw it as his duty to open for the queen windows on to the real world, so that she might understand where her best interests lay and, therefore, the policies which she should pursue. Theirs was an uneasy relationship based, not on affection, but on mutual respect – he for her position; she for his abilities.

> This only thing is wanting in you, that you write more at length and more fully respecting the state of the times and the dispositions of men;

and this the rather, in proportion as the times in which we live are abounding in dangers, and the dispositions of the men with whom we have to contend, are not without their infinite recesses and deep concealments.[4]

So Walsingham wrote in 1577 to his old friend, the Strasbourg scholar, John Sturmius, and this typical snippet from one of his thousands of letters helps to explain the reasons for his promotion to a place among the nation's political leaders. He lost no opportunity to keep himself abreast of current affairs. In December 1573 Francis Walsingham was sworn a member of the Council and joint principal secretary. Burghley had resigned five months earlier on his appointment as Lord Treasurer (though he remained active in all areas of policy) and had been replaced by Walsingham's erstwhile colleague, Sir Thomas Smith. Smith was regarded as one of the most upright diplomats of the day but he could not match Cecil for mental agility and sheer stamina. He was sixty years of age, experienced indifferent health and found attendance on the procrastinating queen (especially on progress) a severe trial. 'I can neither get the other letters signed nor the letters already signed sent away,' he once complained. Elizabeth was always putting him off with 'anon' and 'soon' and 'tomorrow'. We will soon need a horse or an ass to carry the mounting volume of unfinished business, he grumbled. 'I would some other man occupied my room who had more credit to get things resolved in time.' At last Walsingham was appointed to help him.

The letter to Sturmius reveals a man with extensive contacts throughout Europe; a man gifted in intelligence-gathering; a perceptive intellectual who saw the bigger picture in a world 'abounding in dangers', a diplomat experienced in dealing with duplicitous and devious foreigners, and, above all, an evangelical who viewed time through the magnifying lens of eternity. All these qualities appealed to the moderate Puritan majority on the Council who were anxious to have Walsingham among their number.

Elizabeth's delay in ratifying the appointment may suggest that she did not share their enthusiasm. She and most of her advisers came at the problems of international and internal affairs from very different angles. Cecil, Dudley, Bedford, Walter Mildmay and Warwick all shared a basically 'theological' interpretation of politics. They were defenders of biblical truth against the demonic forces emanating from Rome. They recognized in Walsingham a fellow spirit who was more forthright than any of them in his Puritan zeal. And he had witnessed the perfidy and cruelty of Catholic leaders at first hand. Could anyone be a more effective advocate than the ambassador who had been through the refining fire of St Bartholomew's? Walsingham's straightforward, black-and-white understanding of the responsibilities of a Protestant monarch were easily stated:

> What juster cause can a prince that maketh provision of the Gospel have to enter into wars than when he seeth confederacies made for the rooting out of the Gospel and the religion he professeth. All creatures are created to advance God's glory. Therefore, when his glory is called in question, no league nor policy can excuse if by all means he seek not the defence of the same, yea with the loss of life.[5]

Elizabeth was no less a conviction politician but her convictions were different. Fundamental to her philosophy was the principle of divine right. Monarchs were ordained by God and drew their authority from him. Rebellion, even in the name of religion, was anathema. It could not but throw the whole created order into confusion. This was why she hesitated to aid Protestant dissidents in France and the Low Countries. It was why she refused to hand Mary Stuart over to her own people for trial. She declined to incur the expense of foreign war because wars cost money and money meant raising taxes and taxes necessitated the calling of parliament and parliament was sure to raise issues which were none of their business – marriage, succession and the fate of the Scottish ex-queen. Behind such impertinences, as Elizabeth well knew, lay the Calvinist doctrine that sovereignty is vested in the people; that rulers may be held to account by their subjects; that, in the last analysis, those adjudged tyrants can be removed from office.

These conflicting humours in the body politic which would, in the next century, bring the patient to death's door, were held in balance by the quite remarkable relationship Elizabeth created with the other elements in the political nation. She never attended Council meetings and thereby avoided arguing out tricky subjects with her advisers. By distancing herself from her councillors she obliged them to pay court to her, presenting the results of their deliberations for her approval. By making them wait for answers she put them in their place. Delaying difficult decisions was sometimes disastrous but it kept her ministers on their toes and occasionally the problems went away of their own accord. The fact that she was a woman had the advantage that she could get away with things no king would have dared attempt. Her speeches to parliament were well-rehearsed masterpieces of mild chastisement mingled with heart-melting protestations of love. Closing the session of 1567, for example, Elizabeth rounded on the House of Commons for meddling with the succession and claiming to do so by the right of free speech:

I have in this assembly found so much dissimulation, having always professed plainness, that I marvel thereat – yea two faces under one hood, and the body rotten, being covered with two visors: succession and liberty . . . they thought to work that mischief which never foreign enemy could bring to pass, which is [my] hatred of my Commons.

Having delivered her rebuke, Elizabeth changed the mood of her oratory. She would not send MPs home muttering, with their tails between their legs.

[D]o you think that either I am unmindful of your surety by succession, wherein is all my care, considering I know myself to be mortal? No, I warrant you. Or that I went about to break your liberties? No, it was never my meaning, but to stay you before you fall into the ditch. For all things hath his time. For although perhaps you may have after me one better learned or wiser, yet I assure you, none more careful over you.[6]

Specifically, Elizabeth was determined to retain the Crown's control of all matters religious which had been won by her father. Henry VIII had freed the English church from papal shackles. She would not permit it to be fettered by manacles manufactured in either Rome or Geneva. Given these fundamental differences, the relationship between sovereign and principal secretary was never going to be easy.

One problem facing the holder of the secretary's office was that it was undefined. It was whatever its holder chose to make of it. Since 1530 there had been thirteen principal secretaries, some serving jointly. Of these, the majority had been little more than senior bureaucrats, preparing Council agendas, recording decisions, obtaining royal signatures or seals to documents, despatching messengers, receiving reports and, in fact, oiling the machinery of government. The two great exceptions had been Thomas Cromwell and William Cecil. They had used their unique position of intermediaries between sovereign and royal Council to become framers of policy.

It was not in Walsingham's character to be any less influential. Strong convictions coupled with integrity and a tireless capacity for hard work meant that he would, if he remained in office, play a leading role in the Council. The next five years witnessed the steady development of his influence, assisted by the strong bond he enjoyed with the Earl of Leicester. It was a formidable alliance, forged for both ideological and pragmatic reasons. No one was a better conduit to the queen than her old and closest friend, Robert Dudley. When bad news or unwelcome advice had to be conveyed from the Council the earl was usually the appointed messenger and his persuasive powers were formidable. As the 1570s progressed Leicester committed himself increasingly to the Puritan interest. He used his patronage, particularly in the Midlands, to insinuate radical ministers and lecturers into churches. In view of the fact that Protestant zealotry was the one subject on which Dudley and Elizabeth fundamentally disagreed, the extent to which he was prepared to go in support of his radical protégés is remarkable. During the years Walsingham had spent in France battle royal had raged between Leicester and the Bishop of Peterborough, Edmund Scambler, over the behaviour of Percival Wiburn. This ardent preacher had already been deprived of his benefice in London for refusing to wear 'popish rags' when Leicester appointed him to a living in Northampton. Within months Wiburn had set up a Presbyterian style of church order in which clergy and magistrates worked together to uphold a regime of enforced moral standards and attendance at sermons. As soon as the bishop intervened Wiburn turned to his patron for aid. Poor Scambler was in an invidious position. 'Although your lordship doth like the substance of his doctrine – or the most part thereof, even so do I,' he patiently explained to the earl, 'yet know you not . . . as I do, the contentions and [discord] that is in Northampton . . . about matters, ceremonies and things indifferent, about which he showeth as much vehemency as about the principal grounds of religion.'[7]

By the time Walsingham received a knighthood in December 1577 the quadrumvirate which would guide English affairs for the next, crucial, decade had come into being. Elizabeth ruled with the guidance of her closest confidant, Robert Dudley, her most trusted political adviser, William Cecil, and Francis Walsingham, whom she valued because of his unique grasp of international affairs. Professor Collinson has suggested that we might think of Walsingham as foreign secretary to Burghley's prime minister. However, the mid-seventies to mid-eighties were to be a period of constant anxiety and frustration and more than once Walsingham came close to resigning.

In works of period fiction and also in some popular non-fiction accounts Francis Walsingham has become 'her majesty's spymaster'; a sinister figure who created an intelligence web for trapping those he regarded as enemies of the state. It is not difficult to see why this Machiavellian image finds such ready appeal. Puritans are never popular and critical commentators always enjoy pointing out flaws in religiously earnest 'hypocrites'. Sympathy for the hapless Queen of Scots inevitably spawns animosity for the man who was her nemesis. Walsingham lacked star quality. He was a dour workaholic, not a court exotic like Dudley or Hunsdon, or a political genius like Cecil. It is easy, therefore, to force him into the mould of a dark master of intrigue. Such an oversimplification obscures his real contribution to the middle years of Elizabeth's reign.

Francis Walsingham certainly did head up an official intelligence and counter-intelligence service. But we must be careful in using such terms. England in the 1570s and 1580s bore some comparison with England in the 1970s and 1980s. The country was in a state of cold war in a world where powerful ideological rivals were counterposed. Suspicion, anxiety and fear coursed like stimulants through the bloodstream of international relations, keeping diplomats and states-men on the alert. This is the climate in which espionage most luxuriantly flourishes. Governments desperately need to know what their potential enemies (and, indeed, their allies) are planning. Accurate intelligence has to be gathered as rapidly as possible. If communication is unreliable or too slow the results may be disastrous. But we must not allow our conception of Walsingham's activities to be coloured by the cloak-and-daggery of twentieth-century espio-nage. Elizabethan intelligence-gathering was unsophisticated, hapha-zard and non-specialized. Today's MI5 and MI6 agents are subordinate to their political masters. They are charged with gathering information by employing informants, moles and high-tech surveil-lance technology. They make reports to their political masters. It is the latter who decide what action if any should be taken. Billions are lavished by the major powers on the gathering and analysing of intelligence (and they can still make the most appalling mistakes).

Sixteenth-century methods were different, not only in being, inevitably, more crude, but also more diffuse. There was no specialist body at the service of the queen and her councillors. The queen and her councillors *were* the ones who gathered and assessed intelligence and acted on it. Elizabeth, Dudley, Burghley, Walsingham, the leaders in church and state – all had their own networks. Nor should we assume that news about the activities of foreigners and potential native troublemakers was always pooled for the good of the state. Individual Council members were not above carrying on their own negotiations without the knowledge of their colleagues and Elizabeth certainly went behind the backs of her advisers. For example, in 1581 the queen and Leicester spent several months in secret correspon-dence with d'Aubigny, James VI's favourite, at the very time that official policy was bent on undermining the Frenchman's influence. And there were certainly occasions on which Walsingham withheld from the queen information which, be believed, would provoke an unhelpful response.

Intelligence-gathering was only one of Walsingham's many activities. We can learn a great deal about the scope of his responsibilities and his handling of them from a treatise written by Robert Beale, someone who knew Walsingham and his methods better than most. Beale was ten years younger than the man who became his patron. Like Walsingham he had a legal and bureaucratic background but, more importantly, he shared Francis' Puritan faith. If anything, he was even more extreme in his views. In Mary's reign, though he was only a teenager, he went into exile in Strasbourg and Zurich. By the time of his return Beale was well versed in law and theology. In 1564 he went to Paris where he later found employment with the English ambassador, Sir Henry Norris. Walsingham inherited Beale when he took over the embassy in 1570 but was certainly acquainted with him before then for it must have been sometime in the 1560s that Beale married Walsingham's sister-in-law, Edith St Barbe (Ursula Walsingham's sister). Beale acted as his brother-in-law's secretary in Paris and shared with him the harrowing events of the St Bartholomew's Massacre. Shortly afterwards, doubtless on Walsingham's recommendation, Beale was advanced to the position of clerk to the Council. When Walsingham was secretary Beale was his right-hand man. Theirs was more than just a professional relationship. When Walsingham moved to a more commodious London residence in Aldgate Ward, called the Papey, Beale built himself 'a fair house' in nearby St Mary Street. When in 1579, Walsingham was granted by the queen the lands of what he modestly called a 'cottage' at Barn Elms on the Surrey bank of the Thames near Richmond Palace as his principal country dwelling, Beale also relocated there. The two families were obviously very close. Professionally, Beale enjoyed his superior's complete trust. He deputized for Sir Francis when the latter was absent from the Council board and was often employed as Walsingham's emissary in sensitive situations.

In 1592, the seasoned diplomat, Sir Edward Wotton, was angling for the post of principal secretary (vainly, as it transpired) and Robert Beale wrote for him an account of what was involved. As well as providing a list of the senior bureaucrat's duties, it also provided an insight into Walsingham's methods, not all of which Beale approved.

The secretary's usefulness – and his power if he chose to wield it – lay in his omniscience. As the framer of the Council's agenda he knew (theoretically, at least) all its business and could manipulate discussion. He received diplomatic despatches, correspondence from foreign courts and the hundreds of letters which arrived weekly from all sorts and conditions of men and women, most of them suing for royal favours. The secretary had to use his judgement to sift the wheat of important affairs from the chaff of matters to be delegated to other government officers. Items for Council debate had to be skilfully arranged so that pressing affairs could be dealt with promptly. The secretary had to make digests of complex documents 'lest the rest of the Lords will not have them all read, or shall not have leisure'.[8] Meticulous records of Council business had to be kept by the clerks – as much for the secretary's own security as for general efficiency. If resolutions were not signed as having been approved by the members present, the secretary could find himself stranded; his colleagues denying knowledge of any decision which might prove unpopular with the queen.

The first and easily overlooked characteristic of Walsingham's tenure of office is that the Council emerged as a government parallel with the monarch. Technically its role was advisory and administrative but in that it gave long and detailed consideration to all important issues and in that the queen was never present at its deliberations there was an inevitable separation between Crown and Council and the authority of the latter grew. Before Walsingham's time it was normal for the group to converse three or four times a week. By the Armada year Council meetings were almost a daily phenomenon and lasted several hours. This, doubtless, reflects the growing complexity of international affairs but also indicates Walsingham's diligence. Inevitably, councillors, who were busy men with household and other responsibilities, could not maintain 100 per cent attendance and the secretary was, at times, hard pressed to ensure a quorum. In these years there were about twenty Council members but normally between six and nine turned up for meetings, the most regular being Leicester, Burghley, Walsingham, Sir Francis Knollys (Treasurer of the Household), Sussex (Lord Chamberlain), Lord Howard of Effingham (Lord Privy Seal) and Sir James Croft (Controller of the Household). These men constituted a kind of executive cabinet. As Professor Collinson has observed 'at times there were two governments uneasily co-existing in Elizabethan England: the queen and her council'.[9]

Elizabeth was determined to maintain her supremacy and she never allowed her advisers to forget that that was exactly what they were – advisers. She could and did on occasion countermand their decisions. This could be incredibly frustrating for Walsingham and his colleagues, who believed, usually correctly, that having debated a subject at length and taken account of all the relevant facts, they knew better than their mistress what was needed. 'My Lords here have carefully and faithfully discharged their duties in seeking to stay this dangerous course, but God hath thought good to dispose otherwise of things, in whose hands the hearts of all princes are.'[10] So the long-suffering Walsingham wrote to the President of the Council of the North in April 1581. The colleagues had authorized a force of 1,000 men to cross the border. Subsequently Elizabeth had sent instructions that this force be reduced by half. Only hours later she had decided that there was to be no military action at all.

It is hardly surprising that Beale's advice included stratagems for handling the equivocating queen. He should keep a list of important things that needed to be done in order to be able to advance them whenever his mistress was in a good mood. Forewarning of that mood was vital: 'Learn before you access her Majesty's disposition by some in the privy chamber with whom you must keep credit . . . When her highness is angry or not well disposed trouble her not with any matter which you desire to have done, unless extreme necessity urge it.' Since Elizabeth had an almost pathological aversion to committing herself to any course of action, her secretary should be ready with diversionary tactics: 'When her highness signeth, it shall be good to entertain her with some relation [i.e. anecdote] or speech whereat she may take some pleasure.' As Beale knew, such subtleties did not come easily to Walsingham. Though cunning in his dealings with adversaries, he preferred plain speaking in court and Council. Because he was a man of strong convictions he tended to feel personally affronted when the queen rejected his advice. Beale doubtless had his old friend's difficulties in mind when he counselled:

> Be not dismayed with the controlments and amendments of such things which you shall have done, for you shall have to do with a princess of great wisdom, learning and experience . . . Princes themselves know best their own meaning and there must be time and experience to [become acquainted with] their humours before a man can do any acceptable service.

Walsingham may have paid lip service to that principle but he never really believed it. He frequently grumbled at Elizabeth's indecisiveness, spoke about resigning and absented himself from court with pleas of ill-health. He suffered from a variety of ailments, foremost among which was a longstanding urinary disorder, but there were times when it was only weariness of spirit that kept him from court. So far from accepting that the queen always knew best, Walsingham did not flinch from protesting to her in person. In September 1581, driven to distraction by Elizabeth's dithering over marriage with Anjou and her declining, for financial reasons, to enter a Protestant league, Walsingham delivered himself of a long more-in-sorrow-than-anger homily:

> I cannot deny but I have been infinitely grieved to see the desire I have had to do your Majesty some acceptable service . . . so greatly crossed . . . I will leave to touch my particular [circumstances] though I have as great cause as any man that ever served in the place I now unworthily supply, being at home subject to sundry strange jealousies and in foreign service to displeasure . . . If either ambition or riches were the end of my strife my grief would be the less. But now to the public [matters] wherein if any thing shall escape my pen that may breed offence, I most heartily beseech your Majesty to ascribe it to love, which can never bring forth evil effects, though sometimes it may be subject to sharp censures. And first, for your Majesty's marriage. If your

Majesty mean it, remember that by the delay your Highness useth therein, you lose the benefit of time . . . If you mean it not, then assure yourself it is one of the worst remedies you can use. And as for the league we were in hand withal . . . Common experience teacheth that it is as hard in a politic body to prevent any mischief without [expense] as in a natural body diseased, to cure the same without pain. Remember, I humbly beseech your Majesty, the respect of [expense] hath lost Scotland and I would to God I had no cause to think that it might put your Highness in peril of the loss of England . . . It is strange, considering in what state your Majesty standeth, that in all the directions that we have now received, we have special [instruction] not to yield to anything that may be accompanied with [expense] . . . Heretofore your Majesty's predecessors, in matters of peril, did never look into the [expenses], when their treasure was neither so great as your Majesty's is, nor subjects so wealthy nor so willing to contribute . . . If this sparing and unprovident course be held still, the mischiefs approaching being so apparent as they are, I conclude therefore, having spoken in heart of duty, without offence to your Majesty, that no one that serveth in place of a Councillor, that either weigheth his own credit, or carrieth that sound affection to your Majesty as he ought to do, that would not wish himself in the farthest part of Ethiopia rather than enjoy the fairest palace in England.[11]

Elizabeth found it hard to stomach outspoken criticism, especially when it came from the likes of Walsingham, Archbishop Grindal or Paul Wentworth, Puritans who claimed that their high allegiance to God justified their 'froward' attitude towards their sovereign. When the queen was in a bad mood Walsingham was often the first to feel the rough edge of her tongue. Beale's advice in such circumstances was: 'Bear reproofs, false reports and such like crosses, if they be private and touch you not deeply, with silence or a modest answer. But if it be in company or touch your allegiance, honour or honesty mine advice is that you answer more roundly lest your silence cause standers-by to think ill of you.'

Walsingham also had to be conscious of his relationships with other Council members. He was their social inferior and, therefore, vulnerable. Beale pointed out the danger of the secretary becoming embroiled in personal and group rivalries. 'Take heed you do not addict yourself to any faction that you may find among the councillors. You shall find they will only use you for their own turns and, that done, set little by you afterwards.'

Walsingham was fortunate in that the majority of leading councillors were united on most issues. He naturally gravitated towards Dudley, the leader of the Puritans and the champion of a more aggressive foreign policy. Burghley's voice was more often heard urging caution but the differences between the two noblemen were differences of degree rather than kind. However, in the claustrophobic atmosphere of court and Council chamber, it was impossible that personal rivalries and clashes over policy would not occur.

Between Leicester and Sussex there was a long-established and deep-seated animosity. They quarrelled over most major policy issues – religion, Ireland, the Anjou marriage, relations with Spain and the Netherlands. Early in the reign the two nobles had openly headed court factions and their supporters had worn coloured favours. By the 1580s they confined themselves to heated exchanges across the Council table but even these could turn nasty. In July 1581 Elizabeth had to order them to their rooms like squabbling adolescents and six months later Burghley had to separate them when they came to blows. It should be the secretary's concern, Beale suggested, to smoothe over disagreements rather than take sides.

Unity in the face of political crisis and a termagant queen was vital. Walsingham made sure that he never found himself stranded between Elizabeth and her Council. His caution was endorsed by Beale. 'When there shall be any unpleasant matters to be imparted to her Majesty from the Council . . . let not the burden be laid on you alone but let the rest join with you.'

It is in his reference to Walsingham's intelligence-gathering responsibilities that Beale reveals to us his brother-in-law's fundamental dilemma. His restless diligence and ingrained sense of duty, combined with his conviction that England stood with its back to the wall, facing packs of baying Catholic hounds, drove him to extend his energies and his purse beyond their limits. He lost no opportunity to acquire sources of information. These included 'honest gentlemen in all the shires cities and principal towns'; diplomats; merchants, mariners and others whose work took them abroad; Huguenots and other Protestant friends; foreign courtiers who could be bribed to be Walsingham's eyes and ears; as well as a handful of trained agents placed strategically in over forty centres throughout Europe. Maintaining this network, as well as paying self-appointed informants who thronged Walsingham's office hoping to profit from items of gossip they had for sale, was enormously expensive. As well as the agents, Walsingham had to pay a large staff of clerks and scribes, some of whom were linguists or codifiers. Accurate figures for espionage work are notoriously difficult to come by. Privy Seal warrants suggest a steady increase in payments from £750 in 1582 to more than £2,000 in 1588. But Beale intimates that Walsingham received other payments from the Privy Seal of which he kept no adequate record. An estimate of 1610 makes the figures leap from £5,753 to £13,260 over the same period which suggests that Walsingham received royal funds via other channels. In addition he did not shrink from making payments from his own pocket. Beale commented that the queen was far from pleased with the scale of secret service expenditure and he added his own observation that Walsingham employed too many office staff. He seems to suggest that an unnecessary number of clerks were privy to confidential information and there can be little doubt that foreign spymasters were as adept as he at planting moles. It would be safe to say that, during Walsingham's tenure of office, expenditure on the intelligence services trebled or quadrupled. Beale writes approvingly:

> In the time of the ambassages of M. La Mott and Mr Mauvesieur [Bertrand de Salignac de la Mothe Fénelon and Michel de Castelnau, Seigneur de la Mauvissiere, French ambassadors 1568–75 and 1575–85 respectively] he had some of [their] secretaries that betrayed the secrets both of the French and Scottish dealings. In Scotland he was well beloved of many of the nobility, ministers and others, whom he relieved when they were banished into England. With money he corrupted priests, Jesuits and traitors to betray the practices against this realm.

Walsingham's labours in this aspect of his job demanded Herculean fortitude combined with Minerval wisdom. The torrent of information pouring on to his desk had to be sifted and assessed, as did the trustworthiness of those who supplied it. 'Be not credulous, lest you be deceived,' Beale advised. 'Hear all reports but trust not all. Weight them with time and deliberation and be not liberal of trifles. Observe them that deal on both hands [ie double agents] lest you be deceived.' And when the intelligence had been assimilated and the necessary letters written to forward it elsewhere, messengers had to be despatched, for which purpose Walsingham kept a stable of sixty horses.

Beale's final advice was couched in pious terms:

> Beware that before God and the whole world you can give a good account of your councils and actions to be void of impiety, covetousness, envy, maliciousness, injustice and fraud.
>
> Wherefore you must be circumspect and pray to God, from whom every good gift proceedeth, to direct you by his holy Spirit. Do nothing against his word, which ought to be your lantern, way and direction. First, briefly examine all your Councils and actions according to the rule of the Ten Commandments, doing nothing that is prohibited in any of them, for (as the Apostle sayeth), 'no evil action can produce a good result'.
>
> And the Prophet cryeth out a woe unto them that take council without him and [do] grievous things, who shall not escape in the day of the visitation of the Lord.
>
> Grieve not your own conscience and keep yourself as near as you may to the maintenance of the laws and liberties of the land. Decline from evil and do good. Beware of too much worldly policy and human wit.

Walsingham certainly kept his inner eye focused on such sound evangelical advice but in the hard world of devious sixteenth-century politics it was not always easy to live by it.

Viewed from the point of national religion there is a common misconception that Elizabeth's reign presents us with a mirror-image of Mary's: there was an official national church and those who opposed it were persecuted. Mary burned Protestants. Elizabeth had Catholics hanged, drawn and quartered. Under both regimes men and women of conscience took themselves into exile. Succoured by their co-religionists, many engaged in propaganda attacks on the land of their birth and a few indulged in political action. Such a simplistic analysis may appeal to the British instinct of sympathy for the underdog and that variety of toleration which appeals to an agnostic age – a toleration born of expediency out of indifference. In the sixteenth century few, if any commentators believed (or were bold enough to state openly) that all faiths are equally valid or invalid and may, therefore, coexist peacefully within the state. When Walsingham complained to Catherine de Medici about the 1572 massacres, she responded that King Charles was determined to have only one church in France – just as, she cannily pointed out, Elizabeth would only tolerate one English church. In the closing years of Elizabeth's reign Richard Hooker asserted in his *Laws of Ecclesiastical Polity* what his royal mistress certainly took as axiomatic, that an Englishman and a Christian were the same animal viewed from different perspectives. Political loyalty and religious devotion were intertwined and demonstrated in conformity of worship.

What does not follow from this is that Catholic and Protestant regimes dealt in the same way with dissidents or adopted the same strategies for world mission. Rome's religion was power based. Its procedures for dealing with heretics had been honed over centuries. The Inquisition ferreted them out. The Index identified books possession of which was proof of enmity towards the truth. Ecclesiastical courts tried and condemned suspects. Pressure was brought to bear on princes and aristocrats to see sentences carried out. By such well tried processes almost 300 Protestants went to the stake in Mary Tudor's reign. During the forty-four years that Elizabeth was on the throne, 183 Catholics were executed. And, of course, the figure pales into insignificance compared with the severe campaigns of repression carried out by Catholic regimes in Spain, France, Italy, the Netherlands and some of the small central European states.

Catholic and Protestant mindsets concerning the eradication of heresy were very different. Their attitudes had both political and theological aspects. All sixteenth-century rulers of church and state removed dissidents in order to preserve unity and uniformity. For centuries this had been the motive, whether openly acknowledged or not, for disposing of stubborn heretics. But there had to be justification for imposing a capital sentence. The Catholic mantra which vindicated the decision to hand over a condemned heretic to the secular arm for execution was: 'We destroy the body to save the soul.' The errant member was removed from the world of men so that he could lead no more of them astray and despatched to purgatory where he could atone for his sins and, perhaps, ultimately attain blessedness. Protestants did not believe in purgatory. The individual had to make his peace with God in this world, for beyond it there awaited only the final judgement. Therefore, to put someone to death was to remove from him the possibility of salvation once and for all. The church had no 'licence to kill'. No one could be cut off from the living on the grounds of faith. Vengeance belonged only to God. Elizabeth and even her more radical councillors were not prepared to do his job for him. They prided themselves that they did not descend to the barbarity of the auto da fé and the government-sponsored lynch mob.

But it *was* their duty to preserve the integrity of the state. The Act of Uniformity had required clergy to use the Book of Common Prayer on pain of forfeiting a year's salary and the laity were instructed to attend divine service or pay a fine of one shilling. For the first ten years of the reign this legislation was enforced sporadically and without the vigour that a centrally directed campaign would have provided. Then had come Pius V's declaration of war in the bull *Regnans in Excelsis* and the Ridolfi plot. Following these scares, parliament tightened the recusancy laws in 1571. Yet, as far as English Catholics were concerned, life went on much as before. Occasionally an order went out from the Council to magistrates and bishops to draw up lists of people who absented themselves from their parish churches but any 'persecution' was for the most part half-hearted. It took the terrorist and invasion scares of the 1580s for the government to tighten the screws on English Catholics.

★   ★   ★

Walsingham could not have reached the pinnacle of his public career at a more critical time for the nation. It was not just that the French massacre sounded a wake-up call for all who had reason to fear a reinvigorated Roman Catholicism. The pontificate of Gregory XIII saw the centralization of papal power and the energetic application of the Counter-Reformation. The new pope urged Philip II to lead a crusade against the heretic island and encouraged the plots of free-enterprise zealots. Confronted with the anxieties of English Catholics who had no desire to seek the queen's death, Gregory absolved them from active conspiracy, but he did not backtrack from his conviction that the removal of Elizabeth was a major plank of papal policy.

> Since that guilty woman of England rules over two such noble kingdoms of Christendom and is the cause of so much injury to the catholic faith, and loss of so many million souls, there is no doubt that whosoever sends her out of the world with the pious intention of doing service, not only does not sin but gains merit.[12]

So wrote Gregory's secretary of state in his master's name.

But the pope understood well that state-sponsored terrorism was not the only effective means of reclaiming lands lost to Rome. It had to be accompanied by a campaign for winning hearts and minds. This missionary endeavour he entrusted to the Society of Jesus. Under his patronage the Jesuit College at Rome expanded rapidly to become one of the major educational institutions of Europe, and similar training establishments sprang up elsewhere. The most significant for England was the English College at Douai in the southern Netherlands. It was founded in 1568 by William Allen, an Oxford graduate who had dedicated himself to the reconversion of his homeland. Allen knew that time was not on his side. Natural wastage and government activity were steadily removing the stock of priests prepared clandestinely to teach the old religion. Failing a successful Catholic rising (something for which he also worked), it would be necessary to look to the next generation to keep the faith alive. Douai College (removed to Rheims in 1578) received young Englishmen to be trained as priests to restock the Catholic church. The first such was ordained in 1574. From this beginning sprang the English Mission. Year on year groups of priests were smuggled into England to succour the small communities of recusants (those who 'recused', ie refused, to worship according to the reformed English rite) and to preach and baptize in secret conventicles. The hunting down of these immigrant priests became a major difficulty to government throughout the rest of the reign. It provided the Catholic cause with martyrs and a wealth of romantic cloak and dagger legends about brow-beating Protestant vigilantes being cleverly outwitted by householders who concealed priests in secret rooms.

'Oh, that the Lord would bow the heavens and come down, and bridle the mouths of the papists, Turks and schismatics!'[13] So Bishop Cox of Ely apostrophized his friend Heinrich Bullinger in January 1575. Wherever England's leaders looked they saw trouble on every side. The Islamic threat still seemed very real. Suleyman the Magnificent had died in 1566 and thereafter the Ottoman Empire went into a slow decline but Europeans had grown accustomed to fearing the Turk, and defence of the eastern boundary and the Mediterranean littoral still consumed large quantities of blood and treasure. The fact that Cox bracketed the activities of Catholic and Puritan propagandists together with the mullahs of a totally alien religion indicates how aggravated the leaders of England's religious establishment were with those of their fellow countrymen who claimed to espouse the same Christian faith but who refused to accommodate themselves to the Elizabethan settlement. Catholic infiltrators and Puritan preachers were alike anathema to those of the moderately Protestant Church of England, by law established. Members of the establishment were, by definition, those who craved that permanence and stability which was represented by the queen and the bishops. Elizabeth certainly regarded the English Reformation as a done deal. Religious controversy was a thing of the past and those who sought to rake it up – whether Catholic or Puritan – were enemies of the state. An increasing majority of English men and women supported this point of view, if for no other reason than that they wanted a quiet life – and after forty years of religious turmoil who could blame them?

But the fury of Bishop Cox betrayed a complete lack of understanding for the enthusiasts of either side. His thinking was not spiritual or even theological, but political. Here is this establishment man in full flood against the Puritans:

> These disputants of ours are so shuffling and so tenacious of their own opinion, that they will give way to no one who opposes their judgment . . . To give you an instance of their candour, they are zealously endeavouring to overthrow the entire order of our Anglican church. Night and day do they importune both the people and the nobility, and stir them up to abhorrence of those persons who, on the abolition of popery, are faithfully discharging the duties of the ministry; and they busy themselves in everywhere weakening and diminishing their credit. And that they may effect this with greater ease and plausibility, they bawl out to those harpies who are greedily hankering after plunder . . . that the property and revenues of the cathedral churches ought to be diverted to I know not what other uses . . . At first they attacked only things of little consequence; but now they turn every thing, both great and small, up and down, and throw all things into confusion; and would bring the church into very great danger, were not our most pious queen most faithful to her principles, and did she not dread and restrain the vanity and inconsistency of these frivolous men.[14]

Cox was bothered about the challenge to royal and episcopal authority (and, the cynic might add, to his own status and economic wellbeing). Ultimate authority was the essential point at issue. For Catholics and Puritans it lay not in the queen but in the pope and the Bible respectively.

The new secretary found himself walking a tightrope. He was a member of the political establishment, sworn to be loyal to the queen and her religion. But he was also a Bible-based Protestant with a tender conscience who believed passionately that England's safety and its very existence as a holy nation depended on completing the Reformation. He extended his patronage to preachers and writers and even supported an underground press which attacked the continued use of mass vestments and the 'unscriptural' rule of the church by bishops, priests and deacons. Walsingham soon came to be tarred by his enemies with the brush of Presbyterianism and it was only royal favour which saved him from being openly attacked by members of the religious establishment. When the fellows of Magdalen College, Oxford complained about one of Walsingham's protégés whom, they said, wanted to strip the ancient foundation of some of its 'papistical' assets, they acknowledged that their real quarrel was with Walsingham, though they did not dare to say so openly. The minister's overt Puritanism drew him closer to the Dudley circle. Indeed, to a large extent he sheltered under Leicester's wing. One of the more remarkable aspects of England's remarkable governing quadrumvirate was the fact that Elizabeth trusted and worked with men whose religious convictions she loathed. However, by no means did the queen abdicate her responsibility to her church. On occasions she could and did act in defiance of her closest advisers.

Matters came to a head for Walsingham very early on. In May 1575, Matthew Parker, the moderate Archbishop of Canterbury, died. The man backed by Burghley and Walsingham to become senior primate was Edmund Grindal, Archbishop of York. Unlike Parker, Grindal had been a Marian exile and returned to England a thoroughgoing Calvinist. Elizabeth was wary of accepting the advice of her leading councillors and it was not until Christmas Eve that she finally signed the warrant for Grindal's appointment. Walsingham and his colleagues were in no doubt about how tricky the relationship between Elizabeth and her archbishop was going to be. As soon as his appointment was confirmed, Grindal received a cautiously unsigned letter, probably from Walsingham, which set out the expectations of those who had supported his candidature:

It is greatly hoped for by the godly and well-affected of this realm that your lordship will prove a profitable instrument in that calling; especially in removing the corruptions in the Court of the Faculties [the ecclesiastical body which granted dispensations from such canon laws as those aimed at preventing such customs as pluralism and marriage within the prohibited degrees] . . . I could wish your lordship to repair hither with as convenient speed as ye may, to the end that there may be some consultation had with some of your brethren how some part of those Romish dregs remaining in [the Church and] offensive to the godly, may be removed. I know it will be hard for you to do that good that you and your brethren desire. Yet . . . somewhat there may be done. Herein I had rather declare unto your lordship at your repair hither frankly by mouth what I think than to commit the same to letters.[15]

Grindal was not slow in embarking on a reforming programme. He set out to remove some of the practices Puritans considered offensive. He put his weight behind a strengthening of the recusancy laws, and he inaugurated an initiative designed to win hearts and minds but also to introduce Calvinist teaching and practice by the back door. This was the publication of the Geneva Bible, a move in which Francis Walsingham was heavily involved. The version of the holy text beloved by the returned exiles had never found favour with many of the bishops, who objected to the radical glosses which adorned its margins. Though not suppressed, the Geneva Bible was not enthusiastically endorsed by the establishment. Now that the Puritans had a friend at Lambeth they were determined to make good this omission. Walsingham recommended for the task Christopher Barker, a protégé whose printing premises were located in St Paul's Churchyard, where the proprietor proudly displayed the Walsingham heraldic device of a tiger's head. In 1576 Barker immediately set about producing four editions of the Bible, some in pocket format for personal use, others designed to be read in households or set up in churches. These were followed by a version which was more explosive.

Laurence Tomson, a fine scholar and linguist, was a member of Walsingham's secretarial staff. He was now set to make a fresh translation of the New Testament incorporating glosses by Theodore Beza, who had taken over leadership of the Geneva church after Calvin's death in 1564. Beza was much more forthright in asserting what he believed to be the form of church polity sanctioned by Scripture and which, needless to say, did not square with the structure of the English church. As if that was not pointed enough, another edition of the Geneva Bible appeared in 1578 which incorporated a Puritan version of the Prayer Book. In this every ceremony and even every word offensive to Puritans (e.g. 'priest') was expunged. It would be impossible to overestimate the impact of this missionary endeavour. The aim to place a 'sound' version of the Bible in every home was, in large measure, successful. Two books above all were formative of the national psyche until well into the seventeeth century – Foxe's *Acts and Monuments* and the Geneva Bible.

But Elizabeth was by now quite convinced that anything that smelled of Geneva was a threat to good monarchical government. She refused to be hustled along the path which, she was convinced, had as its destination the establishment of a dour Calvinist republic. Surrounded by councillors and church leaders who espoused a theology to which she was emotionally and intellectually disinclined, she dug her heels in. The *casus belli* between the queen and her Puritan advisers was 'the godly exercises of prophesying'. These were regular weekday meetings of Puritan clergy held for mutual instruction and encouragement. They took the form of a sermon which members of the public were urged to attend followed by discussion and prayer among the ministers themselves. The objectives were raising the standards of preaching and creating a unified body of biblical teaching. As such there could be little objection to them and the exercises were supported by several noble and gentry families. Many of the meetings were financially supported by municipal councils and rural landowners. However, reactionary elements in church and state, among which the queen was definitely included, were always worried about potentially disruptive conventicles. The prophesyings were outside episcopal control and, in several cases, were addressed by radicals who had been deprived of church office. There were instances of Presbyterian teaching and criticism of the established order but these were exaggerated by opponents and alarmists. There was a long and uncomfortable tradition of parish priests stirring their people to revolt. The Pilgrimage of Grace (1536–7) and the Prayer Book Rebellion (1549) were still vivid in the memory of many of the queen's subjects. Elizabeth decided that the prophesyings were to cease.

She was becoming increasingly sensitive to criticism and had recently had more than enough of that from her parliament. Peter Wentworth, Walsingham's brother-in-law, was despatched to the Tower for a speech made on 8 February 1576, which has gone down in the annals of the long struggle for parliamentary freedom. Wentworth exposed two stratagems used by the court to stifle debate:

> One is a rumour that runneth about the House, and this it is: take heed what you do, the Queen's majesty liketh not of such a manner. Whosoever preferreth it, she will be much offended with him . . . The other is sometimes a message is brought into the House either of commanding or inhibiting very injurious unto the freedom of speech and consultation. I would to God, Mr Speaker, that these two were buried in Hell, I mean rumours and messages.

The shocked house heard Wentworth go on to attack the queen directly for overruling parliamentary decisions.

> Her Majesty hath committed great faults, yea dangerous faults to herself and the state . . . It is a dangerous thing in a prince unkindly to entreat and abuse his or her nobility and people as her Majesty did the last Parliament, and it is a dangerous thing in a prince to oppose or bend herself against her nobility and people.

He concluded by assuring his hearers that he was motivated by

> the advancement of God's glory, our honourable sovereign's safety and . . . the sure defence of this noble isle of England, and all by maintaining the liberties of the honourable council, the fountain from whence all these do spring.[16]

Wentworth never asserted in as many words that sovereignty was vested in the people rather than in the Crown but the queen might be forgiven for concluding that his zealous oratory tended in that direction.

Wentworth was only detained for a month (although this would not be his only sojourn in the Tower). However angry Elizabeth was, there was not much she could do by way of punishing the outspoken MP. She was wise enough not to risk a direct confrontation with the House of Commons. The Archbishop of Canterbury was a different matter. She had made him and she could break him. She was determined to have her own way in the church. In the summer or autumn of 1576 she ordered Grindal to put an end to the prophesyings. She went further. So concerned was she about the influence of the 'enthusiasts' that she told Grindal that three or four preachers per shire were quite sufficient for the education of the people. The rest of the ministers could read approved homilies.

Grindal was dismayed and indignant. In his lengthy response he did not water down his feelings with flattery or false humility. He was astonished, he said, that her majesty should advocate reducing the number of preachers when both the Bible and common sense urged the need for energetic proclamation of the Gospel. As to the exercises, he had discussed them with his diocesans and concluded that most of the ministerial meetings were not only above reproach but 'profitable to increase knowledge among the ministers and [tend] to the edifying of the hearers'. Therefore, Grindal declared,

> I am forced with all humility, and yet plainly, to profess that I cannot with safe conscience and without the offence of the majesty of God give my assent to the suppressing of the said exercises . . . Bear with me, I beseech you, Madam, if I choose rather to offend your earthly Majesty than to offend the heavenly majesty of God.[17]

But Grindal did not stop here; he delivered to the queen a lecture on spiritual and temporal authority: 'If you consult your ministers in matters of finance, it is surely more fitting that you should consult the bishops of the Lord on matters of religion . . . In a matter of faith . . . it is the practice of bishops to judge Christian [rulers], and not [rulers] bishops.'[18] And the end of his letter got very personal. He commended the queen for supporting true religion, then added:

> Ye have done many things well; but except ye persevere to the end, ye cannot be blessed. For if ye turn from God, then God would turn away

his merciful countenance from you. And what remaineth then to be looked for, but only a terrible expectation of God's judgements, and an heaping up of wrath against the day of wrath?[19]

Elizabeth was not accustomed to such forthright defiance. She was surrounded by ladies who catered to her every whim, gentlemen and lords who played the game of courtly love, councillors who addressed her with obsequious respect and deferred to her wishes even when they disagreed with her. Grindal's diatribe pierced her ego like naked steel. She was so furious with him that all reason deserted her. She sent all her bishops a royal fiat to suppress the prophesyings and she instructed her Council to arrange for the archbishop's dismissal from office.

This put the advisory body and particularly its Puritan caucus into a quandary. They managed to wriggle out of sacking Grindal on the grounds that they lacked legal warrant for such an unprecedented task but they did oversee the action that was taken against him. Walsingham and his colleagues do not emerge with much credit from their part in the long-drawn-out confrontation between queen and archbishop. Grindal was not deprived but he was sequestered, that is to say that, for the remaining six and a half years of his life, he was not allowed to carry out any of the duties pertaining to his office. Walsingham, Burghley and their allies were fully in sympathy with the archbishop and when they saw the domestic issue in the light of international events they could only deplore the queen's action. By turning so violently against the primate and the ecclesiological position he represented she could only raise the hopes of those labouring for the reintroduction of Catholicism. Walsingham was profoundly convinced that the queen was wrong. He wrote as much in a private letter to Burghley: 'you see how we proceed still in making war against God, whose ire we should rather seek to appease that he may keep the wars that most apparently approach towards us from us. God open her majesty's eyes that she may both see her peril and acknowledge from whence the true remedy is to be sought.'[20]

Walsingham believed that only a royal U-turn would regain divine favour. Yet he did not remonstrate with the queen nor did he stand

four square behind Grindal and put his own position at risk. In later
years he would speak his mind frankly to the queen whatever the
consequences but his position was not yet sufficiently secure for that.
He explained the delicacy of his position and his own sense of
priorities in a letter to his diplomatic colleague, William Davison
in Antwerp. The Merchant Venturers in that city were proposing to
use a 'puritanized' version of the Prayer Book in their worship.
Walsingham advised against it:

> I have thought good therefore, as one that wishes you well, to let you
> understand that if it should come to her Majesty's ears it would greatly
> kindle offence as well against the Company of the said Adventurers for
> yielding to such a connivance as also against yourself for the furthering
> of the same. I do not write this as one that misliketh of such a form of
> exercise of prayer; only I would have all reformations done by public
> authority. It were very dangerous that every private man's zeal should
> carry sufficient authority of reforming things amiss . . . If you knew
> with what difficulty we retain that we have, and that the seeking of
> more might hazard (according to man's understanding) that which we
> already have, you would then, Mr. Davison, deal warily in this time
> when policy carrieth more sway than zeal. And yet have we great cause
> to thank God for that we presently enjoy, having God's word sincerely
> preached and the sacraments truly administered. The rest we lack we
> are to beg by prayer and attend with patience.[21]

A flattering correspondent once informed Walsingham: 'You are
thought in Spain, France and Italy to govern that noble ship [i.e. the
queen] and guard her from danger of shipwreck.'[22] Those words must
have brought a wry smile to Mr Secretary's lips.

Chapter 6

'GOD OPEN HER MAJESTY'S EYES'
FOREIGN AFFAIRS
1578–80

Satan is roaring like a lion, the world is going mad, Antichrist is resorting to every extreme, that he may with wolf-like ferocity devour the sheep of Christ: the sea is full of pirates, the soil of Flanders is wet with the blood of Christians: in France, Guise is reported to rage in his new slaughter-house against the Protestants. England, by the favour of God, is yet safe; but how can she be secure from human malignity? For it is greatly to be feared that the flames of our neighbour's house may reach us; the Tridentine fathers enforcing that bloody decree of theirs, and our daily sins deserving the execution of it.[1]

So wrote Dr Laurence Humphrey, President of Magdalen College, Oxford, to a friend in Zurich, in August 1578. Many people in political and diplomatic circles shared his gloomy interpretation of international affairs. The peace England had enjoyed for the greater part of twenty years could not be relied on to continue. If one took a cosmic view, as devout Puritans, of course, did, England did not deserve the blessing of continued tranquillity. The diplomat Dr Thomas Wilson, an envoy in the Low Countries, witnessed at close quarters the miseries of a country where Protestant and Catholic forces were engaged in armed struggle. The lesson to be learned was clear to him, as he told Walsingham in April 1577: 'never will I think that ever any perfect or assured amity will be amongst any that are divided in religion. The queen's Majesty may perhaps mislike my plain writing in these matters after so bold a manner.'[2] In fact,

Elizabeth would have agreed with her diplomat's assessment. Every state should have one religion. She had made up her mind what England's ought to be. The trouble was that her church was under attack from both Catholic ritualists and Protestant evangelicals.

Walsingham and his associates had clear policy objectives. With the world as it was England could not pursue an isolationist religious policy. At home the Protestant state should be built up by sound preaching and the establishment of a ministry able to exercise moral discipline. Catholic infiltrators should be rooted out and severely dealt with. Mary Stuart should be neutralized as a political threat, by whatever means were available. Beleaguered Protestants in France and the Netherlands should be succoured. And England should join with other Protestant states to withstand the Catholic League which, according to Walsingham's sources, had been formed.

No development in the sphere of European diplomacy could induce Elizabeth to espouse such a clear cut manifesto. She was incapable of being proactive. The only consistent element in her approach to foreign affairs was the desire to avoid commitment. Policy was decided on a day-to-day basis and might change on the instant at the arrival of the latest despatch. There was an element of wisdom, albeit small, in the queen's attitude. Relations between the continental states were so multi-faceted and changeable that an element of short-termism and flexibility was sometimes necessary.

It may be helpful to provide a quick overview of international events in these years. Rome had discovered in Gregory XIII an energetic and industrious administrator. His most lasting innovation was the introduction of the Gregorian Calendar to replace the inaccurate Julian Calendar but his management skills extended to the foundation of several seminaries for the training of missionary priests. In 1578 he placed the English College in Rome (an offshoot of the Douai-Rheims College) under the control of the Jesuits and it became the power source for the reconversion of England. Winning back the Protestant island state remained a priority for the pope who was always ready to receive Catholic adventurers with some bold and invariably impractical invasion plan.

Any realistic scheme would require massive support from Philip II.

Sir Francis Walsingham c.1585, attributed to John de Critz the Elder.

NON SINE SOLE
IRIS.

Queen Elizabeth I. *The Rainbow Portait* by Isaac Oliver. The gown of the ever-wary queen is spangled with eyes and ears. Vigilance and desire for peace (symbolized by the rainbow) go together.

One of the main objections Protestants had about the papacy was its assumption of worldly power. As early as 1526 Hans Holbein made this engraving satirizing the pope's presumption in receiving homage from the emperor.

Vt quibus excepti domibus mysteria Christi
Egerunt, quósque à funestro schismate sanctæ
Iunxere Ecclesiæ, pródant, et talia multa
Distendunt miseros diris cruciatibus artus

Racking of Catholic priests by Sebastiano Martellini. Like much religious propaganda of the period, this image, commissioned by William Allen, contained many inaccuracies.

Queen Elizabeth with Burghley and Walsingham by William Faithorne, 1655, in D. Digges *The Compleat Ambassador*. By the mid-17th century the two men were assessed as having been equally influential in the Elizabethan regime.

FRANCISCVS VALESIVS D.G.DVX ALENCON. ET BRA.COM.FLAN.PROT

Francis duc d'Anjou (formerly Alençon) in a distinctly flattering portrait of Elizabeth's 'Frog'.

The St Bartholomew's Massacre, 1572 – a hideous memory which remained vivid for Walsingham for the rest of his life.

The burning of Thomas Cranmer as illustrated in John Foxe's *Actes and Monuments*. Foxe's version of church history kept alive the memory of the martyrs, especially those who died in the reign of Mary Tudor, the victims of savage Catholic repression. Walsingham, who lost friends and mentors in the Marian persecution was passionate about preventing another Catholic regime ever being established in England.

William Allen, founder of the Catholic seminaries at Douai, Rheims and Rome and organizer of the mission to England. Had the armada succcceeded Elizabeth would have been deposed (and probably executed) and Allen would have been nominated as regent.

The assassination of William the Silent, 1584, leader of the Dutch revolt, one of the few Catholic atrocities which moved Queen Elizabeth to look to her own security.

The Funeral of Sir Philip Sidney, 1586. The death of Walsingham's son-in-law in the Netherlands was a personal tragedy and plunged the ageing minister into debt. From Thomas Lant, *Sequito celebratas pompa funeris*, 1587.

The trial of Mary Queen of Scots. Walsingham is one of the seated figures facing away from the viewer (No 28, 3rd from the left).

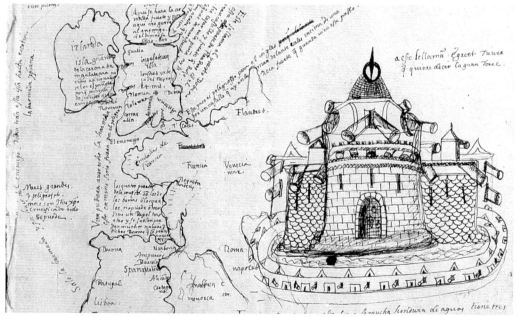

Bernardino de Escalante's plan for the invasion of England, 1586. He recommended a feint against Ireland to draw off the English navy and a major strike at Kent across the Channel. The invading Spanish force would, he suggested, only have one major obstacle to face – the Tower of London, of which he offered a poorly-remembered drawing.

He remained emotionally committed to the Enterprise of England but he was preoccupied with the seemingly endless debilitating wars in the Mediterranean and the Netherlands. The naval triumph of his half-brother, Don John of Austria, over the Turks at Lepanto in 1571 was a great morale boost but three years later Spain was driven out of Tunis and, in 1575, Philip's treasury declared itself bankrupt. Appointing the charismatic and belligerent Don John as Governor of the Spanish Netherlands in 1576 could not disguise the fact that the position of the occupying force was precarious. Then, in 1578, there came a massive change of fortune. The young, headstrong and childless King Sebastian of Portugal was killed in battle. After the brief reign of the Cardinal, King Henry, Philip II became heir apparent by virtue of being the senior male relative of Sebastian (Philip's nephew) and he asserted his claim, backed by a swift military intervention. With the Portuguese possessions in Brazil and the Orient added to his own empire, Philip now became awesomely powerful. A celebratory medal struck in 1580 modestly declaimed 'The World is Not Enough'. This coincided with the arrival of news about Francis Drake's circumnavigation (1577–80) during which he had harried the Pacific coast of South America, despoiled a Spanish bullion ship of a vast treasure and established commercial contacts in the 'closed' markets of the Spice Islands. This effrontery quickened Philip's Anglophobia. Henceforth the Enterprise of England remained at the top of his agenda.

In any potential confrontation between Spain and England affairs in France added repeated complications. The life of the nation, of the court and of the royal family was crazed with rivalries and factions. France was, in fact, ungovernable. In May 1574 Charles IX died, the second of Catherine de Medici's ill-fated brood, doomed to expire before the age of forty without siring an heir. His place was taken by his fanatical brother, Henri, duc d'Anjou. The youngest boy, Francis, duc d'Alençon, now assumed his brother's title of Anjou. But he would rather have assumed the kingship. Of all Catherine's sons Anjou was the most ambitious. He craved a crown – any crown. This rivalry at the very centre further weakened an already brittle political situation. Henry III kept his brother at court, a virtual prisoner. Also detained there was Henry of Navarre, next in line to the throne after Catherine's sons and married to her daughter, Marguerite. Navarre had been brought up a Protestant and had fought with the Huguenots in the earlier wars of religion. In September 1575 Anjou escaped and cynically threw in his lot with the Protestants. Six months later he was joined by Navarre. Henry averted another major military confrontation by making a humiliating peace which granted the Huguenots an unprecedented degree of toleration and negated the Catholic advances made in the wake of the St Bartholomew Massacre. It was never going to work. Catholic leaders in Paris and the provinces simply refused to accept the peace terms and, within months, civil war had broken out again. This time Anjou fought alongside the Guises and other leaders of the Catholic Holy League. Navarre was excommunicated by the pope and debarred from the royal succession. Chaos persisted year in and year out, France's royal government being neither able to win a war nor to sustain a peace. Social and economic dislocation followed political and religious strife. Sporadic peasant revolts and bourgeois anti-government demonstrations became a regular feature of French life.

In 1578 the duc d'Anjou grabbed the headlines again. For a second time he escaped the confines of his brother's court, travelled north and offered himself to the rebels in the Low Countries as their leader and protector. At the same time he sent envoys to London with avowals of undying love for Elizabeth and a serious marriage proposal. With all this going on it is not surprising that Walsingham, along with his colleagues, was bewildered. 'We are in consultation,' he wrote on 11 May, 'what were fit to be done in the Low Country causes, which we find subject to so many difficulties as we know not what to resolve.' He could not decide whether Anjou's move was part of a French plot to annexe the Netherlands or a stratagem by the duke to carve for himself an independent kingdom. Nor could he conclude what the impact would be on the Low Countries or on Franco–Spanish relations.[3]

To the outside observer events in the Netherlands were, indeed, as confused and confusing as those in France. Don John arrived in 1576, intent on winning reputation by subduing the province and using it as a springboard for the invasion of England. His master in the Escorial was more pragmatic. With an empty purse and worrying despatches from all over the empire regularly keeping him at his desk long into the hours of darkness, he ordered his half-brother to make peace at all costs, even if it involved extending religious toleration to the Calvinists. Reluctantly, Don John disbanded the Spanish army of occupation and entered negotiations with the native government, the States General. The result was the Pacification of Ghent (1577). William of Orange (aka William the Silent) took up residence in Brussels as, eventually, a Spanish viceroy. (He removed to Antwerp the following year.) But the situation was very far from being a simple conflict between imperial power and nationalist rebels. Catholic nobles, who were in a majority in the States General, looked for religious unity. The Protestant areas – mainly Holland and Zeeland in the north-west – were interested in nothing less than complete independence from Spain. Don John sulked in his new headquarters in Nassau and took every opportunity to sow discord. Philip II had abated none of his religious zeal and prayed earnestly that God would reverse his fortunes and enable him to complete his holy mission to his troublesome province.

In 1578 Don John died and his place was taken by Allesandro Farnese, Duke of Parma. For the next six years affairs in the Low Countries were dominated by two men who were military and political equals. Parma united the Catholic southern states and William of Orange headed the United (Protestant) Provinces in the north. Philip declared William an outlaw and offered a reward to anyone who would assassinate him. The United Provinces deposed Philip and expunged all reference to Spain from currency and official records. Then fate played a cruel trick on the rebels. An almost bloodless coup gave Philip control of Portugal and its empire. His fortunes changed overnight. Once more he was able to take up the sword as Catholic champion. This was also the point (1580) at which the crown of the United Netherlands was offered to the duc d'Anjou. The French prince enjoyed his position for two and a half years. Then, with Parma nibbling away at his territory and the Dutch politicians squabbling among themselves, he quit.

It was not only events beyond the Narrow Seas that called for vigilance on the part of Elizabeth and her Council. As well as the subversive influence of Catholic priests succoured by recusant families the country was vulnerable to attack from Scotland and Ireland. 'The state of Scotland,' Walsingham wrote in 1581, 'may well be re-sembled to a diseased body, that one day yieldeth hope of life, and another utter despair of recovery.'[4] The problems Walsingham faced in dealings with the northern kingdom were essentially the same as those which confronted him in England's continental neighbours – competing factions and the queen's refusal to be proactive. During the civil war that raged in Scotland between 1567 and 1572 Mary Stuart had fled to England and the regent, James Stewart, Earl of Moray, had been assassinated. The man who emerged from the crisis to restore order and a measure of peace was James Douglas, fourth Earl of Morton, who reigned as regent in the name of the infant James VI from 1572 to 1578. He was pro-English and Protestant without being bigoted. He was quite clear about his aims and objectives. His dearest wish was for an offensive and defensive league between the two kingdoms. This would involve a major financial subvention from Elizabeth and her open involvement in the trial and execution of Mary. In all this he had the support of Walsingham and the majority of the Council. The situation, as they saw it, could not have been more favourable. Morton had the measure of his aristocratic enemies and France was in no position to interfere. There was no guarantee and, indeed, no likelihood that this state of affairs would survive indefinitely. Firm support from the queen might have secured Scottish peace and friendship but, true to form, Elizabeth made no commitment.

A coup in 1578 only removed Morton temporarily from his position of power but it did formally put an end to the king's minority. This meant that anyone who could worm his way into the affections of the twelve-year-old James VI could subvert the government. That man now appeared in the person of Esmé Stuart, Seigneur d'Aubigny. Stuart, soon to become Earl, then Duke of Lennox, was a distant cousin of the king, had spent all his life in France, was a friend of the Guises and now came to strengthen the pro-French party in Scotland and, if it could be managed, to whisk young James across the sea to be married to a suitable Catholic princess. The teenage king was captivated by his kinsman and his tales of sophisticated court life – so different from that of his own household, dominated by dour Presbyterian councillors and tutors. By the beginning of 1581 Morton was in prison. Within six months he had been tried, convicted on perjured evidence and beheaded by the 'maiden', a prototype guillotine that he himself had introduced into Scotland.

Elizabeth had not lifted a finger to help Morton. She was, at the time, pursuing her love affair with Anjou and had no desire to upset the Anglo-French apple cart. But even she could see the danger of allowing James to fall further under the spell of his favourite. She allowed Walsingham discreetly to encourage the pro-English lords to carry out a coup. The young king was snatched and held a virtual prisoner at Ruthven Castle. So far from solving anything, the abduction only turned up the heat under the witch's cauldron of Scottish politics. It took some feverish activity by Walsingham and his agents to save their mistress from a diplomatic scalding. By now French influence north of the border was increasing and Walsingham was at his wit's end.

> The French bring crowns and we bring words . . . I hold Scotland for lost unless God be merciful unto this poor island. How unseasonably the same is like to fall out, or rather dangerously, all the world may see, if the state of things at home and abroad be duly looked into. God open her Majesty's eyes to see her peril and not to prefer treasure before safety.[5]

In June 1583 the young King of Scotland escaped from his minders. Henceforth a new element entered the complexities of Anglo-Scottish relations. As well as the balance of noble factions, Elizabeth's Council had to consider the personal relationship between their queen and her 'brother' of Scotland.

If Scotland was the postern gate which had to be guarded against French infiltration, the back door for Spain into Elizabeth's kingdom was Ireland. In 1558 Ireland was not a Catholic country in any meaningful sense of the word. If the people and their leaders resisted the Reformation it was not out of loyalty to the old faith. Catholic priests, where they were to be found, despaired of parishioners who rarely if ever attended mass and did not bring their children for baptism. The loyalties of the Irish people were to their clan leaders, independent warlords whose constant bloody feuding kept much of the country in constant turmoil. It was the attempts by Elizabeth's deputies to impose order and religious unity on chieftains who were a law unto themselves which gave rise to a defiant Catholicism and opened doors to the agents of Spain and Rome.

The Desmond Rebellions (1569–73 and 1579–83) were the latest in a series of risings by the men of Munster and Leinster in southern Ireland against English rule. They can scarcely be said to have taken on the character of religious wars but the rebels did seek the aid of Catholic powers and did hold out to those powers the prospect of an Ireland united by allegiance to the pope. The military leader of the Desmond Clan in 1569 was James Fitzmaurice Fitzgerald. Before launching his campaign he sent envoys to Philip II, Pius V and Don John of Austria. He offered the crown of a united Ireland to Don John. At the same time an altogether more colourful representative of the Irish cause appeared at the Escorial. Thomas Stukeley had been, by turns, a mercenary soldier, a pirate, an English official in Ireland, a self-appointed Irish freedom-fighter and, now, a conspirator in league with de Spes and Roberto Ridolfi. Stukeley's bravado and zeal impressed Philip, who promised 5,000 men for the invasion of Ireland. However, the Stukeley raid came to nothing because of squabbles in the Irish camp. Fitzmaurice's man, the Archbishop of Cashel, arrived and cast serious doubt on the adventurer's credentials. With the Irish falling out among themselves Philip preferred to put all his eggs into the basket of the Enterprise of England. With no foreign aid the rebels were steadily driven back into the mountains of Kerry in the far south-west. After a long resistance they were forced to surrender. English reprisals were vicious and counter-productive.

Fitzmaurice next tried his fortune in France and Rome. He was well received by Gregory XIII and with the papal funds placed at his disposal was able to charter a ship in Lisbon and embark a small force of Spanish and Portuguese troops. This vessel got no farther than St Malo where Fitzmaurice's captains deserted. In the interim Stukeley had not been inactive. Having redeemed his reputation fighting alongside Don John at Lepanto in October 1571, he devoted the next six years to touring Catholic courts and dreaming up various schemes to unseat Elizabeth and restore her realm to the Catholic faith. Eventually, it was the pope who took Stukeley sufficiently seriously to provide him with a ship and 600 armed men. But this hair-brained adventurer was better at conceiving grandiose plans than at overseeing the necessary organization. His vessel was so unseaworthy that, once in the Atlantic, it had to make for the nearest port. At Lisbon Stukeley appealed to King Sebastian for another vessel. Sebastian, even more gung-ho than his visitor, diverted Stukeley into joining him in an expedition against Morocco. Both men perished at the Battle of Alcazar in August 1578. Once again the Irish were on their own.

Fitzmaurice had finally reached Ireland only weeks before with the remnant of his foreign troops. The second Desmond Rebellion was marked by two massacres. In August 1580 an English force of 800 men, led by the Lord Deputy, Earl Grey de Wilton, was cut to pieces at Glenmalure. Weeks later, papal reinforcements landed at Smerwick in the far south-west and were besieged in a fort at Dun an Oir. After surrendering they were slaughtered to a man. Fighting dragged on for a further three years. Eventually the remaining rebels were brought to heel. Fitzmaurice fell in battle. The victors thoughtfully sent his head as a present to the queen.

It is small matter for a historian to provide an overview of the international situation such as has occupied the last few pages. No such convenient analysis was available to the Elizabethan government. The kaleidoscope of foreign affairs was constantly changing and the queen could only respond on a day by day basis. She had no grand strategy. What Walsingham was acutely aware of was that England was surrounded on all sides by the forces of Antichrist. The devil had at his disposal the richest and most powerful empire in the world, a religious leader in Rome urging state-sponsored terrorism and despatching his mullahs into England to deflect Elizabeth's subjects from their loyalty. Catholic preachers, pamphleteers, soldiers, desperadoes and assassins were everywhere. And the only person who seemed ignorant of or indifferent to the queen's peril was the queen herself. Walsingham was often in despair at the deluge which seemed likely to break over England at any moment. Increasing age and a daunting workload played havoc with his health. Yet, despite everything, he kept his nerve, held to his convictions and handled his royal mistress as best he could. Just how he set about this and with what results we must now consider.

As far as foreign affairs were concerned Walsingham had a fairly quiet first year in which to ease himself into his new responsibilities. Affairs in Scotland and Ireland were stable. In France, the queen mother and her acolytes were adjusting to the change of regime from Charles IX to Henry III and the Huguenots were still reeling from the shock of the St Bartholomew Massacre. Philip II was too preoccupied to respond warmly to the entreaties of Catholic warmongers, whether Gregory XIII or Thomas Stukeley. The Dutch rebels were engaged in talks with their Spanish overlords (though Philip's refusal to tolerate Calvinist worship preordained their failure). All in all, Elizabeth saw no need for robust policies which might upset the apple cart. She had negotiated a commercial treaty with the Duke of Alva which restored North Sea trading relations, much to the delight of the English mercantile community. She even refused to take defensive measures when Philip sent a fleet to reinforce his Netherlands garrisons. With the alarm of the Northern Rebellion and the Ridolfi plot behind her and Mary Stuart detained where she could do no harm, Elizabeth felt that she and her realm were secure, as she would tell parliament in March 1576: 'These seventeen years God hath both prospered and protected you with good success under my direction and I nothing doubt but the same maintaining hand will guide you still and bring you to the ripeness of perfection.' She bade the parliamentarians to compare England's state with 'the bitter storms and trouble of your neighbours'. Then, aware that her hearers might learn the wrong lessons from the tribulations of France and the Netherlands, she added that she would not attribute to rulers the causes of dissension. 'God forbid I should, since these misfortunes may proceed as well from sins among the people.'[6]

Walsingham did not read the signs of the times in the same way. Both religious conviction and the clear evidence he frequently received from his informants of the hostile intent of Catholic powers made him reject the policy of appeasement. 'We seek neither to conserve friends nor to provide for withstanding our enemies,' he complained to Burghley. 'If this kind of government might carry continuance withal, then should we have less cause to lament, but surely it is so loose as in reason it cannot last. God be merciful to us.'[7]

For the moment he could do little to help the Dutch rebels beyond receiving emissaries from William the Silent and commending his cause to the queen. In France, where he knew personally those most closely involved in the politico-religious conflict, he had more latitude. Charles IX was dying and England could look for nothing good from the man who would soon be Henry III. Elizabeth maintained a desultory flirtatious correspondence with Alençon and felt some concern for his virtual imprisonment at Vincennes. Walsingham was more interested in the hostility of the youngest Valois to his older brother and the possibility of backing him as leader of the Huguenot opposition. Walsingham despatched two agents, Jacomo Manucci and Thomas Wilkes, to make contact with Alençon and Henry of Navarre with a view to setting them free and renewing havoc in France. It was a hazardous undertaking and Manucci spent several weeks in a French prison. However, Walsingham did make contact with the prisoners and a plan was concocted for their release. Elizabeth even seriously considered sending Alençon money to bribe his guards. But for the moment Catherine de Medici outwitted them. She moved the prisoners to the Louvre in June 1574, where they could be more closely watched. When, more than a year later Alençon (now Anjou) and Henry of Navarre did make their escape it was without English help.

The first round in the conflict of royal and secretarial diplomatic styles went to the queen. Huguenot morale was raised by the leadership of Anjou and Navarre and also by the appearance on

France's eastern border of 20,000 German Protestant mercenaries. Henry III and Catherine could not risk England being drawn into a Protestant league and made a great show of friendship towards Elizabeth. Philip II, fearing an Anglo-French alliance, also courted her by sending one of his senior diplomats, Bernardino de Mendoza, to repair the damage done by de Spes. He came as a special envoy in 1574 and as resident ambassador in 1578. The queen warmly entertained him and also the French ambassador, Fénelon, and continued her old policy of playing off France and Spain against each other.

In relationships with the Low Countries it was confusion which aided Elizabeth's parsimonious policies. Walsingham saw the struggle of the freedom-fighters in crisp black and white. He sometimes referred to it as a contest between Christ and Belial. In fact, the situation consisted of numerous overlapping shades of grey. William of Orange, the Estates General, Philip II, his governor and various splinter groups of Dutch nobles all had their own agendas. One indication of the Dutch desperate but vain search for cohesion can be seen in their quest for a leader. Within the space of three years they offered their sovereignty to Elizabeth, the Duke of Anjou and the Archduke Matthias (the emperor's brother). Walsingham begged the queen to support Orange financially but he begged once too often. Elizabeth gave him such a public dressing down that he felt obliged to complain to Leicester about his treatment. But it was not only the queen with whom the secretary fell out. Burghley, too, was opposed to a partisan approach to the Dutch problem, as were other members of the Council. In fact, no single issue caused such a division in their ranks. Even Sussex found himself on the same side as Leicester and arguing against Burghley and his allies.

The danger in a policy of non-intervention was that it might allow either Spain or France to take undisputed control of the Netherlands. All the councillors could see this but they were so bemused by the twists and turns of events in the Low Countries that they could not agree on what to do. In effect, England had no policy with regard to the fate of a country which had for centuries been one of its main trading partners. Even when Orange's intelligence officers intercepted a letter of Don John asking Philip to endorse an invasion of England this did not lead to a major shift in royal policy. Walsingham was so worried and angry at the situation that he took a grave personal risk and one that could, at the very least, have put an end to his political career. He went behind the queen's back. He communicated directly and privately with William the Silent. In one letter, sent in the autumn of 1576, he urged the prince to write to those councillors closest to Elizabeth, begging them to intercede with her on his behalf and to explain, in simple terms, the difficult situation in which he found himself. The bottom line of his appeal should be, Walsingham suggested, that, without significant aid from England 'he must either be enforced to abandon the cause by retiring into Germany, or to reconcile himself with Spain upon any conditions, or to yield those countries absolutely to the French king's hands.'[8]

In the whispering gallery of the court where every man needed to watch his own back such impropriety could not go unnoticed. There were in Walsingham's large staff those who, for a price or to curry favour with some great lord, were not above leaking documents or telling tales. The secretary's enemies used information gleaned in this way to try to undermine him. Fortunately for Walsingham Elizabeth chose not to hear or to act upon such tittle-tattle. She never tired of making clear to those around her that she formed her own opinions of men's worth and it may have been to demonstrate this point that, on 1 December 1577 she conferred a knighthood on her secretary. The following April he was granted the prestigious post of chancellor of the Order of the Garter.

One of Elizabeth Tudor's more impressive characteristics was that she was an excellent judge of character. She surrounded herself with men of talent and, unlike her father, she did not falter in her loyalty towards those who served her. She found Walsingham irritating and would have no truck with his religious opinions, because, as she rightly divined, extreme evangelicalism was ultimately inimical to episcopal (and, by implication, to monarchical) good order. But she recognized her secretary's talents and his invaluable network of contacts. By the spring of 1578 Mendoza could mournfully report to his master: 'Some of the councillors are well disposed towards your majesty, but Leicester, whose spirit is Walsingham, is so highly favoured by the Queen . . . that he centres in his hands and those of his friends most of the business of the country.' This common perception missed the subtleties of the relationships at the centre of England's power politics. Leicester had, by now, become more a consort than a favourite. The queen trusted him and his 'spirit' and allowed them considerable political latitude but she always stayed in control and if her reason – or, more commonly, her intuition – told her that they were wrong she simply rejected their advice.

This is well borne out by the Grindal affair, which came to a head at the same time as Elizabeth and her advisers were dealing with the bewildering complexities of the Netherlands. The archbishop's sequestration took place in the spring of 1577 and Walsingham may well have felt some relief that he was away from court at the time. A recurrence of his urinary complaint (possibly a kidney stone) kept him out of his office for two or three months. He, therefore, did not have to confront Elizabeth face to face with the news that her instructions to set Grindal's deprivation in motion were of dubious legality. As he lay in his chamber, slowly recovering his health, Walsingham may have hoped that his mistress, by temperament so changeable, would come round to a more reasonable frame of mind. He knew from personal experience that she could be thunderous storms one day and smiling sunshine the next. But in this instance she was utterly implacable. The archbishop's reproach had stung her to the quick because it exposed the very limited nature of her own Protestantism. This is clear from the speech Sir Nicholas Bacon (Lord Keeper of the Great Seal) was deputed to give at a special hearing before the Council (which did not, in fact, take place due to Grindal's illness). If the queen had not intervened, Bacon's written address stated, 'it was like that religion, which of his own nature should be uniform, would against his nature have proved milliform, yea, in continuance nulliform, specially in rites and ceremonies and sometimes also in matters of doctrine.'[9] Unhindered exposition of the word of God was not at the top of the queen's religious agenda. The importance of the church for Elizabeth was its adhesive quality. It was the cement which held society together. Weaken it, and the structure, including the Crown, would tumble.

For Walsingham and his friends this attitude was incomprehensible because in their view the real danger to state and monarchy came not from Puritan preachers, who proclaimed their message openly, but from Catholic priests who worked insidiously in secret to destroy the religious settlement. To them this was so obvious that it was a matter of real astonishment that Elizabeth could not see it. The wake-up call came in June 1577 at about the time that Walsingham returned to court.

In April of that year a young man called Cuthbert Mayne took up the post of steward to Francis Tregian of Wolvedon, Cornwall. In fact, Mayne was a priest come hotfoot from Douai to spearhead the English mission. His activities soon aroused suspicion. He was arrested and tried before Sir Roger Manwood at the next Michaelmas assize. Manwood seems to have been something of an expert at dealing with religious dissidents. He was a commissioner for examining immigrants – not in search of Catholics but of Anabaptists, two of whom he sentenced to death by burning. He was also a scourge of Puritans. Mayne presented something of a problem for him since it was difficult to discern any capital crime with which to charge the man. However, he had been found in possession of a papal bull. Since this implied introducing foreign jurisdiction into England it counted as a treason and the priest was condemned to be hanged, drawn and quartered. The judgement had to be submitted to the Council for approval. It was not until the end of November that the sentence was carried out. Even then Mayne might have had an eleventh-hour reprieve. He was offered his life if he would acknowledge Elizabeth as supreme governor of the Church of England. He not only refused but asserted what was official Vatican policy: that, one way or another, England should be returned to papal obedience and that loyal English Catholics should be ready to enlist under the banner of any foreign prince who would lead a crusade against the heretical island.

The threatened revival of Catholicism presented a quandary to the government. Reports coming in to Walsingham and his colleagues from their various networks indicated a growth of recusancy and the Council was aware that, despite diligent watch being kept at the ports, young zealots from Douai were slipping into the country disguised as merchants, tradesmen, artisans and students. Their numbers were, so far, small (some thirty to forty since 1574) but their influence, through the gentry and noble patrons who supported them, was out of all proportion to their numerical strength. 'The heretics are as much troubled at the name of the Anglo-Douai priests – which is now famous throughout England – as all the Catholics are consoled thereby.'[10] So one of William Allen's young men reported in 1576. It was the kind of excited bravado that might be expected from front-line troops engaged in an ideological war but it did highlight the fact that a new stage had been reached in the struggle for the soul of England.

We might expect that committed Protestant radicals such as Walsingham would have demanded a thorough offensive against underground sedition and subversion. Images of Catholic persecution against Protestants were seared into Walsingham's memory. It would have been understandable if he had believed that payback time had come. In fact, he did not urge severe repression and the reaction of the government was mild by any contemporary standards.

If any religious group in England was hounded in the early to mid-seventies it was the Puritans or, at least, those of them who were presbyterially inclined. The contrast of Elizabeth's attitude towards Puritans was demonstrated in a cause célèbre which excited nationwide attention some two years after the Mayne affair. John Stubbe was a young zealot who was appalled at the prospect of Elizabeth's marriage to a Catholic prince. In August 1579 he expressed his pungent views in a pamphlet whose title left no doubt about his position: *The Discovery of a gaping gulf whereinto England is likely to be swallowed by another French marriage if the Lord forbid not the banes [banns] by letting her majesty see the sin and punishment thereof.* Stubbe made much of the queen's age and the unlikelihood of her bearing children. As for Anjou, Stubbe could scarcely have been more scathing. He likened the Frenchman to 'the old serpent . . . in the form of a man, come a second time to seduce the English Eve and ruin the English paradise'.[11] That being the case, marriage to Anjou would increase Catholic influence with no counterbalancing advantage. Elizabeth was incensed and her response was swift. She issued a proclamation forbidding circulation of the *Discovery* and ordered the arrest of Stubbe, his printer and publisher. She was all for having the offenders summarily hanged but eventually agreed to their being tried for sedition. They were sentenced to having their right hands cut off. (It took three blows with a butcher's knife to sever Stubbe's wrist.) Their condemnation was a travesty of justice because the Marian statute invoked was a temporary measure designed to protect Philip II, the queen's husband from libellous attack. When Robert Monson, a prominent judge of Common Pleas, pointed this out he was packed off to the Fleet and dismissed from his post. Elizabeth remained deaf to all pleas on Stubbe's behalf. She was determined to leave no one in any doubt that she would not be lectured to in matters of religion by anyone, be he archbishop or vulgar scribbler. She can scarcely have been unaware that Stubbe's reservations were shared by many prominent men, including her principal secretary

Meanwhile, bishops had the queen's wholehearted support in suppressing the prophesyings. Elizabeth took the view that most of her people were, like her, not extremists and that, if she and the episcopal shepherds of the flock protected it from the influence of Rome and Geneva, the *via media* would triumph in the long term. Complacency ruled.

> The purity of the Christian religion is flourishing and prosperous among us, and can neither be overturned nor defiled by any devices of Satan. For although we are unable to banish from the church . . . those *new* men whom we call Puritans, who tread all authority underfoot, or the *veteran* papists, who celebrate their divine service in their secret corners, or the profane disputants who deride the true worship of God, such, however, is the number and influence of the truly faithful, that both in numbers and appearance it very far takes the lead of all the separatists.[12]

So the Archbishop of York reported to a friend in Zurich.

It was not an attitude Walsingham could share. Writing to John Sturmius in Strasbourg he grumbled:

One evil attending prosperity, which, if not the only one, is certainly a very grievous one, [is] that it makes us forget or at least be very indifferent . . . to those events and calamities by which others are oppressed. If in these circumstances you would arouse us who are in deep sleep and heedlessly secure, and by your more frequent letters would warn us of impending danger, you would show most honourable zeal and do us a most useful service.[13]

Walsingham shared the queen's disinclination to religious persecution *per se* because he had witnessed at first hand what happened when people were whipped into action by unholy zeal. He was well aware that the making of martyrs was no way to kill a religious movement. He was convinced of the importance of winning hearts and minds and this is why he was so depressed at the suppression of Puritan preachers. He well understood that the majority of his fellow countrymen were ignorant of or indifferent to the fundamentals of the Christian faith. He regarded an educational programme as vital to the creation of a truly godly commonwealth. Most importantly of all, he had a pan-European perspective. No one in English government circles had stronger personal connections with the movers and shakers on the continent or was better informed of events there.

The infiltration of priests trained in the Low Countries, France and Rome was precisely the kind of activity he had long feared. As soon as reports from Cornwall reached his desk Walsingham set about planning countermeasures with Burghley. While William Allen at Douai was using the story of Mayne's suffering to inspire other young men to seek death or glory in England, Walsingham was despatching letters to senior bishops summoning them to a conference. The colloquy considered various measures for the apprehending of immigrant priests and denying them succour. These included placing under house arrest prominent members of the Catholic community such as Thomas Watson, the Marian Bishop of Lincoln and John de Feckenham, ex-Abbot of Westminster; rigid scrutiny of school teachers and any who had influence over children; and the imprisonment of stubborn recusants. To proceed efficiently against those who persisted in 'papistical error' it was proposed to turn ten secure castles into detention centres. In these places the inmates would be subjected to a programme of re-education. Those who persisted in their error and refused to swear the oath of supremacy might then be punished with confiscation of property and continued imprisonment.

The ensuing investigation produced an alarming amount of evidence of Catholic resurgence. Leicester reported that in the Midlands 'papists were never in that jollity they be at this present time'. John Aylmer, Bishop of London, told Walsingham 'the papists marvellously increase both in numbers and in obstinate withdrawal of themselves from . . . the services of God.' Similar information came from diocesan bishops and from Walsingham's own agents throughout the country. Faced with this situation the government did – nothing. No new laws were enacted. Few if any reported recusants were prosecuted under the existing laws. The detention centres did not materialize. Walsingham had collected a large volume of information and painstakingly filed it. It remained unused. Worse than that, in 1579 he was obliged to write the following extraordinary and humiliating letter to several of his contacts in the shires:

[T]hough, in due and necessary policy, it were fit that Papists who will not conform themselves to resort to public prayer should receive punishment due to their contempt according to the laws provided in that behalf, yet the time serveth not now to deal therein, and therefore I cannot but advise you and such others of the best affected gentlemen in that shire to forbear to persecute by way of indictment such as lately were presented, whose names you certified us; for that if you shall proceed therein, you shall not prevail to do that good you desire, but shall rather fail through some commandment from hence, prohibiting you to surcease in proceeding in that behalf, which would breed no less discredit unto you than encouragement to the papists.

Walsingham explained that he was writing personally and confidentially in order to save both his correspondents and himself from public embarrassment.

If I had not prevented the same, there had been written unto you a general letter from my Lords of the Council to inhibit you from prosecuting the matter against the parties presented and by you certified, which things assuredly will follow if you shall not take profit of this secret advertisement I give you, which I shall request you that the same may be so used as my name be concealed, for that otherwise some may take occasion to make some curious construction of this my good and sincere meaning to other end than by me is meant.[14]

Why was it that 'the time serveth not'? The answer is not just that the queen had changed her mind. Her advisers were well used to that by now. A kind of policy paralysis afflicted the government because Elizabeth was undergoing the worst emotional and mental turmoil of her life. Over several issues she could not make her own decisions and she would not take advice. She fancied herself betrayed by some of those closest to her and when she did turn to her Council for support she found that body so divided as to be useless. Under the strains of the years 1577–80 there were times when the Burghley, Leicester, Walsingham caucus fell apart. This was the period when the deluge Walsingham had long prophesied finally burst forth. In foreign affairs disaster followed hard on the heels of disaster and Elizabeth's personal relationships mirrored events abroad.

A series of ominous occurrences within a few weeks in 1578 provided the first act in the tragedy. In January Don John won a spectacular victory over the army of the Estates General. In February the Duke of Anjou opened negotiations with the Dutch rebels. In March the Earl of Morton was dismissed as Scottish regent. Simultaneously, news arrived that Thomas Stukeley had embarked papal troops in Italy for his proposed assault on Ireland.

But it was not fresh complications in English relations with her neighbours that immobilized the queen. That was down to her own intimate relationships with two men. As we have seen, it was in March 1578 that Anjou revived in earnest his marriage offer to Elizabeth. The ambitious prince still entertained visions of himself in an English crown or, at least, a regent's coronet. Failing that, he hoped that Elizabeth would bolster his position in the Netherlands.

For her part, the queen welcomed his overtures because it gave her a lever with which to manipulate Anjou's behaviour in the sensitive Dutch situation. Yet there was more than that to her response. In September 1578 she celebrated her forty-fifth birthday. If marriage and, more specifically, motherhood were to be realities for her, it was a case of now or never. She entered into negotiations with enthusiasm, even − or so it seemed to her advisers − with abandon. Walsingham followed Leicester's lead in opposing the match. As well as his religious objection to Anjou and his suspicion of the prince's motives, he was concerned about Elizabeth's safety. Childbirth could only be risky for her and if it should result in her death England would be left at the mercy of Anjou and the French royal house.

However, the real reason for the queen's obduracy over the marriage was a crisis in her relationship with Robert Dudley. Her love for the widower earl ran deep and had evolved over the years from youthful passion to emotional reliance. This parsimonious woman showered gifts on her favourite. She listened to his advice on matters of state. She tolerated his opposition to her decisions on religion and foreign affairs. She winked at his passing love affairs. The other side of the coin was her utter possessiveness. She could not tolerate the merest suggestion that another woman might replace her in Leicester's affections. When, therefore, she learned that her 'Sweet Robin' had clandestinely married she was completely devastated. For Dudley, his relationship with the queen was a trap. He was dependent on her for everything − estates, political status, social position, luxurious lifestyle − but the price he was expected to pay for all this was remaining single. Elizabeth would not marry him but he could not marry anyone else. Not only was this sexually frustrating; it was dynastically disastrous. He could not sire a legitimate heir; the Dudley line was doomed to extinction. After twenty years of this increasingly intolerable situation Robert Dudley was married in September 1578 to Lettice, daughter of his conciliar colleague, Sir Francis Knollys. She was already pregnant with their first child.

The news was kept secret as long as possible and it is not clear when or under what circumstances Elizabeth heard it. According to one story she did not discover Leicester's 'betrayal' for over nine months. It is, however, difficult to believe that the information would not have leaked earlier, that the earl's enemies would not have grasped the opportunity to discredit him, or that Elizabeth would not have pricked up her ears at rumours flying round the court. What is important is that when she did hear the devastating news she was thrown into a rage of self-pity and indignation. What particularly galled her was that while Leicester was opposing her marriage he was himself entering into a clandestine union with one of her own attendants. She reacted by pursuing the Anjou relationship with ostentatious vigour, by refusing to hear any criticism of it and by launching on a vendetta against Leicester's 'friends', the Puritans, especially those who presumed to criticise her actions.

Walsingham had already incurred the queen's displeasure over negotiations with the Netherlands. In order to obtain a clear picture of what was happening in that troubled country, in the summer of 1578, she decided to send her secretary on a high-level diplomatic mission. In June Walsingham arrived at Antwerp in the company of Henry, Lord Cobham (presumably included in the mission to give it more social prestige). Their instructions were to find out what Anjou was up to, to offer their services as negotiators between Don John and the Estates General and to spy out the military situation. The diplomats spent three and a half arduous months in the Netherlands. In the height of summer, when plague haunted the cities and waterways, they scuttled back and forth between the regent, the Estates General, the Prince of Orange and the Duke of Anjou. It was an exhausting, frustrating and ultimately fruitless business.

Walsingham and his colleague were kept waiting by all the interested parties, each of whom was watching the situation to see how it could be exploited to best advantage. When discussions did take place it proved impossible to find any compromise acceptable to the regent and the rebels. As for Anjou, Walsingham had the annoyance of his advice being rejected. He had concluded that the duke was a factor to be reckoned with. He recommended that Elizabeth should circumvent him by providing financial aid to Orange. So pressing were the Dutch and so convinced was Walsingham of the rightness of his advice that he raised £5,000 for Orange as an earnest of his government's good faith. When news of this reached the queen she was distinctly unamused. She had decided that the best way to handle Anjou was to play the marriage card. With the Frenchman fighting her battles for her there was no need to part with a single penny for the rebels' cause. She berated Walsingham for exceeding his commission and instructed him to recover all monies which had been advanced to the Netherlanders. This was a body blow to the diplomats. They now had to face the wrath of the Estates General and Prince William and to be accused of being the envoys of perfidious Albion. Walsingham reported that Elizabeth's credit was exhausted and that she would never be trusted again. He did not hesitate to express his feelings to a conciliar colleague:

> It is an intolerable grief to me to receive so hard measure at her Majesty's hands, as if I were some notorious offender. Surely sir, it standeth not with her Majesty's safety to deal so unkindly with those that serve her faithfully. There is a difference between serving with a cheerful and languishing mind. If there had lacked in us either care, faithfulness, or diligence, then were we worthy of blame . . . When our doings shall come to examination, I hope the greatest fault we may be charged withal is that we have had more regard to her Majesty's honour and safety than to her treasure, wherein we have dealt no worse with her than with ourselves, having for her services' sake engaged ourselves £5,000 thick; which doing of ours, being offensively taken, doth make the burden the heavier.[15]

As if this was not bad enough, Walsingham discovered he was caught up in the murky and sordid events surrounding the death of Don John. The thirty-three-year-old regent died of typhus at Bouges on 1 October. His last weeks had been rendered distressing by military failure and by the suspicion of his half-brother, the king. Relations between them were so bad that John's secretary, Juan de Escobedo, was assassinated on Philip's orders. Walsingham became involved because members of the late regent's suite suspected him of complicity in Don John's death. Although Walsingham stoutly denied this aspersion he could not distance himself entirely from the seamy events at the regent's court. The man who was accused of poisoning Don John and who was executed for it in December was Egremont Radcliffe, half-brother of the Earl of Sussex, a young ruffian who occupied the shadowlands of espionage and intrigue where many of Walsingham's agents had their abode. A headstrong Catholic who had taken part in the Northern Rebellion, Radcliffe was forced to flee overseas and put his services at the disposal of Philip II. In the Netherlands and at the Spanish court he mixed with other English malcontents, among them the Earl of Westmorland and Thomas Stukeley. In 1575 he returned to England, apparently repentant of his earlier crimes and offering to place his knowledge and contacts at the disposal of the English government. Walsingham did not trust him and Radcliffe soon found himself shut up in the Tower. While there he translated from the French a tractate entitled *Politique Discourses* which advocated unquestioning loyalty to appointed authority. This work, designed to demonstrate his complete change of heart, he dedicated to Walsingham. In May 1578 Radcliffe was secretly set free and sent out of the country, a circumstance which the Spanish ambassador regarded as not a little suspicious. According to a witness who testified some years later, the released prisoner had been seen with the secretary at Hampton Court. It is difficult to avoid the suspicion that Radcliffe was sent over to the Netherlands in advance of Walsingham's mission as a useful gatherer of intelligence.

Two other names appear in the fragmentary records of events taking place in the late summer and early autumn of 1578. Alfonso Ferrabosco was an Italian musician who had been until recently in the household of Philip Sidney (soon to be Walsingham's son-in-law) and was now on his way home to Bologna. He was carrying messages for the English government and, according to diplomatic sources, Radcliffe intended to join him on his journey. Thomas Harrison was an agent of Walsingham who, years later, claimed that he had acted as a go-between for Radcliffe and Walsingham and was lucky to have avoided sharing the latter's fate. Since Don John was not murdered the question of Walsingham's complicity does not arise but his need to be kept informed of everything going on in the Netherlands inevitably involved him with unsavoury characters and the hatred he aroused in Spanish court circles was enough to ensure that the worst was readily believed of him.

Having achieved nothing and suffered much, Walsingham could scarcely wait to be recalled. In September he grumbled to Burghley:

> He had need to be furnished with patience that shall deal in such sour service as we are employed in, being almost ashamed to show our faces abroad, having entertained them here with hope of the continuance of her Majesty's favour, and now, in the end, when they stood in greatest need of her assistance, to be as it were quite abandoned. Besides the alienation of this country people's hearts from her Majesty, which cannot but be perilous both unto herself and her realm, it will render her Highness hateful to the world, many hard speeches being given out against her, which as we hear with grief so cannot your Lordship but also read with grief, if we should set down the same . . . How unpleasant it is to be employed in so unfortunate a service I leave to your Lordship's good judgement.[16]

He fully intended to return home as soon as possible and then resign his office.

Of course, he did no such thing. He was soon back in harness at court and involved in the royal marriage fracas. Anjou expertly pursued his courtship, first through his representative, the utterly charming Jean de Simier, then, in August, through a personal visit. Elizabeth demanded of her councillors that each should put his verdict in writing. Walsingham responded with his usual crisp-mindedness. He set out the pros and cons of the union as he believed it would be perceived at home and abroad. The debit side of his balance sheet far outweighed the credit. He rehearsed all the obvious objections, including the disparity of ages and the health risk. He cast serious doubt on Anjou's motivation and his sincerity. But his principal argument was the religious one. For a Catholic and a Protestant to be yoked together was asking for trouble. He cited the marriage of Henry of Navarre and Marguerite de Valois – the result of which was that 'most horrible spectacle [of which] I was an eye witness'.[17]

Elizabeth was not oblivious to the arguments but she was emotionally committed to Anjou. Her 'Frog', as she nicknamed him, was
a lusty young man and an ardent wooer. He offered her her last
chance of romance and she grabbed it. In the face of her determination the majority of the Council prevaricated. When the prince
arrived for what was supposed to be a secret visit to his beloved there
was general embarrassment at the undignified spectacle of dalliance
between the middle-aged queen and her ugly suitor. Mendoza
relished their difficulties: 'The councillors themselves deny that
[Anjou] is here and, in order not to offend the queen, they shut
their eyes and avoid going to court, so as not to appear to stand in the
way of interviews with him only attending the Council when they are
obliged.'[18]

Walsingham may well have been the only one who did not cloak
his disapproval. Leicester certainly felt it necessary to offer his friend
some words of warning:

> You know her disposition as well as I, and yet can I not use but
> frankness with you. I would have you, as much as you may, avoid the
> suspicion of her majesty that you doubt Monsieur's love to her too
> much, or that you lack devotion enough in you to further her
> marriage, albeit I promise I think she has little enough herself to it.
> But yet, what she would others think and do therein you partly have
> cause to know . . . You have as much as I can learn, for our conference
> with her majesty about affairs is but seldom and slender . . . For this
> matter in hand for her marriage there is no man can tell what to say. As
> yet she hath imparted with no man, at least not with me nor, for ought
> I can learn, with any other.[19]

Unfortunately, where religious sensibilities were concerned, discretion was not a card that Walsingham played skilfully or with
conviction. During a conversation with him in early October the
queen flew into a rage. She told him his advice was worthless and that
all he was good for was protecting heretics. This was almost certainly a
reference to the red-hot issue of the hour, the arrest of John Stubbe
and his associates. It may be that Walsingham had interceded for the

writer. Elizabeth certainly believed, as did others, that *The Discovery of a gaping gulf* emanated from the Leicester-Walsingham circle. It answered with remarkable precision pro-marriage arguments advanced by Sussex and which can only have been leaked by someone in the queen's inner circle. The pamphlet was printed by Hugh Singleton who only avoided Stubbe's fate by virtue of a last-minute pardon. He was noted as a disseminator of Puritan literature and simultaneously with *The Discovery* he published *The Shephard's Calendar* by Edmund Spenser, one of Leicester's protégés. This poem, dedicated to Philip Sidney, was a much more refined piece of literature but it, too, was critical of the Anjou match. Both works were part of a campaign engineered by councillors opposed to the French marriage. Having failed themselves to change the queen's mind they used their clientage networks of preachers and writers to work on public opinion, a stratagem which was ultimately successful. It did not help Walsingham in the short term. Elizabeth, furious at the propaganda campaign being mounted against her, banished Walsingham from court. He did not return until the end of the year. Even then he was not granted access to the queen, 'being still entertained as a man not thoroughly restored to her favour'.[20]

Very soon after his return Walsingham showed himself to be a man converted. He actually supported the queen's marriage plans. Had he been chastened by his exile from court? Had friends prevailed upon him not to ruin his career? Had he decided that if Anjou became consort Elizabeth would need advisers around her to counteract his influence? Possibly all these considerations were at work but more important was the fact that events forced foreign policy to lurch in a new direction. The year 1580 saw the union of the Spanish and Portuguese crowns, the ascendancy of d'Aubigny in Scotland, a resurgence of Spanish power in the Netherlands under the leadership of the highly accomplished regent, Alexander Farnese, Duke of Parma, the formal acceptance by Anjou of the sovereignty offered by the Estates General, and early successes for the Irish rebels. Catholic morale was hugely boosted by the growth of Spanish power. More priests were smuggled into England, the most prominent being Edmund Campion and Robert Persons. Mary Stuart's hopes were resurrected by messages from her co-religionists in Scotland which hinted at Spanish assistance for an armed rescue bid. In this changed situation old, well-tried English policy principles forced themselves to the fore: avoid isolation, encourage Franco-Spanish hostility and prevent the French gaining the upper hand in Scotland. An alliance with France now seemed the most pressing necessity. If that involved a Tudor-Valois marriage, even Walsingham conceded that it might be the lesser of two evils.

In his experience England had never been in a more critical position. The existence of so many Catholic threats only confirmed his conviction that a master plan existed for the overthrow of the English Protestant state. Now he stepped up – almost in desperation – his intelligence-gathering activities. It is no accident that most of the evidence for Walsingham's activities as Elizabeth's 'spymaster' comes from the 1580s. His first recorded payment for espionage is the £750 he received in 1582. Six years later he was receiving over £2,000 per annum, and these could well be underestimated figures.

No longer did Mr Secretary rely almost entirely on scraps of information gleaned from correspondence, rumours from the Elizabethan underworld or chance arrest at the ports. He had gathered a team of reliable agents who could be put to work on specific projects. The clandestine activities of Charles Sledd give us some indication of what begins to look like an espionage network. In July 1579 this shadowy figure was despatched to the newly founded English College at Rome, posing as an eager potential Catholic missionary. On his return to London ten months later he provided his patron with a long, detailed written report. It has to be read with caution because there was always a tendency for spies to embellish their information in order to enhance their own importance and, thereby, remain employed. But, if Sledd is to be trusted, his report confirmed Walsingham's conspiracy theories. The agent assured his employer that the students in Rome did not confine themselves to planning the reconversion of their countrymen. They discussed invasion plans and concluded that a landing at Milford Haven would enable them to march eastwards, gathering support as they approached the capital from the thousands of secret Catholics eagerly awaiting their deliverance. Their own informants had reported that the royal armoury at the Tower of London held inadequate stocks of powder and ordnance to quell an organized rebellion. This was no more than the excited babbling of zealots eager to become cannon-fodder in a holy cause but we know, and Walsingham certainly knew, how frightening and – given the right circumstances – how effective such fundamentalist covens could be.

Sledd returned to England with a list of names and a memory for faces. It did not take long for his knowledge to bear fruit. Within weeks he had busted one cell of immigrant priests in London and arrested two of its members. Sledd was not the only agent set to track down Jesuit priests arriving from their foreign training camps buoyed up with hatred for Elizabeth and her supporters. As a result of the vigilance of Walsingham's bloodhounds, more than a dozen covert Catholic activists were apprehended within a year. It was then a matter of deciding whether torture or bribery would best serve the cause of tackling the terrorist threat. Walsingham certainly managed to turn some of the captives. As one priest reported to his mentor in Rome, the worst threat to their security came from 'false brethren' in Walsingham's employ.

When it came to provocative acts the English could not claim innocence. This was dramatically demonstrated by the biggest single item of national news for 1580. On 26 September Francis Drake arrived in Plymouth harbour with his ship, the *Golden Hind*, laden to the gunwales with the spoils of one of the greatest voyages in maritime history. Since setting out at the end of 1577 he had rounded Cape Horn, attacked Spanish settlements on the Pacific coast, cap- tured a treasure-laden galleon and crossed the ocean to trade in the Moluccas, the preserve of Spanish and Portuguese merchant ven- turers. Sporadic information about the hispanophobe *El Draco's* circumnavigational progress had reached Europe in preceding months and, understandably, Philip II was furious. Mendoza, his ambassador, demanded restitution and the public punishment of Drake. Eliza- beth's reaction was to welcome Drake as a hero, confer a knighthood on him and scoop her share of the expedition's proceeds. Drake's pioneer voyage and his audacious challenge to Iberian maritime supremacy was a diplomatic embarrassment and one on which the Council was divided. Burghley was furious with Drake's piracy and declined a gift of ten gold ingots and Sussex told the captain to his face that he was an ill-bred braggart. They were sore because Drake's provocative exploits ran counter to their preferred policy of maintaining good relations with Spain. But as far as the queen was concerned money talked. Out of Drake's massive haul she received something in excess of £150,000. There was no way she was going to relinquish that.

Where did Walsingham stand in all this? If Drake is to be believed, he was the *fons et origo* of the whole project. According to a manuscript account of the 1590s the secretary summoned Drake to discuss ways in which the Crown might recoup losses inflicted by Spain through the disruption of Netherlands trade, the seizure of ships and goods, and assistance given to enemies of state. 'He showed me a plot,' Drake recalled, 'calling me . . . to note down where I thought [King Philip] might be most annoyed.'[21] The two men roughed out a plan for harassing the Pacific coast settlements and seeking a north-west passage by which to return. In a subsequent meeting the two men presented their scheme to the queen, who approved it. Another version of events credits Hatton with initiating the venture but agrees that Walsingham was brought in at an early stage. The clandestine arrangements were covered by a smokescreen of false information. It was given out that Drake's ships were being fitted out for a trading venture to the Levant. One thing Elizabeth – and doubtless Walsingham – insisted on was that Burghley should be kept in the dark.

This was a daring and risky operation for the backers to be involved in. The shared costs were not inconsiderable and the navigation of the Straits of Magellan, vital to the plan, was hazardous in the extreme. Few ships had accomplished it since Magellan's pioneering transit half a century earlier. Walsingham and his co-conspirators could not know that the 1577–80 voyage was going to be one of the most famous of all time, nor can they have dreamed of the financial rewards it would yield. It was nothing more nor less than a breathtaking act of piracy. How was Elizabeth persuaded to give it her blessing? She was certainly impressed by Drake – his macho bravado and his formidable record in transatlantic ventures. She saw the opportunity of staging an important diplomatic coup. Although she studiously avoided provoking Spanish hostility, she was annoyed at Iberian dominance of long-distance trade routes. If it could be shown that English ships could reach the Pacific and return home round the northern passages of the Americas this would show Spain and Portugal that they no longer enjoyed a monopoly. Moreover, if things turned out badly she could always disown Drake and claim that his was a private venture.

But the clincher, as Walsingham knew it would be, was the prospect of golden rewards. The trail of precious metal from New World mines ran from the Peruvian coast across the Panama peninsula to the Caribbean ports, where the annual treasure fleets loaded the cargoes for the transatlantic crossing. Spanish settlements on the Atlantic seaboard were well garrisoned but their counterparts on the other side of the continent were poorly protected because they were not under threat. Elizabeth was never averse to laying her hands on Spanish gold as she had shown by the seizure of Philip's ships in 1568. If the confident mariner could, as he claimed, return with a good haul of precious metal this would go a long way to reimbursing the treasury for such expenditure as the suppression of Irish revolt. Walsingham could also have pointed out that the shock of English interlopers in the New World would affect Philip's opportunity to make mischief in the Netherlands. Spain was bankrupt and her troops in the Low Countries had mutinied over pay arrears. Walsingham welcomed anything that would further embarrass Philip and aid the Dutch rebels.

The circumnavigation voyage and its unexpectedly massive financial success was one of Walsingham's great coups. It illustrates well the main thrust of his foreign policy and its divergence from that of Burghley and the queen. He never doubted that Spain was the great enemy and that an eventual showdown was inevitable. On 4 April 1581 Elizabeth cocked a diplomatic snook at King Philip. Amidst jubilant celebrations at Deptford, where the *Golden Hind* had been berthed, she not only conferred a knighthood on Drake, she asked the French ambassador to perform the dubbing ceremony. There could have been no more graphic demonstration of Anglo-French amity and the solidarity of both countries against Spain.

Of course, the marriage was still at the heart of relations between the two countries. After their recent disagreement Elizabeth had refrained from involving Walsingham in the protracted negotiations. But now she determined to send him on a top-level mission to Henry III. Bearing in mind his last ambassadorial adventure, Walsingham was far from enthusiastic. 'Her majesty,' he informed a colleague, 'hath some intention to send me over the seas, notwithstanding I will labour by all the means I may to break the journey off. Yourself can tell how hardly I was used in my last voyage and, as this is a matter of more danger than that, so have I cause to fear to be served with harder measure than I was.'[22]

But once again duty outweighed personal inclination.

Chapter 7

'SHE SEEMETH TO BE VERY EARNESTLY BENT TO PROCEED'

1581–4

'I content myself, Monsieur, that you assure yourself of me as of the most faithful friend that ever prince had. And if you trust to such a rock, all the tempest of the sea will be far from shaking it, nor will any storm on the earth turn it aside from honouring and loving you.'[1] So Elizabeth assured Anjou in March 1581. He cannot possibly have been taken in by the image of the queen as an example of granite immutability. He and his brother, Henry III, knew that the protestation of unshakable amity was a smokescreen behind which Francis Walsingham would bargain, bluff and bluster to obtain for England maximum diplomatic advantage at minimum cost. The ambassador's instructions were to bring about an Anglo-French defensive treaty while making no final commitment to marriage. Elizabeth had come round to the point of view that Walsingham had always advocated; the creation of a league with France which would hold Spanish ambition in check. Her hot-and-cold response to Anjou's wooing continued to keep everyone guessing but it seems that, by now, Elizabeth had resigned herself to the fact that marriage to the French prince was impracticable.

Perhaps the realization dawned that she had, all along, been in love with the *idea* of marriage, rather than the reality. In times of sober reflection she could not but acknowledge the practical difficulties pointed out to her by Walsingham and others – the differences of religion and age and the potential danger to her own health. She had no need to read the radical Puritan propaganda that poured from the presses to realize the widespread resentment marriage to Anjou would cause. In London there was much sympathy for men like John Stubbe. When the executioner, with three blows, cut off the pamphleteer's right hand, the large crowd in the Westminster market-place watched the event in sullen silence. When parliament was convened in 1580 the mood of opposition was plain. Yet Elizabeth remained the consummate actress, able to switch roles at a moment's notice. When it suited her she continued to revert to that of the lovesick bride-to-be. Not for the first or last time Walsingham found himself having to guess not only the intentions of foreign princes but also of his own mistress.

He was perhaps encouraged to receive, via Leicester, one of those heart-warming messages at which Elizabeth excelled. Dudley reported that the queen had spoken very warmly of her secretary. She acknowledged that Walsingham was a man of unshakable principles and opinions. She knew that her 'Moor' could not 'change his colour' but assured him that she valued his faithful service and that he would always enjoy her favour. It may have been a throwaway comment but it does go to the heart of the unique relationship the queen maintained with her closest advisers. Through all the frustrations, differences of opinion and downright confrontations, Elizabeth's charisma and loyalty to her closest servants held them willingly in thrall.

Walsingham set off for France on 22 July and was there for two months. As he had feared, he found himself in an impossible situation. Henry III, Catherine and Anjou were at odds among themselves but on one principle they were united: marriage must come before treaty. But Elizabeth's emissary was instructed not to commit her to marriage before treaty terms were agreed. The French feared – quite reasonably – that, if she were not matrimonially linked to Anjou, she might 'slip the collar' and leave him 'in the briars'. As with most diplomacy it was all a question of which side would crack first. For hour after hour in various meetings Walsingham argued the English case and, considering his own difficult position, he did it remarkably well. Every time he reported back on the problems he was encountering he received fresh instructions either to advance or withdraw the marriage proposal. 'I would to God,' he complained to Burghley, 'her highness would resolve one way or the other touching the matter of her marriage . . . when her majesty is pressed to marry, she seemeth to affect a league, and when a league is proposed, then she liketh better of marriage.'[2]

Anjou was determined that, if he could not access Elizabeth's person, he might at least access her purse. He desperately needed money for his campaign against Parma. Meanwhile Henry and Catherine, not wishing to provoke Spain, were trying to deflect Anjou from his Netherlands enterprise. Elizabeth, of course, wanted to encourage her Frog's adventures for much the same reason – she wanted to avoid direct confrontation with Philip II.

The same motivation lay behind another aspect of the negotiations. There was a pretender to the Portuguese throne in the shape of Dom Antonio of Avis, an illegitimate son of the former king. He travelled to Paris and London during the first half of 1581 attempting to hire ships and men for an assault on the Azores. He was well received by Walsingham and Leicester, who put him up in Bayard's Castle and argued his case in Council. Philip, meanwhile, informed the queen via Mendoza that assistance given to his rival would be construed as an act of war. Elizabeth, like Catherine, was in a quandary. Both queens were not averse to tweaking the lion's tail but both were wary of the lion's claws. Walsingham enthusiastically advocated Dom Antonio's cause but was inhibited by Elizabeth's insistence that any English aid must be given in secret. He did, however, work out a way of squaring the circle. This was yet another occasion on which Walsingham, the conviction politician, went ahead on his own initiative. If the word 'Puritan' suggests to us people with a drab, negative attitude to life then Walsingham fails to fit the stereotype. He was a venture capitalist who relished risk-taking and thrilled to the exploits of bold mariners and merchants. He had proved this in his sponsorship of Drake's 1577–80 voyage. He now took another gamble, laying his career on the line and re-investing a substantial chunk of the profits of the circumnavigation expedition. He backed the hero of the hour in a yet more audacious and provocative raid on Spanish interests.

Drake was to take a small fleet to Terceira in the Azores (currently loyal to Dom Antonio) and use it as a base to attack the silver fleet. He would be sailing under the pretender's flag in order to preserve the fiction of Elizabeth's non-involvement. In reality she and Walsingham would be major backers of the venture and hoped for a pecuniary return similar to that of the previous expedition. Walsingham knew his mistress well enough to be sure that she would be dazzled by gold. He, himself, was not averse to making money but his major concern was to nudge the queen ever closer to open confrontation with Spain. Much as she liked the idea of the Azores expedition, Elizabeth was not prepared to go it alone. She made her consent conditional on French involvement. Thus the Portuguese venture became firmly entwined with the marriage and treaty negotiations. It was put on hold until, as Drake pointed out, it was too late in the season to be feasible, because the treasure fleet had safely reached Spain. He paid off his men and sold his provisions.

The end results of weeks of hard bargaining were muddle and compromise. Elizabeth supplied Anjou with £10,000 for the Netherlands and agreed to receive a further visit from him. Ultimately, Dom Antonio was able to assemble a fleet of sixty Dutch and English ships which set out the following year. Elizabeth's contribution was a few supply vessels. Philip's navy confronted it off the island of São Miguel and inflicted a heavy defeat. In 1583 the last vestiges of resistance in the Azores were crushed. Walsingham, who once again had backed a daring enterprise with his own money, once again found himself seriously out of pocket. Anjou departed for the Netherlands in mid-August and conducted a two-month campaign. But after an early success in the capture of Cambrai, his expedition faltered for lack of funds. By the end of October he was back in Paris busily preparing for his second visit to England.

Anjou now desperately needed Elizabeth's support if his Low Countries adventure was not to collapse ignominiously. At the end of October he arrived once again in London to pursue his courtship with renewed vigour. He understood well that Walsingham was a key player in the formation of policy and he deliberately courted the secretary. He expressed a warm regard for Walsingham's honesty and his political acumen. He even asked if he might be a guest in Walsingham's house for a few days before moving on to the court. (Walsingham wriggled out of this expensive honour by pointing out

that the plague was rampant in his quarter of the capital.) It is difficult
to know with what size pinch of salt to take Anjou's protestations of
friendship and regard but what is evident is that he earnestly desired
Walsingham's support. He knew that Mr Secretary did not, in his
heart of hearts, favour the marriage but that he might be brought to
advocate it on pragmatic grounds.

Walsingham was certainly committed to giving maximum support
to the French prince in the Netherlands. It was vital, in his view, to
take advantage of Parma's currently weak position. About Elizabeth's
attitude to the marriage Walsingham was probably as much in the
dark as anyone. He certainly shared the shock which reverberated
round the court as the result of an event which took place on 22
November. According to Mendoza:

> At eleven in the morning, the Queen and [Anjou] were walking
> together in a gallery, Leicester and Walsingham being present, when
> the French ambassador entered and said that he wished to write to his
> master, from whom he had received orders to hear from the Queen's
> own lips her intention with regard to marrying his brother. She
> replied, 'You may write this to the King: that the Duke of [Anjou]
> shall be my husband', and at the same moment she turned to [Anjou]
> and kissed him on the mouth, drawing a ring from her own hand and
> giving it to him as a pledge. [Anjou] gave her a ring of his in return, and
> shortly afterwards the Queen summoned the ladies and gentlemen
> from the presence chamber in the gallery, repeating to them in a loud
> voice in [Anjou's] presence what she had previously said.[3]

Breathtaking as this development was, Walsingham had other pressing
concerns in those autumn days. His campaign against the infiltrated
priests was bearing fruits and his secretariat was heavily employed in
sifting the reports of informers and organizing searches. To set the
scene for the dramatic events of November and December 1581 we
must go back to the beginning of the year. Parliament had last met in
1576 and, in subsequent years, it had been prorogued twenty-six
times. Elizabeth was more than happy to do without it while the
Anjou courtship was on her agenda. She did not want her freedom of

movement compromised by forceful expression of public (or, at least, parliamentary) opinion. But trouble in Ireland, with its concomitant costs, and the mounting activity of the Jesuit fifth column made it necessary for the state to fortify itself with financial and statutory backing. Walsingham was to the fore in urging the summoning of parliament which met, in January, against a background of nation-wide anxiety about a major Catholic threat.

Now it was the radical Protestants who were in tune with the popular mood. On the first day of business Walsingham's brother-in-law, Paul Wentworth, proposed a national fast, accompanied by the preaching of sermons, to unite the queen and her subjects and stiffen their resolve against the papistical onslaught. 'Prayer and fasting' was a biblical principle eagerly espoused by the Puritans. Elizabeth squashed the proposal firmly. She saw it – probably correctly – as an attempt by the radicals to grab the initiative. Such important religious matters, she reminded members, were for the queen and her bishops to decide, not a secular body. And she did not let the opportunity pass without singling out the Wentworth brothers for her especial disapprobation.

It was another of Walsingham's brothers-in-law, Sir Walter Mild-may, Chancellor of the Exchequer, who set out the business desig-nated by the Crown for the session. His indignant rhetoric about the Catholic threat could not conceal his, and the government's, anxiety:

> The obstinate and stiff-necked Papist is so far from being reformed as he hath gotten stomach to go backwards and to show his disobedience, not only in arrogant words but also in contemptuous deeds. To confirm them herein, and to increase their numbers, you see how the Pope hath and doth comfort their hollow hearts with absolutions, dispensations, reconciliations, and such other things of Rome. You see how lately he hath sent hither a sort of hypocrites, naming themselves Jesuits, a rabble of vagrant friars newly sprung up and coming through the world to trouble the Church of God; whose principal errand is, by creeping into the houses and familiarities of men of behaviour and reputation, not only to corrupt the realm with false doctrine, but also, under that pretence, to stir sedition. In consequence, not only former

recusants, but many, very many who previously conformed, now utterly refuse to be of our Church.[4]

The escalation of Jesuit infiltration, the second Desmond Rebellion and the alarming rumours of Spanish invasion preparations had provoked another reversal of government policy. The softly, softly approach was laid aside – for the time being, at least.

Mildmay called for tougher anti-recusancy laws and the taxation necessary to put the nation's defences in good order to meet any foreign threat. His rousing peroration urged members to do their duty:

> The love and duty that we owe to our most gracious Queen, by whose ministry God hath done so great things for us – even such as be wonderful in the eyes of the world – to make us more careful for her preservation and security than for our own: a princess known by long experience to be a principal patron of the Gospel, virtuous, wise, faithful, just; unspotted in word or deed, merciful, temperate, a maintainer of peace and justice amongst her people without respect of persons; a Queen besides of this realm, our native country, renowned through the world, which our enemies gape to overrun, if by force or sleight they could do it. For such a Queen and such a country, and for the defence of the honour and surety of them both, nothing ought to be so dear unto us that with most willing hearts we should not spend and adventure freely.[5]

The man who stood to second Mildmay's speech was Thomas Norton, veteran parliamentarian and pamphleteer whom we have already met. The co-author of *Gorboduc* and the translator of Calvin's *Institution* had consistently busied himself in religious and constitutional issues. He was no fiery-eyed extremist, demanding the abolition of offensive items of clerical dress or the merciless harrowing of all suspected Catholics, but he held very clear opinions that were close to those of his friend and patron Francis Walsingham. Without wanting to see a change of church government he was critical of episcopacy – or, at least, the halfway-house stance of most of Elizabeth's bishops.

He disapproved of the Anjou marriage on religious grounds. He was committed to the rooting out of recusancy and the apprehension of immigrant priests. In 1578–9 he had been one of the secretary's intelligence agents in Rome and he was one of the most skilled interrogators of Catholic prisoners, a task which earned him the nickname of 'Rackmaster' among his enemies.

We will return shortly to the subject of torture in the war on terror. First let us hear what Norton himself had to say about the appropriate way to handle Catholics:

> Touching toleration to papists, I have ever holden, and have published this opinion, that her subjects holding popish heresies upon persuasion of conscience were to be borne withal and relieved by the instruction and the leisure of God's Spirit to be attended, so long as they did not disturb the church, and held them within allegiance and loyal affections to the queen.[6]

Walsingham was of much the same opinion. Those whose religious convictions had not yet been reformed could not be coerced into faith. They needed to be educated. He favoured more biting recusancy fines as a means of encouraging offenders to attend their parish churches where they might be brought to truth, in Norton's words, by 'instruction and the leisure of God's Spirit'. Underground sacerdotalism was a more urgent problem The priests who flitted about the shires from hiding place to hiding place were the subjects of a foreign ruler who had set himself to removing Elizabeth Tudor from her throne. However much they disavowed political motives, there was no escape from the logic that they were emissaries of a regime which was financing invasions in Ireland and fomenting plots in England and Scotland. Converts were, by the terms of *Regnans in excelsis*, expected to pray for and give support to military intervention by a Catholic invader. The remembered images of 1572 were still vivid to Walsingham. He had seen what frenzied mobs could do when stirred by their priests and had no reason to doubt that the same would happen in England if Catholics were to gain the upper hand.

Thanks to the energy and efficiency of magistrates, informers and spies, several of these ecclesiastical 'runagates' were being arrested but that only solved one part of the problem. The government still had to decide how to proceed against them. An analysis Walsingham committed to writing in 1586 showed a pragmatic and essentially secular understanding of the problem. He dismissed a policy of wholesale execution. Not only was it morally indefensible, it was counter-productive. Creating martyrs had never been an effective way of halting a religious movement. Walsingham recommended that a few priests should suffer the penalty for treason, 'for example's sake'. The rest should be banished or held in secure detention centres (an old idea now resurrected). He even, briefly, advocated a scheme to allow priests and Catholic laymen to emigrate to America.

In the early months of 1581 parliament struggled to come up with legislation which would give the government powers to deal effectively with the Catholic threat. The draconian first draft was considerably watered down in committee and, though we do not know whose guiding hands were the strongest, the statute that eventually emerged enshrined Walsingham's principle of dealing with proselytization as a political offence. Recusancy fines were swingeingly increased. From one shilling a week they rose to £20 a month. The basis for prosecuting priests was defined as deflecting English people from their allegiance or converting them to Catholicism *with the intention* of undermining their loyalty. The Act made clear that religious belief and even the effort to spread that belief were not *per se* punishable by the state, unless it could be shown that political subversion was intended. The final wording of the 'Act to retain the Queen's Majesty's subjects in their due obedience' was a piece of masterly lawyerese; it avoided the opprobrium of being an instrument of religious persecution while enabling the courts, whenever they wished, to interpret religious zeal as treasonable intent.

The Act fell a long way short of the measures the parliamentary draftsmen had initially proposed and it has customarily been assumed that the modifications were made on the queen's insistence. Elizabeth was temperamentally disinclined to 'make windows into men's hearts and secret thoughts'. She was also instinctively wary of measures initiated in her Puritan-dominated House of Commons. But the Council – and this certainly included Walsingham – were also involved in steering the bill to its final form. It was all very well for MPs to indulge in anti-papal oratory but the government had to come up with workable legislation. Any law depended for its effectiveness on the willingness of local courts and magistrates to implement it. Any attempt to impose widespread persecution would have been resented and thwarted in the shires, particularly in those farthest from London. If Walsingham ever needed to be reminded that politics is the art of the possible he had only to reflect on his long and tortuous relationship with the queen. As it was, the new Act allowed Walsingham the freedom to proceed against apprehended priests on an individual basis. No one knew more than he about the men his agents (and other vigilantes) tracked down and other members of the Council frequently deferred to his judgement on the best way to deal with them. Thus it was that Walsingham decided who might be 'turned' into government agents, who should remain under lock and key, who ought to be banished and who should suffer the dramatic and sanguinary penalty imposed on traitors.

In the parliament of 1572–83 Walsingham sat as a member for Surrey but there is very little evidence of his involvement in its proceedings. However, he remained in close contact with Thomas Norton who was very active in the 1581 session. He was a principal draftsman of the Recusancy Act and when a new sedition bill came before parliament he tried to turn it into a second specifically anti-Catholic measure. The bill, as proposed, toughened the law on slandering the sovereign and also made it an offence to cast horoscopes or 'by prophesying, calculation or other unlawful act' try to determine how long the queen would live or who would succeed her. As the years passed, Elizabeth's subjects became increasingly anxious about the future and this provided opportunity for necromancers and preachers to impress the gullible with claims of hidden knowledge on the sensitive subject. The proposed Act was not directed against Catholics. Indeed, it was more likely to catch Puritan pamphleteers and preachers. (The memory of Stubbe's fate was still vivid in people's minds.) Norton now proposed an amendment which would make it an offence to proclaim that the doctrine of the English church was heretical or schismatic.

Norton had, by this time, interrogated several captured priests. He had been involved in the examination of Cuthbert Mayne and knew at first hand how tricky it had been to secure a safe conviction. The priest had been offered a way of escape: all he had to do was swear allegiance to Elizabeth as supreme governor of the church. This he could not, in conscience, do. Was it then that Norton had the idea of applying a doctrinal litmus test to all suspected Catholics? By whatever route Norton arrived at his amendment, it amounted to bringing religious belief firmly under the umbrella of civil law. So much for Norton's insistence on toleration! In the event his ploy failed and, within months, this most loyal of the queen's subjects found himself in the Tower for incurring the queen's displeasure.

These complex parliamentary manoeuvrings indicate how tense and divisive the Catholic problem was. Faced with the mounting likelihood of invasion and the present fact of infiltration, Walsingham and his colleagues might have responded by creating draconian laws which would have filled the prisons and kept the executioners busy for years. This was, in reality, not an option. Firstly because of the size of the problem. The arrest of thousands of Englishmen on suspicion of treason – even if the courts could be induced to prosecute – would have been intolerably divisive and would have played into the hands of England's enemies. But pragmatism was not the only, or the main, reason for pursuing a more cautious policy. Massive state persecution was morally indefensible. The proof of that lay ready to hand. Spain had gone down that route and ended up as a police state. France had gone down that route and ended up in ungovernable chaos. So Walsingham, who shared Norton's abhorrence of popery and his longing to cleanse England of Romish defilement, refused to accept his friend's apparently simple solution.

The Commons – or, at least, its Puritan majority – could not allow the session to end without continuing to press the need for further church reform. Even those who were prepared to accept episcopal government were scandalized by the abuses which remained to be addressed, such as non-residence, the poor educational quality of many clergy, and heavy-handed discipline of radicals. After much earnest debate the house deputed four councillors – Walsingham, his co-secretary Thomas Wilson, Hatton and Mildmay – to present their grievances to a committee of bishops. Reporting back to the house, Mildmay acknowledged, on behalf of the queen, that earlier parliamentary complaints had been ignored by the clergy. He assured members: 'her Majesty would eftsoons commit the same unto such others of them as with all convenient speed, without remissness and slackness, should see the same accomplished accordingly, in such sort as the same shall neither be delayed or undone.'[7]

Elizabeth did, indeed, take the matter up with the bishops and exhorted them to redress such grievances as they should decide needed to be dealt with. The result was, of course, that nothing happened. Inevitably, several members felt that, once again, they had been fobbed off by the queen with empty answers. Norton was reported to the Council as one of the malcontents. In his defence he insisted that, while being highly critical of the bishops, he had not spoken ill of the queen.

Norton, like Walsingham, now belonged to the older generation of Puritans. If some of his opinions and actions seem to be mutually contradictory it is probably because he was sensitive to the challenge of younger Puritans who were more extreme and more demonstrative. They viewed their elders as compromisers and yesterday's men. Norton was anxious to show that he yielded nothing to the young Turks in zeal but, in fact, he had inevitably mellowed and had learned that confrontation was not the most effective way of securing change – certainly with a queen like Elizabeth. Walsingham found himself in much the same position. His attitude towards impatient reformers was still: 'If you knew with what difficulty we retain what we have and that seeking of more might hazard . . . that which we already have, you would then deal warily in this time when policy carrieth more sway than zeal.'[8]

As we have seen, part of Walsingham's strategy in dealing with the Jesuit menace was to make examples of the more notorious offenders. In July 1581 his agents achieved a major coup. Acting on information received, a local magistrate arrived at Leyford Grange, near Wantage, the home of a known recusant, with an armed posse. They subjected the house and outbuildings to an inch-by-inch search but it was only after many hours that they discovered three priests cowering in a secret room. One of them was Edmund Campion, a star of the English mission, a man of considerable intellect who, before his defection to Rome, had been marked out by the queen for special favour. Walsingham was just about to embark for France and it was from beyond the Channel that he wrote urging Campion's prosecutors to throw the book at him.

The captives were conveyed to London and, because the Council ordered that their arrival should be made into a public spectacle, they were paraded through the streets of the capital, tied securely to their horses. Campion bore a placard bearing the words 'Edmund Campion the Seditious Jesuit'. After a few days in the Tower Campion was brought to the house of the Lord Chancellor, Sir Thomas Bromley, to be examined on behalf of the Council by Leicester and Hatton. They were doubtless anxious about the impression he would make at his forthcoming trial, as was the queen. Campion was recognized by all who knew him as sweet-natured, clear-headed and a gifted orator. He was careful not to condemn himself by any unguarded word and his examiners ordered that he be returned to prison and, if necessary, put to the rack. Walsingham, still in France, played no part in the subsequent interrogation which went on for almost three months but Beale deputized for him and Thomas Norton took care of the application of torture.

One remarkable – and probably ill-advised – aspect of Campion's ordeal was public disputation. On four separate occasions he was obliged to debate with Protestant theologians several points of doctrine. If this exercise was devised to draw attention to the pernicious opinions of the accused and the fair-mindedness of his accusers (and we should bear in mind that in no Catholic country were Protestant prisoners permitted to air and defend their beliefs in public), it backfired badly. Norton, one of Campion's adversaries, complained that the prisoner used the events to deliver prepared speeches and that the open invitation to the public enabled the priest's friends and sympathizers to attend. London was soon awash with pro- and anti-Campion tracts.

The Council, therefore, had to consider carefully how they were going to proceed judicially against the Jesuits. They decided not to use the recent Act, which could have seen the trial bogged down in religious issues. Instead they fell back on Edward III's Treason Act of 1351. The prosecution had witnesses, predominantly Charles Sledd, ready to swear that Campion and his colleagues were parties to a plot, hatched in the Rome seminary, to assassinate the queen and stir up rebellion in preparation for an invasion. The trial took place on 20 November in a packed Westminster Hall. The presiding judge was Sir Christopher Wray, Chief Justice of Queen's Bench who had been in charge of Stubbe's trial. The prosecutor was Edmund Anderson, the Attorney-General who arrived fresh from the trials of nonconformists in East Anglia. Both were sound establishment men, pledged to defending the status quo against attack from extremists – of whatever colour. Campion handled the defence well and he enjoyed a wide measure of sympathy, particularly when the audience noted that torture had left him unable to raise his right hand in order to enter his plea of not guilty. Onlookers were divided in their opinions. Not so the jury. Eleven days later Campion and two companions were drawn on hurdles to Tyburn to face death by hanging, drawing and quartering.

Then, while the Campion affair was still a *cause célèbre* being argued about in alehouses and market places, something remarkable happened. Within four days of the Jesuit's death, Thomas Norton, his chief tormentor, was arrested and locked up in the Bloody Tower. His offence was, apparently, having spoken against the Anjou match. If he had offended the queen in this way no evidence survives and Norton was clearly astonished by his sudden arrest. There were certainly sterner critics of Elizabeth's matrimonial proceedings – some in the Council – who were allowed free speech. The timing cannot have been a coincidence. 'Rackmaster' Norton was an unpopular figure and public sympathy for Campion swelled the numbers of those who would have loved to see him behind bars, if not stretched on his own instrument of torture. Norton's arrest looks very much like a sop to the populace, a move ordered by Elizabeth to demonstrate her even-handedness and also to placate the French.

Norton's captivity was far from arduous. He remained in the

Tower until March 1582, but was allowed many comforts and privileges. He was furnished with writing materials and fired off several letters to prominent persons proclaiming his innocence. He also received visitors. Among them was Sir Francis Walsingham. The secretary stood by his old friend as far as he could. He interceded with the queen for the prisoner's release. He promised to take care of Norton's wife, who was in the early stages of a complete mental collapse. And he gave Norton a new literary commission. He proposed that the fifty-year-old author, poet, lawyer and parliamentarian should draw on his long experience to analyse the English church and set forth 'such things as are meet to be considered of for the stay of the present corruption in religion'. The result, known as Norton's *Devices*, was not printed but both Walsingham and Burghley owned manuscript copies and his ideas on reforming, not just the church, but the legal, judicial and educational systems were, we must assume, useful to them in the framing of policy. Norton's conciliar friends secured his complete return to freedom in April 1582, whereupon he resumed his various activities in close association with Walsingham. He had only two more years of life left but they were hectic. He continued to publish his observations on religious matters and to examine Catholic prisoners. He rebutted the attacks of Catholic pamphleteers. In addition, Walsingham set him to write a massive historical review of important events and personalities since the Norman conquest. Whatever the queen might think of Thomas Norton and however he might be perceived by the people, he enjoyed the friendship, support and confidence of Francis Walsingham to the very end. And he had one last significant service to perform for his patron.

The duc d'Anjou left England on 7 February. Elizabeth played her love games adroitly to the last, accompanying her departing guest as far as Canterbury and there making a major production of their tearful adieus. The Frenchman left with a noble escort led by none other than the Earl of Leicester. In fact, during the marriage negotiations over the preceding months, the queen had increasingly upped the ante, even to the point of demanding that Henry III should close down the Catholic seminary at Rheims. She thus made it impossible for the French to agree to her terms. Instead of marrying Anjou she supplied him with more funds for his Netherlands campaigns. Unfortunately, the faction-riven Dutch Protestants were quite ungovernable. Also Anjou was no match for Parma, nor could the money the duke was able to raise in France and England outweigh the Indies gold Philip now had at his command. In June 1583 a humiliated Anjou crossed the border back into France. Elizabeth had nothing to show for her investment.

She certainly had not secured a firm alliance with France. Despite Walsingham's arduous and thankless efforts to manufacture some kind of entente, the Guises and their allies had been working behind the scenes against England. The focus of their attention was Scotland and their aim was to work on the young king and revive the auld alliance. Esmé Stuart, Sieur d'Aubigny, had made an excellent start. The Frenchification of James VI's court and the fall of Morton were severe blows to English policy. They put new heart into Mary Stuart. In 1582 the Queen of Scots was forty and had spent more than a third of her life being shunted around various strongholds in the English Midlands. She knew full well that Walsingham kept a close watch on all her servants and visitors and intercepted her letters whenever he could. One of her few distractions was dreaming up new ways of maintaining contact with her supporters in Scotland and France and the London embassies of Henry III and Philip II. Mary's guardian, the Earl of Shrewsbury, was certainly kept on his toes:

> Good Mr Secretary, This Lady's tailor, Jukes, yet with much ado is [dismissed], and she loth to let him depart. Desiring to retain still all that come to her, she caused him to make sundry things for her, which hath been [the reason for] his stay. I made him to be truly looked unto. Yet, can I not answer but that they might use some [secret] practice with him. I know them so well and their cunning dealings [that] I cannot be of other opinions.[9]

So Shrewsbury reported in April 1581, but for all his vigilance and the beavering of Walsingham's agents nothing seriously incriminating came to light.

This was frustrating for the secretary. Scraps of intelligence coming into his office offered glimpses of fresh plots, plans and alliances directed against England but no coherent pattern emerged and certainly nothing that would tie the Queen of Scots to a conspiracy against Elizabeth. Ironically it was those very events that encouraged England's enemies which provided Walsingham with more valuable information. The fire beneath the pot of Catholic conspiracy was fanned by indignation at Drake's piracy (Mendoza was so angry about Elizabeth's support for her corsair that he refused to attend her court after November 1580), by d'Aubigny's success in Scotland and by the fate of Campion and other priests. Throughout the Catholic world there was an accelerating optimism; a sense that God was about to bring the defiant heretic nation to its knees. Serious plans were discussed at the highest levels. Conspiracies abounded and more and more people were brought into them. This was Walsingham's opportunity. The increasing number of chains being forged meant that there were certain to be weak links.

While he was in France, in the autumn of 1581, Walsingham probed the Guise circle to discover what he could about how their Scottish connections worked and what their plans were. He observed a worrying euphoria amongst the ultra-Catholics at court. Guise policy which, during the early wars of religion had been a flexible mix of dynastic, religious and political interests, had now settled into a determined crusade, not only to exterminate Huguenots, but also to carry the papal offensive abroad, at swordpoint if necessary. They had formed a national Catholic League and were in cahoots with Philip II. This was the collusion Walsingham had always feared. With d'Aubigny in place in Edinburgh the conspirators regarded the re-conversion of Scotland as virtually a done deal. Their plans were both detailed and ambitious. The principal couriers were the Jesuit Robert Persons, who had recently escaped from England following Campion's arrest, and William Crichton, a Scottish Jesuit. Persons was in the process of setting up another English seminary on Guise's estate at Eu in Normandy, about which Elizabeth soon protested in the strongest terms. She instructed her ambassador to demand the closure of the college and not to be fobbed off with assurances that the establishment was for purely educational purposes.

> . . . her Highness certainly knoweth that the foundation of the same seminaries and houses is only to instruct such young persons as may be cunningly allured thither, from whence afterwards they are returned with charge to seduce her majesty's subjects from their true allegiance, due unto her, unto the obedience of such as by bulls and censures have sought and do seek her Majesty's deprivation and ruin; as may be verified by the examinations of sundry of them which have been taken in this realm, and by such writings and instructions as have been taken with them, and therefore her Majesty can in no wise repute them in the number of her good subjects.[10]

Persons was despatched to Lisbon to meet Philip with a request for 8,000 troops. Crichton would return to Scotland with a view to receiving the young king into the Catholic church. Those who knew James well believed that his conversion might be achieved on the offer of a suitably large financial inducement. If necessary, the king was to be brought into France. Mendoza, meanwhile, was in touch with malcontent English nobles in the north, who were to join with a Scottish army once a Catholic regime had been established north of the border. An intercepted letter from Mary Stuart to James Beaton, her representative in Paris, revealed that she was apprised of the general outline of the plot.

This information reaching Walsingham in bits and pieces over the weeks and months led to frenzied and diverse activity. For her part, Elizabeth preferred to deal with her fellow royals. She sent Beale to Sheffield Lodge where Mary was currently being held to see whether it might be possible to reach an accommodation. The Queen of Scots offered a deal: she would recognize Elizabeth as lawful occupant to the English throne and forswear all discussion with foreign powers if she were allowed to return to Scotland to rule jointly with her son. When Beale reported back his royal mistress was disposed to give Mary the benefit of the doubt. Partly to please Anjou, she authorized some lessening of Mary's confinement and assured her of her goodwill. Walsingham, meanwhile, was at his wit's end with Elizabeth's inability or unwillingness to recognize the Scottish queen's duplicity. By now he had a good idea of what was brewing and of Mary's involvement in it. Confirmation came with an important surveillance coup in May. One of the couriers being used by Mendoza was an agent posing as an itinerant tooth-puller. He aroused the suspicion of Sir John Forster, Warden of the Middle March. The messenger was arrested and though he escaped (probably through bribery) he left some of his belongings behind. Concealed in the back of a mirror Forster discovered Mendoza's letters to Crichton. These told Walsingham virtually all he needed to know about the ominous league of forces operating against England. It must have been with an I-told-you-so air that the secretary reported to the queen on the machinations of her enemies and insisted that she intervene in the affairs of young King James and grasp the nettle of dealing with his mother. But any such action struck at the heart of Elizabeth's conviction that the persons of anointed sovereigns were inviolable. She would not countenance encouraging Scottish subjects to defy their king. Walsingham's frustration knew no bounds. Since Elizabeth seemed determined to be her own worst enemy, he now took the policy initiative of personally intriguing with his allies among the Scottish nobility.

As the international situation grew more and more tense and dangerous through the 1580s we find Walsingham increasingly acting alone in his concern for the safety of his queen, his country and his religion. In his official letters he was at pains to indicate to ambassadors and foreign correspondents that he was conveying the instructions of the queen or the 'lords of the Council' but often he was keeping his superiors in the dark and pursuing his own courses. He was at the centre of the widest and most effective intelligence web. He possessed the best overview of international affairs. Therefore he felt he knew better than anyone else the appropriate action that should be taken. The next step, if he could not win his argument in debate, was to go it alone. The temptation to act independently is one that faces many guardians of national secrets. The name J. Edgar Hoover comes very readily to mind. Like the FBI chief, Walsingham was impatient with his political leaders. He regarded the queen as being incapable of consistent action, Burghley as being too cautious and deferential towards Philip II, and the rest of the Council as being too often distracted by factions and personality clashes. Accordingly, he played his cards close to his chest, letting out information to his colleagues, and even his mistress, on a need-to-know basis. Thus, for example, he instructed the English ambassador in France to write certain elements of his report in a 'by-letter and not in your general letter, which I must needs show to divers of my lords, and so either make them privy to the contents of the cipher or vex them if I send it undeciphered'.[11] When Walsingham discovered that the ambassador in Scotland, Robert Bowes, was reporting to Burghley, as well to him, he remonstrated. He ordered Bowes to communicate directly to him, in cipher, so that no one at court could open his letters and read them whenever he was not there. Another diplomat, Edward Stafford, ambassador to France, was so worried by Walsingham's methods that he complained to Burghley:

> I write to you, my lord, as the only friend upon whom I repose trust, to know your advice upon a letter Mr Secretary writ me yesterday . . . he would have me write to him secretly. I know that by his means the Queen has had false advertisements of preparations here from his factors and has been incensed that news of importance should come from others.[12]

As we shall see, Walsingham was keeping a close watch on the ambassador, who had aroused his suspicions. Three years later Stafford was known to be selling information about English naval movements to Guise and Philip. But his dealings with the ambassador are further evidence that Walsingham was a control freak. His unilateral activity was risky and he certainly could not have indulged in it without the support of the Earl of Leicester.

It was clear to him that the key to the Scottish situation was the young king and his bedazzlement with d'Aubigny. Walsingham was in close contact with the anti-French caucus in Scotland and with the fugitive Earl of Angus who was their ally in England. Angus went to

Elizabeth and asked for money to fund a coup. Inevitably the queen declined to be involved. Walsingham, therefore, advanced some of his own capital and helped to organize the plot. All was going well until the secretary heard from Paris that his plans were discovered. He sent messengers galloping northwards to Robert Bowes, who urged the conspirators to accelerate their arrangements. The result was the kidnapping of a king. When James was hunting close to Perth on 7 August a party of horsemen intercepted him and carried him off to the nearby castle of Ruthven, a stronghold of the Earl of Gowrie.

It was round two to the Protestant lords but the match was far from over. D'Aubigny was still at large. He planned a counter-kidnap, which failed. French intrigues were still afoot. Their party was still strong and loyalties on both sides were mutable; that is to say they could be bought. Walsingham urged Elizabeth to open her purse. He received the old answer. In the name of King James his new minders ordered the favourite out of the country. Desperately, d'Aubigny prevaricated. After the counter-kidnap failed he tried to organize support among some of the northern English nobles but his letters were intercepted. Meanwhile, Henry III and the Guises sent a new ambassador, La Mothe Fénélon, to Scotland. He arrived in London en route to take up his assignment, his luggage including chests of French gold. He presented himself at Elizabeth's court and requested a passport to travel overland to Scotland. At all costs it was vital to prevent the diplomat enabling d'Aubigny to turn the tables by financing his cause and assuring him of military aid. There now ensued an almost comic situation. The queen's councillors devised stratagem after stratagem to detain Fénélon, while urging their Scottish confederates to eject d'Aubigny with all possible haste. Eventually the impatient ambassador told Elizabeth that, if his passport was not forthcoming, he would create a diplomatic incident by packing his bags and going home. The passport was duly produced and the diplomat, William Davison, was assigned to accompany Fénélon on his journey – with secret instructions from Walsingham to do everything possible to slow him down. When every means to detain the Frenchman had been exhausted he left London at the end of December. And still no word had been received about d'Aubigny's departure from Scotland. In fact the exiled favourite set out from Dalkeith about the same time that Fénélon quit London. It had been a close call.

But the constantly changing cloudscape of Scottish events allowed the English government no opportunity to relax. In June 1583 King James was snatched out of Gowrie's custody. This time the kidnap was engineered by the captain of the royal guard whom Walsingham had been instrumental in putting in place. This is yet one more indication that in the intricate world of national and international factions almost anyone could be bought. French influence was once more in the ascendant north of the border. Walsingham was driven to distraction by the worsening situation. What he learned from his latest intelligence source only added to his alarm.

He had discovered that the French embassy was the clearing house for the secret correspondence reaching Mary from France and Spain. The ambassador, Michel de Castlenau, Sieur de la Mauvissière was a charming, friendly man whom, on a personal level, Walsingham liked. However he was not very astute and had no inkling that the secretary was soon running two spies in his household. The first, Giordano Bruno, a guest under Castlenau's roof, offered his services to the English government without prompting. Many would-be informants resorted to Walsingham because they knew that he was a willing paymaster hungry for intelligence, and we cannot know to what extent greed and idealism motivated most occupants of the seamy diplomatic underworld. Bruno, however, was in a different category. A Neapolitan scholar, poet and philosopher of distinction, he enjoyed Europe-wide literary and political connections. In religious matters he was a fence-sitter, opposing the pretensions of the papacy without embracing Protestantism. He enjoyed London's intellectual scene because of its atmosphere of free debate and was particularly attracted to the Dudley-Sidney circle. He was a well-informed and also a witty correspondent. For instance the *nom de guerre* he chose for himself suggested that in the opinion of Catholic reactionaries he was a heretic; a brand for the burning. He signed his reports 'Henry Fagot'.

The second agent was a Scottish theologian and poet, William Fowler, who had found himself in an English jail. The price of his freedom was to be Walsingham's mole in the French embassy. So now there were two government spies in Castelnau's palatial residence, Salisbury Court, close by the notorious Bridewell house of correction, among whose inmates were both Puritan and Catholic undesirables. Neither knew of the other's activities and the situation bordered on the comic when Bruno warned Walsingham that Fowler was not all he seemed. In fact, Fowler obviously overplayed his hand and this was actually useful to Walsingham, for, while Castelnau was keeping an eye on Fowler, he was oblivious to Bruno's activities. And Bruno was a real danger to him.

The Italian was a remarkable spy with a real talent for the work. In the summer of 1583 he bribed no less a person than Castelnau's secretary, Nicolas Leclerc, Sieur de Courcelles, to betray his master's secrets. Was it jealousy that prompted Leclerc to turn against his employer? Did he hope to elbow the aged ambassador aside and take his job? Leclerc was certainly ambitious and went on to higher diplomatic service. Whatever the truth of the matter, Walsingham was now receiving a steady supply of reports and copied confidential documents from Salisbury Court. From them he learned how Mary Stuart's communication system worked. Her couriers included Henry Howard, brother of the Duke of Norfolk who had been executed after the Ridolfi plot, and Francis Throckmorton, nephew of the diplomat, Sir Nicholas Throckmorton. Bruno particularly disliked Howard and made him the victim of a savagely witty literary attack. Both men were covert Catholics and Howard was already under surveillance. It was now revealed that they made frequent nocturnal visits to the embassy. Everything was now going well for Walsingham. He was carefully accumulating evidence and had high hopes of being able to secure the big prize – incontrovertible evidence against Mary that would lead to her trial and execution. All he had to do was wait for the appropriate moment to strike.

Then came the bombshell. In late July Elizabeth ordered him to go to Scotland and sort out in person English relations with the king. Walsingham was furious. He did not want to be away from London at such a crucial time and he was convinced that the Scottish mission was a fool's errand. According to Mendoza he actually prostrated himself before the queen, begging her to rescind the order and vowing that he would not drive north even if she threatened to hang him for disobedience. Of course, he did go. It was left for his deputy, Robert Beale, to confide mournfully to England's man in Paris:

> Mr Secretary is to be this day at Berwick. The king goes very violently on with the late change of noblemen, and 'cannot be entreated to stay' by her Majesty's letter praying him not to proceed further until Mr. Secretary's coming. So I doubt whether he will be able to do any good therein. 'I fear we have lost too many good occasions of settling that realm for the general quietness of the whole Isle, which will be hard to bring so well to pass hereafter, if things go outward as they have lately begun. The Lord's will be done.'[13]

Events turned out just as the brothers-in-law feared. In Scotland the sixteen-year-old king was flexing his intellectual muscles. Understandably suspicious of those who sought to manipulate him, he asserted his right to choose for himself whom to trust. At the moment this did not include the emissaries of his 'cousin' Elizabeth. Walsingham was certainly not the wisest of choices as an appropriate person to win over an impressionable, teenage prince. When he was granted an audience he did not hesitate to deliver what, in abstract, reads like a Calvinist sermon. James cannot have enjoyed being told 'that young princes were many times carried into great errors upon an opinion of the absoluteness of their royal authority and do not consider, that when they transgress the bounds and limits of the law, they leave to be kings and become tyrants.'[14]

The Earl of Arran, who now held the reins in Edinburgh, complained to Elizabeth of her envoy's heavy-handedness. This played into the hands of Walsingham's conciliar opponents and exposed the divisions within government. Walsingham was all for plotting yet another coup with his Scottish allies. Elizabeth still hoped to achieve a compromise by direct talks with Mary. Burghley, Hunsdon and the appeasement group favoured doing a deal with Arran. When Walsingham discovered that other approaches were running concurrently with his own he was, understandably, piqued. It confirmed his impression that all his efforts were so much wasted time and energy. Months later he wrote to William Davison in Scotland very frankly describing the state of affairs within the Council. We are fortunate in having the first draft of his letter as well as the finished version, which was toned down. What Walsingham first wrote, and obviously felt deeply, was:

> You know [Hunsdon's] passion, whose propinquity in blood doth somewhat prevail here, especially being countenanced by [Burghley] who doth use [Hunsdon] as a counterpoise to [Leicester] though, God wot, he be but a weak one. [Burghley] hath always liked to entertain [circuitous] courses, which groweth from lack of resolution in him, which, I pray God, may not prove the destruction of England.[15]

The links between Walsingham and Leicester had recently become even stronger by the marriage of the secretary's daughter, Frances, to Dudley's nephew, Sir Philip Sidney. The ceremony took place on 21 September, while Walsingham was still in Scotland. One cannot help wondering whether Elizabeth's determination to send Walsingham out of London was to deprive him of the pleasure of attending the wedding of his only child. (His other daughter had died in 1580.) She had opposed the alliance ever since it had been mooted in 1581. There was no logical reason for disapproval of a match that most regarded as eminently suitable. The prospect of other people's married happiness, especially those connected with the court, often aroused her jealous spite. Castelnau reported that the two councillors now united by their marriage had incurred the queen's 'grande jalousie'. Walsingham, naturally, was very distressed that Elizabeth, despite his long and faithful service, could not bring herself to offer her royal blessing to his daughter and son-in-law. This was yet one more burden piled upon the already overloaded wagon of his loyalty. Philip Sidney had no house of his own. Indeed, as a part of the nuptial agreement, Walsingham paid off his son-in-law's debts. So, the newlyweds moved in with Sir Francis and Lady Ursula at Barn Elms and their town house, now located in Sydon or Seething Lane, at the eastern edge of the City, close by the Tower.

With matters as they were in the English and Scottish courts it is not surprising that Leicester sent word to his friend in September 1583 to return as soon as possible. It was still another month before Walsingham could get back to a desk, doubtless piled with urgent business. Unmasking what would become known as the Throckmorton plot was now his most urgent task but before that he was diverted by the need to examine a madman. A certain Warwickshire gentleman, John Somerville or Somerfield, had been received into the Roman church by Hugh Hall, a priest. He subsequently announced his intention of going to court to assassinate the queen where he hoped to see the head of this 'serpent and viper' set up on a pole. He was, naturally, brought to London where Walsingham examined him to see whether he had any connection with a wider Catholic conspiracy. He concluded that the poor man posed no threat and, had the times been different, Somerville might have been consigned to Bedlam and quietly forgotten. As it was he and Hall and Mr Arden, Somerville's father-in-law (whose only crime was that he had known of Somerville's insane ravings and concealed them from the authorities), were indicted for treason and condemned to be hanged, drawn and quartered.

A few days later, Mendoza reported this and other items of gossip to Parma. His letter is worth quoting at some length because it indicates how jittery the whole court, from Elizabeth downwards, had become. Somerville, he reported, had been committed to Newgate, where he:

> hanged himself with his own garters the day before he was to be executed with his father in law, who suffered accordingly . . . the Earl of Northumberland [is detained], his guard being Captain Laydon. The Earl of Arundel is to remain a prisoner in his own house, and the Countess his wife, who was in the castle of Arundel, being with child, is to come hither; who is a very brave lady, a great Catholic and a servant of [Elizabeth]. Mr. Shelley, a rich gentleman of Sussex, has been arrested on suspicion of having aided the lords who have gone to France in their embarkation. [Lord Paget and Charles Arundel] . . .
> A Jesuit father embarking with great secrecy in an English ship,

which sailed from Rye with a good wind, but six leagues out at sea, it veered so contrary that the sailors were forced to put into Queen-borough, some leagues away, where the inquisitors of the Queen, coming to inspect the ship, took him merely on suspicion and sent him to Lord Cobham, governor of the country, who had him brought before the Council. They, having examined him, ordered him into a prison not so strait of others of this kingdom, all of which are filled with Catholics; all those who had gone away being ordered to be brought back by troops and many others being taken, while the judges of the counties have orders to proceed against the goods of those who are not living in their own houses. This may show his Majesty with what fury [Elizabeth] permits the persecution of the good party daily to increase . . .

A soldier, returned from Terceira . . . [came] to the Court to give a letter to the Earl of Bedford and to see the Queen. [He proceeded with] such boldness that he found his way to the place where the Queen was with two other ladies. She . . . cried out angrily for him to be seized and carried to the chamber of the Earl of Leicester, where he was asked whether I had sent him to kill the Queen and if he bore arms, though he having nothing but a blunt knife. After giving him something to eat, they detained him in the Council Chamber, and questioned him anew, with caresses and promises, whether I had sent him thither, and how many times he had spoken with me about the [Queen], who replied that he had never seen me, nor knew any other person in the Indies or England whom they named. Afterwards examining him about the Pope, and seeing him to be a Protestant, they encouraged him, and the said mariner gave out his entrance to be in order to irritate the people against me, and make them cry out that it was by my intervention that the lunatic desired to kill the Queen; who has said publicly to the ambassador of France that there are three hundred Catholics who have sworn to kill her.[16]

By the time this was written, in mid-December, Mendoza knew that Throckmorton had been arrested and tortured in the Tower. He must have realized that his own complicity in plots against the queen was about to come out, if it had not already. Walsingham pounced on 4 November. The operation was minutely planned. After dark two armed men called discreetly at Throckmorton's house. Within the hour he was locked up in the Tower and Walsingham's men were going through his lodgings with a fine tooth comb. Yet, for all that they had the element of surprise, the raiders failed to discover a casket of letters newly arrived from France, which one of Throckmorton's men smuggled out of the house and took to Mendoza. The next day Mr Secretary had on his desk a bundle of incriminating evidence. There were names – the Earls of Arundel and Northumberland, Lord Howard, Charles Arundel and Thomas, Baron Paget. As we have seen the last two escaped to France but the others were detained. There were plans of south coast harbours which would make good landing places for invading troops. There was a cache of polemical pamphlets directed against Elizabeth and supporting Mary's claim to the Crown. It was useful but it was not enough. Throckmorton knew a great deal more. It was just a matter of inducing him to divulge it and Walsingham knew the best man for the job – Thomas Norton.

Norton was understandably upset by the epithet 'Rackmaster' attached to him by Catholic propagandists. He protested to Walsingham in 1582: 'I was never the Rackmaster but the meanest of all that were in commission and as it were clerk unto them, and the doing was by the hands only of the queen's servants, and by Mr Lieutenant [of the Tower] only direction for much or little.'[17] However, the fact that he was frequently called upon by Walsingham to examine prisoners indicates that he was something of an expert in interrogation techniques. He may not have personally turned the screw but he advised others when the application (or non-application) of physical torture might be most effective. His expertise proved invaluable in the examination of Throckmorton. The prisoner was first interviewed by members of the Council and there is no evidence that Walsingham was among their number. Throckmorton denied everything, claiming in words that have a modern ring that the incriminating papers had been planted on him. After that the councillors withdrew and left Throckmorton to the experts. One reason for Norton's frequent employment in such work must surely be his close relationship with

Walsingham. The secretary could be certain of receiving at first hand accurate accounts of all interrogations before other members of the Council got wind of any significant revelations. On 18 November Walsingham ordered a second racking of the prisoner and, to make sure that he was kept instantly informed, he detailed Council clerk Thomas Wilkes also to be present. Throckmorton's first session of torture had produced little of interest. Walsingham told Wilkes that, in his experience, a second racking usually brought victims to their breaking point. There is something chilling about his insouciant observation, 'I suppose the grief of the last torture will suffice without any extremity of racking to make him more comformable than he hath hitherto shown himself.'[18]

He was quite right. When the prisoner was taken from his cell and marched across the courtyard to the White Tower where the rack was housed (the Tower of London never had a 'torture chamber' of the type beloved of novelists) every terrifying step must have raised the level of fear. From his earlier acquaintance with 'the Earl of Exeter's daughter' (the rack) he knew exactly what lay in wait. The psychological pressure was every whit as bad as the physical. It took little turning of the screw to make Throckmorton gasp out everything he knew and another examinee, William Shelley, a Sussex gentleman, added more details to the plot whose lurid details now emerged. Philip II and Pope Gregory were to finance an invasion led in person by the Duke of Guise which would land at Arundel (and not in Scotland or the north of England, as earlier intelligence had suggested). The way was to be prepared for them by the Earl of Arundel, Lord Paget and the Earl of Northumberland who had extensive estates close to the port. Mary had been apprised of the plan and the principal intermediary between her and the conspirators had been Mendoza (not Castelnau as Walsingham had assumed). Nothing seems to have been said about what would happen to Elizabeth but she would obviously have lost her crown to Mary and, possibly, the head on which it rested.

Was this ever a feasible invasion plan or just another of the extravagant schemes conceived in the fervid imagination of the fanatical duc de Guise? It has to be seen in the context of the long-term, on-and-off Enterprise of England. Philip had for years been committed to the invasion of England – in theory. He had commissioned detailed maps of the south coast and chronicles of the nine seaborne invasions that had taken place since 1066. He had discussed strategic options with Parma and, in the summer of 1583, he had certainly met with Guise, the papal nuncio and various English exiles. It is significant that the Guise faction bypassed Henry III, presumably to prevent serious consequences for France if the operation miscarried. But in October Philip had once more decided that the time was not right. He did not discourage the conspirators but he did make it clear that they could not count on Spanish men and ships. It seems unlikely, in these circumstances, that the Catholic invasion of 1584 was anything more than a scheme which would not have got off the drawing board.

But, of course, Elizabeth's councillors could not know that. They had to decide what action to take based on the information they had. They debated this crucial matter at great length. The serious issues at stake were: the evident *casus belli* which now existed vis-à-vis Spain, the involvement of prominent Catholic nobles who had sizeable followings, the fate of Mary Stuart, and the need not to compromise valuable intelligence sources. It is the complexity of the situation which explains the government's slow, one might almost say leisurely, proceedings. It was important for the ongoing intelligence operation not to alarm potential contacts by precipitate action. Quietly, patiently, Walsingham continued his work of unearthing suspects and fitting more and more pieces into the jigsaw. His most important source continued to be Bruno and, for that reason, no action was taken against Castelnau. The Council drew up a list of charges but the aged diplomat was not molested.

Mendoza was a different matter. He was too astute to leave many chinks in his armour and he was too committed a Catholic for remonstration to have any effect. It was on 19 January that the Spanish ambassador was invited to meet with the Council in the Fleet Street house of Sir Thomas Bromley, the Lord Chancellor. When all were assembled, it was Walsingham, with his command of Italian, who confronted Mendoza with his crimes and conveyed the queen's decision that he quit her realm within fifteen days. The arrogant grandee blustered but had no alternative but to comply. The dismissing of his ambassador (the second in succession to have his residency abruptly terminated) infuriated Philip and when Elizabeth sent an envoy to Spain to explain her conduct he declined to receive him. Mendoza was not replaced and this severance of diplomatic relations was, in effect, the prelude to war. Throckmorton was not put on trial until May 1584 and, even when indicted, it was a further seven weeks before he suffered a traitor's death.

It was not quite so easy to deal with the two members of England's ancient noble houses languishing in prison. Henry Percy, Earl of Northumberland, was placed under house arrest in December and only transferred to the Tower on 9 January. Percy was the brother of the earl executed for leading the Northern Rebellion in 1569 and had been arrested in 1571 for being in communication with Mary Stuart. The Council had no doubt about his involvement in the Throckmorton plot but brought no charges against him. Howard, younger brother of the Duke of Norfolk executed in the wake of the Ridolfi plot, had been in and out of prison several times in the intervening years. He, like Percy, had secretly made contact with the Queen of Scots and was handsomely pensioned by Mendoza. His place of confinement was the cramped and insalubrious Fleet prison. Both men were detained for eighteen months without charge. The government were well aware that two high-profile treason trials would provoke widespread discussion of the religious issue and the real risk of civil disorder. Executions often proved counterproductive and there was also the possibility that juries of the noblemen's peers might not bring in the desired verdicts. All this indecision led up to a tragic conclusion in the summer of 1585. On the night of 20–21 June, Northumberland was found dead in his cell, shot through the head with a pistol and the weapon lying by his side. A jury brought in a verdict of suicide but that, of course, did not satisfy conspiracy theorists. Suspicion fell on Sir Christopher Hatton who, it was alleged, had ordered the Lieutenant of the Tower to change the guard on Percy's cell on the night of his death. It can scarcely be a coincidence that, within days of the earl's death, Howard was released into the custody of Sir Nicholas Bacon, the first stage in his reha-bilitation.

On the diplomatic front the forging of a closer relationship with the United Provinces now assumed paramount importance. If Spain and its Catholic allies were seriously considering invasion it was vital that the Protestant states banded together to defend themselves and to guard the Narrow Sea between them. This was energetically urged by Leicester, Walsingham and their allies. Thus it was that Mr Secretary, although confined to his bed for several weeks in early 1584, painstakingly drafted a naval treaty between the two states. The pattern of international rivalries was beginning to emerge clearly. It was a pattern Walsingham had always recognized. So the news that reached him in mid-July from George Galpin, representative of the Merchant Venturers in the Low Countries, was particularly alarming.

A heavy and lamentable [disaster] is fallen out by the sudden loss of the Prince of Orange who on Tuesday in the afternoon, as he was risen from dinner and went from the eating place to his chamber, even entering out of a door to go up the stairs, the Burgundian that had brought him news of Monsieur his death, making show as if he had some letter to impart and to talk with his Excellency with a pistol shot him under the breast, whereof he fell down dead in the place and never spake word, to the wonderful grief of all there present.[19]

Chapter 8

'BE YOU ALL STOUT AND RESOLUTE'

1584–8

Like the successive eruptions of a long-rumbling volcano, the years we must now consider exploded with shattering events – Leicester's Netherlands campaign, the Babington plot, the execution of Mary Stuart and the coming of the Armada. We know, of course, that Elizabeth's England came safely through these crisis years and our understanding of them tends to be coloured by the nation's fortuitous deliverance in 1588 and the queen's famous 'heart and stomach of a king' speech. For those who lived through this tumultuous period, however, the outcome was very far from certain. For Walsingham it was the Armageddon he had long prophesied and sought to avert. Mounting anxiety drove him and his colleagues to extreme and even desperate measures.

In the dismal summer of 1584 bad news arrived by almost every post. As more details of Orange's assassination came in two worrying facts, though not hitherto unknown, were freshly reinforced. The first was that Philip II had put a price on Orange's head and was ready to reward any denizen of the criminal underworld who would dispose of his enemies for him. The second was that there were Catholic fanatics who needed no such financial incentive. This became clear from the macabre description of the torture of Balthazar Gerard, Orange's killer.

> The same evening he was beaten with ropes and his flesh cut with split quills, after which he was put into a vessel of salt and water, and his throat was soaked in vinegar and brandy; and notwithstanding these

torments, there was no sign whatever of distress or repentance, but, on the contrary, he said he had done an act acceptable to God, by killing a man who had been the cause of the death of more than five hundred thousand persons and that for so doing, he was confident that he should be sanctified and received into the heavens into the first place, near to God.[1]

Three days later Sir Edward Stafford passed on information he had received in Paris from a 'reliable source' close to the Spanish ambassador. Other similar atrocities, he reported, were in preparation, including attacks on Elizabeth. 'There is no doubt that she is a chief mark they shoot at and, seeing there were men cunning enough to enchant a man, and to encourage one to kill the Prince of Orange in the midst of Holland, and a knave found desperate enough to do it, we must think that hereafter anything may be done.'[2] This merely confirmed intelligence Walsingham and other councillors were receiving via their various continental networks.

One such item had recently reached Walsingham from the unstable William Parry, a man he and Burghley had both employed as a spy and who fancied himself as a freelance agent able to play the field – an attitude which resulted in his ultimate downfall. Parry had been in France monitoring the activities of William Crichton and Thomas Morgan, Mary Stuart's agent. He ingratiated himself with the English Catholic community and, in an attempted sting operation, he proposed a scheme for Elizabeth's assassination. The details were forwarded to Rome for the pope's blessing and in March, by which time Parry was back in London, the following carefully worded reply arrived from Gregory's secretary of state: 'His holiness . . . cannot but commend the good disposition and resolution which you write you have towards the public service and benefit: wherein his holiness does exhort you to persevere and to bring to effect that which you have promised.'[3]

Parry triumphantly produced this at court and it had the desired effect. Burghley and Walsingham were impressed and Elizabeth received him warmly. But the intrigue-obsessed adventurer did not receive the material rewards he considered his due and it was this that drove him to fresh scheming. He thought to repeat the stratagem that had proved successful once. This time his victim was Edmund Neville, another of Walsingham's intelligencers who had spent some years in Philip II's Netherlands army. Both sides, not unreasonably, suspected Neville of being a double agent and Parry thought it would be an easy matter to entrap him and, by so doing, further enhance his own reputation. His mistake lay in taking this initiative independently. He drew Neville into another supposed assassination plot. But the prey turned hunter. Neville laid an information against Parry in February 1585. If the stakes had not been so high, the situation would have been farcical. As it was, the Council could not allow such disorderly activity to jeopardize serious espionage activity. Both men were marched off to the Tower. Parry now fell foul of a conciliar plot. The government needed to stir up popular support by giving maximum publicity to assassination conspiracies. They put Parry on trial and Sir Christopher Hatton, the most unscrupulous of the conciliar hawks, concocted a version of the fictional plot which cast Parry in the role of a real, if incompetent, murderer who had already made two unsuccessful attempts on Elizabeth's life. On 2 March Parry went to his death, loudly protesting his innocence. Neville was left to rot in the Tower for fourteen years.

While all this was going on Walsingham uncovered more details of a *real* plot. Fortuitously, William Crichton fell into his hands. While en route from France to Scotland the Jesuit courier's ship encountered a Dutch vessel. He was taken prisoner and immediately put on trial for implication in the death of Prince William. However, news having reached England, the government requested Crichton's extradition and he was handed over. He tried to destroy the evidence he was carrying but enough torn fragments were recovered to enable Walsingham to piece together the overall design. Unfortunately it only related to the earlier Guise plot to attack England via Scotland, which had been aborted by the fall of Esmé Stuart. However, Walsingham, who examined Crichton personally in his own house, was able to gather further proof that Mary was party to the French plans to depose Elizabeth.

It was decided to place her under even stricter surveillance. In the following January she was moved for a whole year to the dank and malodorous castle at Tetbury, Staffordshire, the most depressing of all the eight English residences in which she was held. The Earl of Shrewsbury, who had been her guardian for years, was now considered too easy-going for the job and was relieved of his charge. Walsingham was able to install his friend, Sir Amias Paulet, who took up his post the following spring. A Calvinist and a former ambassador to France who had espoused the Huguenot cause, Paulet well understood the Guise faction and their determination to stop at nothing in the name of international Catholicism. He was not the sort of man to be disarmed by Mary's charm, as she quickly discovered.

Paulet behaved with formal courtesy towards his charge but made it clear that he would stand no nonsense from her. He examined all her incoming and outgoing correspondence. He tore down her cloth of state, answering her protests with the retort that there was but *one* queen in England. And he made spot searches of her rooms. He forbade any contact between Mary's servants and his own staff and submitted them to body searches whenever they left or returned to the castle. He was soon able to boast to Mr Secretary, 'I cannot imagine how it may be possible for them to convey a piece of paper as big as my finger.' There was more to Walsingham's behaviour than a desire to isolate the Queen of Scots. It was also meant to goad Mary into rash, desperate behaviour in trying to communicate with friends and supporters and to provoke her into written indiscretion. Walsingham was determined that she should condemn herself so irrevocably that Elizabeth could not avoid taking the only means left of removing the greatest threat to her security.

Crichton, meanwhile, languished in the Tower. We might have expected Walsingham to subject the prisoner to everything in the fortress's torture armoury but, although Crichton remained in custody for two years, it seems that he was treated with scrupulous correctness. He was a foreign national and so could not, technically, be racked. In all probability this would not have saved him if he had been suspected of any serious plot against the queen's person. He was actually exonerated from that by no less a person than William Parry, who testified that Crichton, when asked for his advice about the assassination of the queen, had counselled against it. Apparently the government believed or disbelieved Parry as it suited them. Crichton was released in 1586 and, of course, immediately resumed anti-English activity. Two years later, when the ships of Philip's stricken Armada were being driven up the North Sea to their doom, Crichton went in pursuit to try to persuade their captains to invade Scotland.

One area of Catholic activity Walsingham was especially interested in was the propaganda machine. Both sides were pumping out pamphlets and broadsheets illustrated with lurid woodblock pictures in a direct assault on public opinion. Some dealt with the central issues of faith and politics but others relied for their impact on character assassination. In 1584 two items from foreign Catholic presses illustrative of both types reached England. William Allen's *A true, sincere and modest Defence of the English Catholics that suffer for their faith* . . . was a 250-page broadside in response to William Cecil's twenty-page pistol shot, *The Execution of Justice in England not for Religion but for Treason*. The other, anonymous, work was a horse of a very different colour. *The Copy of a Letter written by a Master of Arts at Cambridge*, commonly known as *Leicester's Commonwealth* was, simply, the vilest piece of vitriolic libel in the whole history of *La Calumnia*. It sought to deflect indignation from Catholic activists by pointing out that Puritans constituted the most seditious element in English society. It then went on to attack the foremost patron of Puritans, Robert Dudley. It accused him of every crime and moral defect its author(s) could dream up. Leicester was portrayed as a monster who would have rivalled Iago, Rodrigo Borgia, Machiavelli and Don Juan in the pursuance of his ambitious, lustful and vengeful career. His prime objective, according to *Leicester's Commonwealth*, was the removal of all claimants to the throne and ultimately of Elizabeth herself in order to gain supreme power.

As Philip Sidney observed in a hastily written defence of his uncle (never printed), the book was 'so full of horrible villainies as no good heart will think possible to enter into any creature'. But, of course, there were people ready to believe the gist of the book or to assume that there was no smoke without fire. People have always enjoyed salacious gossip about celebrities and the author(s) of *Leicester's Commonwealth* judged their market well. What they misjudged was the government's response. Elizabeth's Council might be afflicted by factions and personality clashes but when one of their number was attacked they were united in their condemnation. The queen issued a proclamation against seditious books and authorized a riposte, probably drawn up by Walsingham, to be sent to the Lord Mayor of London, in which she denounced the libel as 'such as none but the devil himself could deem to be true' and asserted that she regarded the abuse as 'offered to her own self'.[4]

Although she was protected from much of the malicious gossip that circulated at all levels of society, enough reached her ears to act as something of an antidote to the absurd levels of flattery to which she was subjected daily. Did she know that the Earl of Oxford and his cronies swapped jokes about her at their private dinner parties? Mary Stuart certainly made sure that the queen was informed when her hostess, the Countess of Shrewsbury, tittle-tattled about royal sexual adventures and Elizabeth's long list of paramours. The queen had now turned fifty. She had neglected to provide the realm with an heir. The political and religious future was uncertain so it was not to be wondered at if respect and patriotic emotion were on the wane. Given this worrying background, a damage-limitation exercise was vital. Walsingham was instructed to track down the origin of the canard and to suppress its distribution.

Almost immediately his men picked up Ralph Emerson who came to England that summer to further the Catholic propaganda campaign. This was an information coup because Emerson had for the last few years been at the very heart of the Jesuit mission to England. He had crossed the Channel as a servant to Campion in the first wave of the Catholic ideological invasion and narrowly escaped capture. Thereafter he had established himself at Rouen, which was the forward headquarters of the mission presided over by Robert Persons. This was where the streams of Catholic resentment and intrigue converged. Here refugees like Paget and Arundel met up with Mary's envoy, Thomas Morgan, with Allen's latest missionary recruits and with Crichton and other members of the Guise network. 'Little'

Ralph Emerson, as he was known, had made a speciality of discovering new entry routes to England – unwatched coves and creeks
where disguised priests might be landed and byways along which they
might travel to safe houses. Although we have no details of Emerson's
interrogation, it is inconceivable that Walsingham's agents would not
have worked on him to extract all that he had to tell them. Within a
couple of years more than a hundred Catholic activists were being
held in various prisons throughout London, not including the Tower,
an indication that Walsingham's vigilance was bearing so much fruit
that the detention system was under pressure. Emerson was lodged at
the Counter (or Compter) in Poultry, one of the sheriff's jails in the
very heart of the city. He remained in custody for twenty years and
only emerged as a dying paralytic at the beginning of the next reign.

Walsingham seems to have been remarkably successful in his
censorship of *Leicester's Commonwealth*. He exposed another conduit
in the shape of Castelnau's butler who was running a private
colportage enterprise. Agents at the ports were vigilant at sniffing
out smuggled consignments. The book circulated on the continent in
English and in translations but the propagandists simply lacked the
organization to engineer widespread circulation in England. So
unsuccessful was this particular enterprise that, to this day, only a
handful of copies of the original edition survive. Walsingham transferred his energies to tracking down the source of the hate campaign.

This meant probing the activities of the Paris-Rouen exile community, something which immediately presented Walsingham with a
problem. His principal source of information should have been the
ambassador, Sir Edward Stafford, a man for whom he had growing
mistrust. Stafford was unreliable for three reasons. He had a pathological hatred of the Earl of Leicester. By extension, he disliked
Walsingham and, as we have seen, reported to Burghley behind the
secretary's back. His second problem was that his wife was related to
Charles Arundel, one of the leading Catholic activists. Thirdly he had
a gambling problem and was constantly short of money.

Stafford probably owed his appointment to his mother who was
mistress of the robes and one of the queen's closest companions. He
had connections with the Dudley family and when, in 1578, Leicester

wanted to disembarrass himself from a matrimonial entanglement with the Dowager Lady Sheffield, Stafford became involved. The earl's marriage to Lady Stafford had been kept secret and it now suited him to disavow the union in order to espouse Lettice Knollys. Hurriedly, Stafford became the husband of Leicester's discarded wife, much to the queen's displeasure. The whole business was shabby in the extreme, though it must be said that the complex mechanism of deception and covert relationships was driven by the throbbing engine of Elizabeth's jealousy. Stafford was, seemingly, content with his new wife but the whole affair left a nasty taste in his mouth and accounts largely for his animosity towards the Dudley-Walsingham axis. He was from the beginning and remained Burghley's man in Paris.

Walsingham kept a close watch on the ambassador, even to intercepting his private correspondence. He was particularly anxious about Stafford's relationship with Charles Arundel, Lady Stafford's cousin. Arundel had been a gentleman of the privy chamber who had lost his position, he believed, as the result of a personal vendetta by prominent courtiers. The trouble seems to have begun, in 1581, with the disintegration of the Earl of Oxford's coterie, to which he belonged. Oxford and his cronies flirted with anti-establishmentarian – and therefore fashionable – Catholicism but, when news of their illicit activities reached the queen's ears, the little clique fell apart in an orgy of denials and mutual recriminations. Arundel fled to France where he became involved with the Paget brothers and began Catholic plotting in earnest. But he did not forget his personal animosity. A written diatribe against Oxford accused him of atheism, treason, homosexuality and attempted murder. Arundel was a vicious-minded troublemaker who thrived on intrigue, though he was probably unfortunate to get mixed up in the impracticable Throckmorton plot. His story demonstrates that we should be careful of generalizations about Catholic plots. Many ingredients went into the toxic brew of discontent aimed at turning Englishmen against Elizabeth and her court. Indeed, the presence in Paris and Rouen of arrogant, displaced courtiers with their own agendas was more a hindrance than a help to Persons, Guise and all those driven by ideology. Unstable gentlemen and aristocrats with families and sequestered estates in England were vulnerable to bribes. Walsingham was certainly able to turn Charles Paget with promises of restitution in return for information. The alliance of Catholic forces in France was very insecure.

To return to *Leicester's Commonwealth*, whoever concocted it was very knowledgeable about the personalities and intrigues of Elizabeth's court. That and the pungent style point to Charles Arundel as the author but the anti-Leicester bias may well indicate that some of the information and innuendo came from Stafford. The ambassador is unlikely to have been a deliberate contributor to the libel, because its 'revelations' seriously embarrassed his wife, who became quite ill as a result. However it is easy to imagine Arundel voraciously gobbling up every tit-bit of gossip passing across dinner tables and enjoyed in the antechambers of French grandees. Stafford excused his close relationship with Arundel as a means of gathering valuable information. Walsingham suspected that the flow of intelligence was not just in one direction. He was right. By 1586 it was clear to him that Stafford was selling secrets to the duc de Guise and to the Spanish ambassador in Paris – none other than Bernardino de Mendoza. It was very frustrating for the secretary that Stafford was protected by his court connections. Whatever he suspected, Walsingham declined to point the finger at the Arundel-Stafford circle as originators of *Leicester's Commonwealth*. Instead, he identified Morgan as the author. Perhaps this was a ploy to tie Mary specifically to the libellous propaganda which so much annoyed Elizabeth. Walsingham had to tread warily in his relations with Stafford, who always claimed that he only posed as a traitor in order to worm his way into the counsels of the enemy. Whether or not the secrets he passed Guise and Mendoza were vital to English security, he certainly complicated the business of intelligence-gathering. There were two independent and mutually suspicious agencies operating in France.

It is not surprising that Walsingham's expenditure on the secret service rocketed in these years. He sustained a large corps of agents – more than he had ever employed before or would employ after 1588. Every invoice presented to the treasury was likely to provoke royal protest and, in order to do what needed doing without delay, Mr Secretary was often obliged to finance operations out of his own purse. Walsingham's willingness to buy information was widely known and there was no shortage of recruits among footloose adventurers, impecunious hopefuls, ardent Protestants and idealistic patriots.

Men eager to take Walsingham's money might claim the purest of motives: 'I profess myself a spy, but am not one for gain, but to serve my country . . . Whensoever any occasion shall be offered wherein I may adventure some rare and desperate exploit, such as may be for the honour of my country and my own credit, you shall always find me resolute and ready to perform the same.'[5] So wrote Thomas Rogers, alias Nicolas Berden, in January 1584. However, spies were invariably in the game for personal gain, either in the form of cash handouts or, through Walsingham's influence, the chance to take up some lucrative and less hazardous occupation. Berden, for example, became purveyor of poultry to the royal kitchen – a highly profitable enterprise.

It must be said, however, that Berden well deserved his fresh start in life. He worked assiduously to ingratiate himself with the English Catholic community in France and was so successful that he was appointed as their London clearing officer for clandestine correspondence. By early 1586 he could boast to his employer:

By Paget I expect the letters of the lord his brother, Throckmorton, and many others of his party; from Arundel I expect the letters of Sir Francis Englefield, from Brinckley the whole affairs of Allen and Persons, from Foljambe the Scottish Queen's, from Fitzherbert the devices of the Queen Mother together with all occurrents general. And amongst them all, I doubt not but Don Bernardino [de Mendoza], his master's and his own letters will also come to your honour's hands.[6]

In one respect at least Walsingham's work became easier. As the nature and extent of the threat to England's security became increasingly obvious the members of the Council closed ranks. Elizabeth could no longer stop her ears to rumours of plots or dismiss them as anti-Catholic propaganda put out by troublesome Puritans. There could now be no ignoring of the widespread anxiety about terrorism. Nor was it a case of irrational anxiety conjuring up demons.

In the night, imagining some fear,
How easy is a bush supposed a bear![7]

Walsingham kept everyone furnished with hard evidence. The result was the remarkable Bond of Association, drawn up early in October by Burghley and Walsingham, now successfully working in tandem. (Camden suggested that Leicester was the moving force behind the bond.)[8] This, if not exactly Walsingham's finest hour, certainly witnessed the accomplishment of what he had been striving for throughout the last dozen years – the safeguarding of the Protestant state.

The Bond of Association grasped the nettle of what would happen in the event of an attempt on the queen's life. It tried to ensure that such a catastrophe would not lead to a Catholic takeover. It was, in effect, a mirror image of the Catholic League operating in France – a reinforcing of the national religion at all costs. Loyal leaders of the political nation at central and regional levels were invited to set their hands to a document pledging their determination to bring to account everyone in any way connected to such a plot. They were 'to prosecute such person or persons to the death, and to take the uttermost revenge on them for their utter overthrow and extirpation'. Any pretender to the Crown in whose name the plot was devised was to find him/herself along with his/her heirs permanently debarred from inheritance. The Bond was an extraordinary document, conceived in fear and showing little sign of coherent thought. We might think of it as a political thermometer, indicating that the patient was in a state of high fever. It was certainly not, to continue the medical metaphor, a prescription for restoring that patient to full health. It made no provision for the government of the country in the event of the sudden death of the head of state. It was entirely concerned with the nation's reaction to a terrorist outrage. It warned those who might be contemplating such an act that they would gain nothing from it.

Copies of the Bond were drawn up with the utmost haste and distributed throughout the realm, to meeting points where local dignitaries gathered to sign, in some cases with great and solemn ceremony. When the Council arrived at Hampton Court on 19 October to append their names to the document they were joined by scores of church leaders. During the ensuing days a motley of assemblies took place all over the country – mayors and aldermen, members of trade guilds, groups of clergy, noblemen together with their tenants and estate workers, merchant communities – all came together to pledge their undying support for the politico-religious status quo.

And it was a fraud – or, at least, a stratagem very close to fraud. In its desperation the government needed a 'spontaneous' demonstration of national unity. So it set about choreographing such a display. Walsingham inserted the following clause in instructions sent out to conveners of public meetings:

> Your lordship shall not need to take knowledge that you received the copy from me but rather from some other friend of yours in these parts; for that her Majesty would have the matter carried in such sort as this course held for her [safety] may seem to [come more] from the particular care of her well-affected subjects than to grow from any public direction.[9]

Yet, if there was an element of deception in this, ultimate responsibility for it rests with the queen. Underlying the Bond of Association was the old problem – Elizabeth's refusal to conceive or nominate an heir. Her people were increasingly obsessed by the what-would-happen-if question. Their sovereign, in effect, responded that this was none of their business. Her determination, even in these desperate circumstances, to keep her subjects hands off all prerogative matters became clear when parliament assembled. It was essential to give legislative force to the Bond of Association, so writs went out immediately for the first election in twelve years.

The session, which ran from 23 November 1584 to 29 March 1585 with an unusually long Christmas recess (21 December – 4 February), had more than its share of drama. Giving the Bond statutory force raised two constitutional issues. The first concerned the debarring of claimants to the throne. The Council obviously had Mary Stuart in mind, since any likely Catholic plot, whether or not carried out with her connivance, would have her accession as its objective. But the wording of the Bond could also be taken as excluding James from the succession. Elizabeth intervened personally to ensure that the 'Act for provision to be made for the surety of the Queen's most royal person' did not blight the Scottish king's rights unless he had been privy to a plot to remove Elizabeth. The other issue was more fundamental because it concerned the meaning of sovereignty. In the event of the queen being snatched away from them, by what process would her subjects be provided with a replacement? Burghley, doubtless with the support of his colleagues, proposed a bill which would vest power in a 'Great Council', augmented by leading judges to a number of thirty-plus members, who would consider the claims of all rivals and, with the aid of parliament, in effect, elect their next sovereign. This proposal ran quite counter to existing practice and constitutional theory according to which it was axiomatic that on the monarch's death all crown offices became vacant, allowing the new incumbent a completely free hand in filling them. The interregnum solution, a radical, almost republican, proposal, was advocated warmly by most of the Council. Thomas Digges, parliamentarian and one of the scholars of the Dudley-Sidney-Walsingham circle ('the foremost scientific and mathematical writer of Elizabethan England')[10] advocated quite baldly that parliament should be a permanent feature of national life, a new assembly being automatically elected as soon as its predecessor was dissolved, so that the country would never lack a governing body. This was logical, practical and, of course, to Elizabeth quite unacceptable. It was an affront to the holy cow of prerogative. She quashed the draft bill before ever it reached the parliament house.

The queen's stubborn opposition is all the more remarkable given the dramatic circumstances of the time. The extraordinary Parry affair actually began its life on the floor of the House of Commons. William Parry, riding high on the wave of conciliar approval, had acquired a seat. On 17 December, parliament was discussing the second major bill of the session concerned with the expulsion of Jesuits and the punishment of any who succoured them. All members warmly supported harsh measures. Then Parry rose to speak. He not only opposed the bill; he did so in the most extreme language and denounced what he called the base motives of those who supported a measure which would result in nothing but 'blood, danger, despair and confiscation'. He then mystified the shocked house even further by refusing to give his reasons for the outburst. He would, he said, only explain himself to the queen. From this point Parry's dealing and double-dealing unravelled and he was abandoned by Walsingham and others who had originally patronized him.

Religion was now uppermost in MPs' minds, and not only because of the Catholic threat. In July 1583 there occurred an event Elizabeth had long been looking forward to. Archbishop Grindal died. The queen had long since decided on his successor, her leading episcopal yes-man, John Whitgift, Bishop of Worcester. Whitgift was an establishment man, unimaginative, loyal within the narrow confines of his vision and a stickler for rules and regulations. Add to this ambition and an aptitude for impressing the right people and you have the sort of man likely to get to the top of any organization. It followed that the new archbishop was a dedicated enemy of the Puritans. He had spent years locked in intermittent literary warfare with Thomas Cartwright, the acknowledged spokesman of those extreme radicals who campaigned for a root-and-branch reformation of the structures of the church to bring it in line, as they saw it, with the New Testament model. Whitgift's Panglossian view of the Elizabethan settlement was that everything was for the best in this best of all possible churches. Their ponderous disputation was, of course, a dialogue of the deaf. However, it could not fail to commend to the queen the man who ardently championed her authority in church and state. Whitgift wrote:

> I am persuaded that the external government of the church under a Christian magistrate must be according to the kind and form of government used in the commonwealth; else how can you make the prince supreme governor of all states and causes ecclesiastical? Will

you so divide the government of the church from the government of the commonwealth, that, the one being a monarchy, the other must be a democracy, or an aristocracy? This were to divide one realm into two, and to spoil the prince of the one half of her jurisdiction and authority. If you will therefore have the queen of England rule as monarch over all her dominions, then must you also give her leave to use one kind and form of government in all and every part of the same, and so to govern the church in ecclesiastical affairs as she doth the commonwealth in civil.

He deliberately invoked that spectre of republicanism that haunted Elizabeth's imaginings and accounted for her detestation of Puritans:

[I]n this commonwealth it is necessary that one should be over all, except you will transform as well the state of the kingdom as you would of the church; which is not unlike to be your meaning; for not long after you add that the 'commonwealth must be framed according to the church', meaning that the government of the commonwealth ought not to be monarchical, but either democratical, or aristocratical.[11]

As soon as he was installed Whitgift made it clear that his new broom had exceedingly harsh bristles. He issued instructions, with royal backing, to enforce uniformity of doctrine and practice. All clergy were enjoined, on pain of deprivation, to endorse and abide by the Book of Common Prayer in its entirety. This intentionally confrontational approach constituted an assault on tender Puritan consciences and provoked a storm of protest throughout the province of Canterbury. Around 500 clergy declined to make the required subscription to Whitgift's articles. The Council was in despair. At the very time that all Englishmen should be sinking their differences in the face of the Catholic threat it seemed that the senior ecclesiastic was deliberately ripping open old wounds which, given time and patience, might heal themselves. In June 1584, Walsingham joined with Burghley in persuading Whitgift to adopt a more softly-softly approach. Clergy were, as a result, permitted to make a partial subscription.

It was too late. The battle lines had been drawn. Whitgift simply changed his tactics. He prosecuted selected radicals in the ecclesiastical courts and he cultivated Sir Christopher Hatton who, for reasons of personal advancement, adopted the queen's religious policy and became a serious rival to Leicester in the Council. The Puritan clergy similarly organized themselves and presented petitions to their conciliar supporters against proceedings which, as Burghley observed, smacked of the Spanish Inquisition. This was the situation when parliament assembled in November 1584. It was obvious that there was going to be trouble. The House of Commons now included many new members no less zealous for religion than their predecessors but lacking the caution those predecessors had learned from previous encounters with the queen. Foreseeing difficulties, Leicester convened a meeting at Lambeth Palace where the radicals and reactionaries could argue the case. Predictably the debate generated more heat than light. It was the ever-pragmatic Walsingham who played the peacemaker. He persuaded the archbishop to stop hounding incumbents who conformed outwardly and did not draw attention to themselves. Henceforth it would only be new appointees who were obliged to subscribe. It was, however, too late to head off the parliamentary critics.

Promises had been made to previous parliaments concerning further reform of the church. Not only had those promises not been kept; Puritans now found themselves under the cosh of a reactionary regime. The Commons set up a committee to prepare religious legislation. The queen sent to inform them that they were not permitted to meddle in matters ecclesiastical. They ignored the prohibition. Elizabeth authorized a long parliamentary recess as a cooling off period. Parliament came back in February still determined to have satisfaction. Both houses eventually presented two bills. The queen vetoed them. On 29 February she summoned the speaker and told him in no uncertain terms that she would brook no more interference in her governance of the church.

Two days earlier Walsingham had had to endure another of her intemperate outbursts during a meeting of senior churchmen and leading councillors. The queen made ostentatious show of her support for the bishops:

We understand that some of the Nether House have used divers reproachful speeches against you, tending greatly to your dishonour, which we will not suffer; and that they meddle with matters above their capacity not appertaining unto them, for the which we will call some of them to an account. And we understand they be countenanced by some of our Council, which we will redress or else uncouncil some of them.

She grumbled about the behaviour of the London mercantile community:

where every merchant must have his schoolmaster and nightly conventicles expounding Scriptures and catechizing their servants and maids, in so much that I have heard how some of their maids have not sticked to control learned preachers, and say that such a man taught otherwise in our house.

And she made it abundantly clear that her personal animosity was greater towards Puritans than Catholics. She told of a letter received from some foreign correspondent:

who wrote that the papists were [in] hope to prevail again in England, for that her Protestants themselves misliked her, and indeed so [they] do, for I have heard that some of them of late have said that I was of no religion, neither hot [nor] cold, but such a one as one day would give God the vomit. I pray you look unto such men. I doubt not but you will look unto the papists, for that they not only have spite at me, and that very nearly, but at the whole realm and the state of religion. There is an Italian proverb which sayeth, 'From mine enemy let me defend myself, but from a pretended friend, good Lord deliver me.' Both these join together in one opinion against me for neither of them would have me to be queen of England.[12]

And it was those last words that revealed her deepest prejudice. She repeated them a month later when, at the earliest possible moment, she prorogued parliament.

Walsingham may well have breathed a sigh of relief when MPs packed their bags and rode off back to their shires and boroughs. Useless confrontation made the queen more difficult to handle than usual and was a distraction from his principal preoccupation – 'being very careful for the safety of the queen and the realm'. From his letters and reports of others about his conduct we can detect a growing irascibility from 1585 onwards. This was partly due to failing health. Forced absences from court became more frequent because of 'my old disease'. He was wearing himself out with overwork in his attempts to respond appropriately to the worrying situation at home, in Scotland and in the Low Countries. The very volume of intelligence reports constituted a problem. Walsingham's desk must, at times, have been swamped with information, much of it mutually contradictory. Thus, the location of the presumed Catholic strike was a matter for constant assessment and reassessment: would it be Scotland, or Arundel, or Ireland, or the Kent coast? In the ever-difficult internal politics of court and Council he was always having to watch his own back. He could not rely on Burghley's support. The treasurer was still dealing directly with Stafford. On one occasion Walsingham flew into a rage because the ambassador's assessment of the Paris situation differed from that of his own agents and, when reported, humiliated him in front of the queen.

From December 1585 to December 1587 Leicester was, with one interlude, on campaign in the Netherlands. In his absence the Whitgift-Hatton caucus gained strength. Whitgift was admitted to the Council early in 1586 and a year later Hatton was appointed Lord Chancellor (a promotion owing more to royal favour than any experience of the law). At the very time that England found itself on the dizzying rim of the maelstrom of international conspiracy, Walsingham felt his influence waning. Over the years Mr Secretary had perfected the art of bringing the queen round to his viewpoint on many issues. His secret was persistence. Without him nagging at her elbow and refusing to be deflected by her anger, Elizabeth fell prey to her own prevarication and the advice of others. A throwaway line in a letter Burghley wrote to his colleague highlights the role Walsingham so often played and which had become an established feature in the landscape of government: 'I wish your health and presence here, where your ability to attend on her Majesty at all times might greatly further causes . . . by importunity that now, for lack of following, which I cannot do by [reason of] my lameness, remain unperfected.'[13]

In one area of policy Walsingham's advice was, at last, heeded – or it may be that the logic of events prevented Elizabeth reaching any other conclusion. In the summer of 1584 Anjou had died. No longer could Elizabeth's battles in the Netherlands be fought by proxy. Yet the survival of the United Netherlands (the Protestant northern states) still depended on foreign aid. In fact, their dependence was greater than ever. Parma's brilliant and persistent campaign in the south was bringing more and more territory back under Spanish control. Brussels capitulated in March 1585. What was worse from an international point of view was that Antwerp, that great entrepôt, was being systematically starved into submission. By March it had lain under siege for nine months and there was no prospect of it surviving without the intervention of a relief force. (The end came in August and resulted in almost half the city's population fleeing to the north.) The States General turned to both Henry III and Elizabeth as their only potential saviours. They offered sovereignty over their land in return for military aid. By early March it was known in London that the French king had declined. All eyes were now turned on Elizabeth. She had a clear choice: allow the Netherlanders to stew in their own juice and watch Spain seize control of the Narrow Seas and the western trade routes or stand shoulder to shoulder with the rebels, an act which would be, in effect, a declaration of war against Philip.

True to form, she did neither – or rather she tried to do both at the same time, with inevitably disastrous results. Her positive acts were twofold. She entered into a treaty with representatives of the States General, promising men and money for their nationalist struggle and she authorized Drake to harass Spanish shipping in order to distract Philip from the Netherlands and also in the hope of gaining booty to finance the military operation. The second part of the plan was the only one about which the queen could be said to have shown any enthusiasm. The prospect of a cash return on her investment of ships and money was alluring. Also Philip inadvertently came to her aid by seizing some English merchant vessels. Elizabeth could thus claim that she had been provoked into ordering reprisals. Yet even the maritime scheme fell victim to her changeableness. For almost a year it was by turns on and off. Drake, as he gathered and provisioned his fleet, was repeatedly frustrated by the latest order arriving from the court. At last, on 14 September, even though his preparations were not complete, he grabbed the opportunity to set sail. As one of his captains, Christopher Carleill (Walsingham's stepson) explained to Mr Secretary, 'because the wind being fair upon our coming from Plymouth we were loth to lose the same for any small matters, coming so rarely as it doth there, and withal we not the most assured of her Majesty's perseverance to let us go forward'.[14]

Similar dithering hampered relations with the States General. Leicester, Hatton, Burghley and Walsingham handled negotiations with the Dutch representatives. Throughout July and August a series of meetings took place, some at Burghley's town house and some at Walsingham's residence in Seething Lane, and were occasions of exceedingly hard bargaining. The major points at issue were twofold – sovereignty and money. The States General wanted Elizabeth to assume absolute authority and to back it with such a military force as should be able to drive Parma from the land. Such a prospect appalled the queen. She was prepared to *lend* her allies the where-withal to fight a defensive campaign, against the collateral of certain port towns that her troops would garrison. As to sovereignty, that was out of the question since it manifestly implied conquest. She would only consent to send a senior nobleman in charge of her forces in a purely military capacity. Eventually, some sort of agreement was cobbled together and enshrined in the two treaties of Nonsuch.

It must be said that Elizabeth and the States General deserved each other. The leaders of the United Netherlands were hopelessly divided among themselves over their political and religious objectives. While some were insistent on ceding sovereignty to a foreign protector, others were defensive about their freedom and determined to maintain tight control of any army Elizabeth sent over. English aims and objectives were equally divided. The conciliar hawks were, as usual,

Leicester and Walsingham, though on Netherlands affairs they now had the support of Hatton. As the military campaign progressed through 1586 the queen got cold feet and was ready to listen to any scheme which might enable her to disengage honourably. Within the Council an appeasement faction developed of men who, either out of conviction or a desire to curry favour with their mistress, actively promoted peace. There were also those who stood to gain from a cessation of hostilities, men such as Sir James Croft, Controller of the Household, who was receiving a pension from Philip. At one time there were as many as five separate overtures being made to Philip's representatives. Needless to say such parleys were carried out in secret. This gave rise to a situation in which Elizabeth and members of her government were scheming against and even spying on each other. This was the background to the ill-fated Netherlands campaign, which we must now consider in brief outline.

In August 1585 the seasoned general, Sir John Norreys, was despatched with the first detachment of English troops to go to the aid of Amsterdam. He arrived too late but the die had been cast. The Dutch pressed Elizabeth to send Leicester as her deputy and he was eager for the command but it was late September before she could bring herself to agree. Dudley immediately set about making the necessary arrangements. He raised a loan in the City. He requisitioned arms and armour from the royal arsenal in the Tower. He wrote to 200 friends and dependants requesting them to join him with their own bands of armed retainers. Then, in the small hours of 27 September he was awoken to receive a message from Walsingham:

> My very good lord, her majesty sent me word . . . that I should speak unto your lordship that her pleasure is you forbear to proceed in your preparations until you speak with her. How this cometh about I know not. The matter is to be kept secret. These changes here may work some such changes in the Low Country as may prove irreparable.[15]

Ten weeks later uncertainty was still in the air, causing Leicester to appeal to Burghley:

as there can be no good, or honour, fall to this action, but it must be wholly to the praise and honour of her majesty, so whatsoever disgrace or dishonour shall happen (growing for lack of our good maintenance) but it will redound to her majesty also. Her majesty, I see, my Lord, often times doth fall into mislike of this cause, and sundry opinions it may breed in her withal, but I trust in the Lord, seeing her highness hath thus far resolved and grown also to this far execution as she hath, and that mine and other men's poor lives and substances are adventured for her sake, and by her commandment, that she will fortify and maintain her own action to the full performance of that she hath agreed on . . . if her majesty fail with such supply and maintenance as shall be fit, all she hath done hitherto will be utterly lost and cast away and we, her poor subjects, no better than abjects.

Leicester knew full well that his work could be undermined, not only by Elizabeth's half-heartedness and disinclination to spend money, but also by backstabbing colleagues. There was a real note of pathos in his closing appeal to Burghley:

I beseech your lordship have this cause even to your heart . . . have me only thus far in your care, that in these things which her Majesty and you all have agreed and confirmed for me to do, that I shall not be made a metamorphosis [and] that I shall not know what to do.

He added a worried postscript:

My lord, no man feeleth comfort but they that have cause of grief, and no men have so much need of relief and comfort as those that go in these doubtful services. I pray you, my lord, help us to be kept in comfort, for we will hazard our lives for it.[16]

Leicester eventually landed at Flushing on 10 December. He was received with all the glitzy adulation of a visiting potentate. Over the next two and a half weeks he made a stately progress and was feted everywhere with bonfires, banquets, plays, masques and fireworks. Elizabeth and Leicester were extolled in poetry and song as the saviours of the Dutch people. The Netherlanders made it abundantly clear that their expectation was for a semi-regal governor and not just a military commander who, like Anjou, might desert them and leave them to face Spanish retribution. Leicester wrote home for instructions – and for money for garrison troops who were on the point of mutiny over arrears of pay. He received no reply and decided to act on his own initiative. On 25 January, at a solemn ceremony in The Hague, the Earl of Leicester was invested with 'highest and supreme commandment' in the United Provinces.

It is not clear exactly when Walsingham and his colleagues received Dudley's official report of this momentous event. Burghley responded on 7 February but Elizabeth had learned of her representative's flouting of her wishes days before. One of her ladies had heard the news in a private letter and enthusiastically tittle-tattled it round the court. The story grew in the telling and by the time it came to Elizabeth's ears its colourful details included plans being made by the grandiloquent Leicester to bring his wife over to the Low Countries at the head of a sumptuous train that would put Elizabeth's own suite in the shade. Nothing could be better calculated to send the queen into a frenzy than the prospect of the Countess of Leicester, her hated rival for Dudley's affections (she was permanently barred from the court), lording it in princely style. She dictated a scorching reprimand and would have sent it post-haste if Burghley and Walsingham had not done their utmost to delay her. However, if they hoped for a cooling off period they were disappointed. The letter despatched on 10 February expressed the queen's fury at being betrayed by someone 'raised up by ourself and extraordinarily favoured by us above any other subject of this land'.[17]

We may suppose that Dorothy Stafford, mistress of the robes, felt particular satisfaction at seeing the queen's anger kindled against Dudley. Later in the year, when Leicester was seeking permission to return from the Netherlands, Edward Stafford took the opportunity to pour out his venom to Burghley: 'I would keep him where he is and he should drink that which he hath brewed. Her Majesty is not for his tarrying there bound to do more than she should see fit, but I would keep him there to undo himself and sure enough from coming home to undo others.'[18]

The ambassador had, or believed he had, fresh cause for grievance with Leicester's 'spirit', Francis Walsingham. It took the form of a running dispute over Michael Moody, one of Sir Edward's servants. Moody is another of those enigmatic shadowy characters who features in Walsingham's espionage network. He had been employed as courier by Mr Secretary in the early 1580s but was on Stafford's embassy staff in late 1583. Months later he was in London acting as an agent for his master and, when Sir Edward ordered his return to Paris in October, Moody refused, claiming that he was engaged in business for Walsingham. By the following January Stafford learned from a third party that there was quite a different reason for Moody's detention in London. His informant reported, as Stafford explained to Walsingham, that 'the said Michael was a bad man and a conveyor of letters to papists and from papists under the colour of sending to me letters about mine own business'.

Stafford was indignant on two counts. He felt 'greatly wronged' that Walsingham had detained Moody without saying a word to his master. More important, though, was the ambassador's conviction that conspiracy and personal animosity were at work. He suspected that:

> Some evil meaning body [ie person] to me is the cause of it; as since my departure I find not so good dealing as I think I have deserved, by divers bad speeches and rumours spread abroad of me; and that this is but a way invented by some perchance that deceive both you and me, to leave in suspense the cause of the blame of my man, to leave it to men's standing to discourse whether any fault, or part of it, may not be in me. Other bad speeches in mine absence do make me doubt the worst in this: but as they be as false as they that have sowed them be wicked, so I must bear them, and be a pack-horse in that till I be out of this place, and content myself with the faithfulness of my actions, that in the mean time shall give them the lie deep enough.[19]

Was he referring to the Leicester caucus? He was careful to assure Walsingham that he had no doubt of the secretary's honest dealing but such asseveration was no more than the formal courtesy required in official correspondence. We do not have Walsingham's reply but apparently it did not fully satisfy the ambassador. In March he assured Mr Secretary that he had no intention of defending Moody if he had done something wrong but he wanted to know exactly what it was that his servant was accused of.

The historian would also like to know, for two years later Moody's name crops up again in relation to a mysterious assassination plot. And not only Moody's. Sir Edward Stafford had a younger brother, William, who seems to have been little more than a court hanger-on. In 1585 he was pulling whatever strings came to hand in an effort to gain some honourable employment. Edward tried, without success, to obtain a commission for his brother in Leicester's Netherlands army. William seems to have been more successful in seeking Walsingham's patronage, for in June he wrote effusively to the secretary. 'There is no man living to whom I am so beholden,' he claimed. 'If I should live to see my blood shed in your cause I should think it but some recompense for the great good I have received at your hands.'[20] Thereafter, for more than a year, the names of Michael Moody and William Stafford disappear from the records. When they re-emerge it is in a much more sinister context.

Meanwhile, in the fateful year 1586, Walsingham had a multitude of problems pressing down on him. He was increasingly isolated at court in his support for the Netherlands war. Negotiations with Scotland had reached a critical stage. In France the Guise faction was triumphant and Henry III virtually a prisoner in his own palace. That Philip II was making detailed plans for the invasion of England was common knowledge. And over all these disturbing developments loomed the ever-present problem of what to do with Mary Stuart. England in 1586 found itself in a situation not dissimilar to that of England in 1939. An awesome power was spreading across the continent. An English expeditionary force was fighting a losing battle across the Narrow Seas. Fifth columnists were active within the realm and the peace-at-any-price lobby had a powerful voice in government. It has not always been realized just how vital Francis Walsingham's contribution was in holding queen and country to a constant course throughout these dire months.

He used every stratagem at his command – espionage, counter-espionage, overt championing of the international Protestant cause, covert undermining of Catholic endeavours. He confronted the queen openly to her face and worked secretly behind her back. Nor was this duplicity undertaken without personal cost. Walsingham was no amoral Machiavellian. Quite the reverse. As a Puritan he understood the virtues of honesty and plain dealing. As a politician striving to defend those virtues he was only too aware that he often had to muffle his conscience. He periodically gave way to despair and often exploded in fits of hitherto uncharacteristic bad temper. His recurrent physical ailments played their part in his state of mental agitation and this year, 1586, would bring him news which threatened to tip him over the edge of sanity. The character which emerges through all these trials is one deeply coloured with heroism. Walsingham was a man driving himself towards an early grave in the service of a thankless queen who seldom acknowledged how much she was indebted to him.

In the Netherlands English hopes rapidly unravelled. Militarily affairs went from bad to worse. Everyone was to blame for the failure. Leicester was a poor general who antagonized his senior officers and who found liaison with the Dutch very difficult. Military realities, orders from Elizabeth and instructions from the States General pulled him in different directions. His funds and supplies were inadequate because he constantly, and sometimes fruitlessly, had to apply to his laggard paymasters for the necessities of war. If Elizabeth resented his assumption of the governorship of the United Provinces, the States General stripped his title of any meaning by trying to control him and by undermining his endeavours. When Dudley took strong counter-measures to assert his authority, this only provoked more opposition. Town governments, despairing of their English allies, threw their gates open to Parma and Leicester's army was whittled away by the desertion or mutiny of his unpaid troops.

In the Council, Walsingham, Hatton and Burghley continued to support Leicester (though Burghley was not above following his own agenda). They were constantly opposed by Whitgift, Lord Cobham, Lord Buckhurst and Sir James Crofts. Persuading Elizabeth to authorize fresh troops or finance generally resulted in open argument and clandestine audiences with the queen. It was this constant bickering that was largely responsible for the irregularity of treasury disbursements to Leicester. Walsingham found the situation debilitating. 'The opinion of my partiality continueth,' he told Dudley in March, 'nourished by factions, which makes me weary of the place I serve in and to wish myself among the true-hearted Swiss.'[21]

But it was the jittery queen who made his life a real misery. She was terrified of provoking Spanish aggression. Reliable reports reaching London indicated that Drake's activities were proving a valuable distraction to Philip and obliging him to keep a sizeable fleet patrolling the Atlantic and to seek new loans from Italian bankers. Elizabeth was heartened by such news but it only took one contrary report to rouse her anxiety. Once, she had the master of a merchant vessel newly returned from Spain brought before her and quizzed him about what he had seen. He told her of a force of twenty-seven ships being assembled in Lisbon and a rumour that it was to be sent to England. Elizabeth immediately flew into a rage. She threw a string of oaths at Walsingham and, for good measure, hurled her slipper at him as well. She reasoned that one way to prevent Leicester committing acts of aggression was to keep him short of funds but, of course, this only increased the tension. It was in April that Walsingham learned that Elizabeth and some of her councillors had been engaged in secret peace talks through various intermediaries. His response was both indignant and pragmatic. He reported to Leicester:

> I have let her Majesty understand how dangerous and dishonourable it is for her to have such base and ill affected ministers used therein. Morris, the Comptroller's man, is both a notable papist and hath served Monsieur [Anjou] heretofore as a spy. If either your Lordship or myself should use such instruments I know we should bear no small reproach.[22]

But he also advised his colleague that, since peace arias were so much in vogue, he would be well advised to provide himself with a song sheet and out-sing his rivals.

Considering the kind of men Walsingham habitually employed, it was distinctly hypocritical of him to complain about Crofts' agent. In his current dealings with Scotland Mr Secretary was hand-in-glove with one of the biggest blackguards to grace (or disgrace) the world of international diplomacy. Patrick Gray, commonly known as the Master of Gray, first made his appearance at the Scottish court in the train of Esmé Stuart. He was at that time pro-French and a professing Catholic (having originally been brought up a son of the kirk). He was similar to Stuart in being plausible and devilishly handsome – the sort of companion the young James loved. This politico-religious chameleon was driven by insatiable personal ambition. Gray was back in France when Stuart's faction was overthrown and remained there closely in cahoots with the Guises and the Queen of Scots' party. He returned to Scotland in the summer of 1583 and, on discovering that he had really been a Protestant all along, wormed his way into the trust of the reigning favourite, the Earl of Arran. In October 1584 Gray was sent across the border as an ambassador to bring about a permanent settlement of Anglo-Scottish relations.

With the international scene becoming steadily more menacing, Walsingham was more than ever concerned to be rid of the distraction of Scotland and the amoral Gray seemed to be an instrument well tuned for the necessary subtle diplomacy. Gray, putting behind him his earlier commitment to Mary's cause, proposed that James VI would formally exclude his mother from the nominal sovereignty of Scotland and resist further French influence in return for a generous annual subsidy from Elizabeth and her acknowledgement of him as her heir. The queen balked at that last condition but even she could see that it was worth dipping into her purse to secure peace on her northern border and Scottish rejection of Mary's pretensions. From Walsingham's point of view the scheme had another advantage in its psychological impact on the Queen of Scots. She learned of her son's 'treachery' in the spring of 1585 at the time when she was at inhospitable Tutbury and being subjected to Paulet's unsympathetic governance. The news brought on a state of physical collapse. She wrote angrily to James and informed Castelnau that he was not to address her son as king. Cast aside by even her own flesh and blood,

Mary knew that she had become a disposable irrelevance. Walsingham calculated that despair might drive her to throw caution to the winds and give way to some indiscretion which might, at long last, prove fatal.

Getting into bed with the devil was, however, a hazardous pastime. Gray's objective was supreme power in Scotland. While Walsingham was not averse to seeing his ally at the helm of Scottish affairs, he refused to condone Gray's calm proposal that Arran should be assassinated. Gray dropped the sanguinary plan and satisfied himself with playing Iago to Arran's Othello. Once again, Walsingham had to contend with Burghley's different assessment of the political situation. The Lord Treasurer was inclined to back Arran. However, the earl proved no match for his wily opponent. By March 1586 he had been forced into exile. Shortly afterwards the long-drawn-out negotiations reached their culmination in the Treaty of Berwick, a defensive alliance which safeguarded the Protestant religion in both states and ensured joint action in the event of aggression by a third power. The machine oil of this agreement was a pension of £4,000 to be paid to James. This was a major coup for Walsingham and his associates – and it made no mention of Mary Stuart.

By this time Walsingham had spread a net for the captive queen from which she could not escape. He had already isolated her so completely that she was ready to grasp any opportunity to make contact with her friends and supporters. Walsingham hoped that she would be tempted to abandon her habitual caution and so incriminate herself. What turned into the Babington plot did not begin life as a carefully crafted entrapment, planned over several months with military precision. Walsingham did not work that way, nor did his extensive and elaborate 'zoo' of agents lend itself to such organization. There was, of necessity, an element of opportunism about Mr Secretary's espionage activities, which depended for their effectiveness on whatever agents he had available at any given time. Thus it is impossible to discern a beginning of the Babington plot. It emerged from the coming together of various elements. It bubbled up from the steaming cauldron of hatred, fanaticism, internecine rivalry and confused hopes which was the English Catholic community in exile.

Just as English Protestants living abroad in Mary Tudor's reign divided into Calvinist, Zwinglian, Knoxian and Coxian groups, so the Catholic movement fractured along numerous stress lines – Jesuits, secular clergy, laymen, Francophiles and Hispanophiles. Nor was there any common purpose among the zealots who lived abroad or spent some time travelling abroad. While the Jesuits, ever faithful to the incumbent pope, had no problem contemplating or even helping to engineer a Spanish invasion, others balked at the idea of their homeland being overrun by foreigners. The more pragmatically minded considered past failed enterprises and argued that no religious breakthrough could be achieved while Elizabeth remained queen. Whether a change of regime could be wrought by direct action or left to the working out of divine providence was a topic of major discussion among the exiles. Some who fled to English havens fired with the enthusiasm of religious conviction became disillusioned when they encountered Catholic leaders such as Mendoza, Guise, Arundel and Paget whose piety was heavily salted with personal resentment and desire for revenge. It is not difficult to imagine how confused many became, torn between their families back home who were quietly avoiding trouble and their activist peer groups determined on heroic action. Out of this confusion came the turncoats who were ready to betray their fellows and enter the ever-extending pool of Walsingham's counter-conspiracy. Only such an atmosphere of doubt, personal rivalries and divided loyalties explains how the English government was able to penetrate the Catholic communities with comparative ease and recruit double agents.

One such was Gilbert Gifford. He came from a Staffordshire recusant family and between 1577 and 1585 had had a troubled and troublesome career as a member of the English Colleges at Douai, Rheims and Rome. An argumentative and at times violent student, he was a thorn in William Allen's flesh and Edward Stafford later called him 'the most notable double treble villain that ever lived, for he hath played upon all the hands in the world'.[23] In 1585 he met up with John Savage, who had served in Parma's Netherlands army, and John Ballard, a graduate of Rheims, who had travelled extensively in England encouraging the recusant community. One of the projects the trio discussed – at this stage no more than a dream – was the feasibility and desirability of murdering Elizabeth. All three men were known to Walsingham and it was now that his massive intelligence expenditure bore fruit. When Gifford returned to England in December he was picked up and conveyed to Seething Lane. He seemed to have no problem in transferring allegiance, though doubtless Walsingham made him an offer he was in no position to refuse. What interested the secretary was that Gifford had arrived from Paris charged with finding some means of re-establishing a communication system between Mary and her supporters.

Enter Anthony Babington, a twenty-four-year-old Derbyshire gentleman of Catholic sympathies. Some six years earlier he had met Mary Stuart in his capacity as page to the Earl of Shrewsbury, her guardian. Subsequently he had travelled to Paris, met Thomas Morgan, Mary's agent, and conveyed letters between them. Around 1583–4 his activity ceased, probably in the wake of the Throckmorton plot. In August 1585 Castelnau, the French ambassador, was recalled and replaced by Claude de l'Aubespine, Baron de Châteauneuf. The new envoy was a member of the Guise party and much more astute than his predecessor. Walsingham thus lost his most important source of information about French activity and contacts with English Catholics. Moreover, this happened at a time when France was plunging back into religious war and the Catholic League seemed invincible. Guise's followers denounced Henry III and Catherine for their edicts of religious toleration, refused to acknowledge Henry of Navarre as heir presumptive and bound themselves by solemn oath 'to use force and take up arms to the end that the holy church of God may be restored to its dignity'. Once again a crusade was launched to annihilate French Protestantism. It seemed inevitable to Walsingham that Mary Stuart would once more feature prominently in the plans of her kinsmen. Removing her from the equation became a matter of top priority. Even with good luck and a following wind that would take time. Meanwhile he had to find out what the French were up to. That meant opening up a fresh channel of communication between Paris and the Queen of Scots – a channel to which he had access.

Walsingham's instructions to Gifford were very simple: he was to do precisely what Mary's friends had sent him over to do – well, not quite precisely. Gifford easily won the confidence of the ambassador and the captive queen when he proposed a system for smuggling messages in and out of Mary's latest lodging, the Staffordshire manor house of Chartley, concealed in beer barrels. What the sender and the recipient did not know was that their letters were opened, copied and re-sealed in transit. Their contents were deciphered by Walsingham's crack code expert Thomas Phelippes. Mr Secretary knew all the plans of the Catholic network often before the members of that network knew them themselves.

In May 1586, John Ballard, back in England on another tour of recusant houses, made contact with Anthony Babington and attempted to recruit him in an assassination plot whose details he and his co-conspirators had already worked out. Was this a sting operation, set up by Gifford on Walsingham's instructions, or a ham-fisted attempt by Ballard to draw a coterie of young English gentlemen into a genuine plot? Ballard certainly knew that no Catholic rebellion could succeed without the leadership of the leading families of the shires and Babington had many valuable contacts. Whether or not Ballard and Babington were set up, little that passed between them was unknown to Walsingham. The basic elements of the plan as they emerged at subsequent meetings were that Savage would undertake the murder of Elizabeth. Once this was accomplished, Babington with a posse of friends would effect Mary's escape.

Babington was not taken in. He knew how heavily the odds were stacked against the success of the venture. He understood the mood of recusant gentry better than Ballard and realized that the vision of a Catholic uprising had more to do with wishful thinking than reality. Furthermore, he did not relish the idea of a Spanish invasion. As clandestine meetings continued through the early summer the young man continued to be in two minds. Eventually he decided to escape the conflict of conscience by going to live abroad, where he hoped to enter a religious order and devote himself to the contemplative life. He asked one of his confederates, Robert Poley, to approach Walsingham for a passport. Here there is a double irony. Poley had been insinuated into the household of Frances Sidney (Walsingham's daughter-in-law) by the Catholic underground but soon concluded that it was more profitable to work for Mr Secretary. Walsingham's response was to interview Babington and press him for information about the conspirators (presumably as a quid pro quo for travel documents). It seems that, at this point, Walsingham had no thought of using Babington to incriminate Mary.

However, it was this which enabled the idealistic young man to resolve his crisis of conscience. It obliged him to choose once and for all whether to be loyal to his country or his faith. Spurred on by his confessor, he chose the latter. This meant that he threw all his efforts into the plot which came to bear his name. On 6 July he wrote to Mary the letter which would seal the fate of them both. It set out all the elements of the scheme and sought her permission to proceed. Mary's impatiently awaited reply was penned by her secretary on 17 July and, to Walsingham's delight, it was a long letter explicit about her acquiescence in the conspirators' treason. She advised them how to go about their several tasks, even to proposing the most effective PR slogans for winning public support. Babington and his friends should give out that their intentions were to protect the realm from Puritans and prevent Leicester coming back from the Netherlands to usurp the crown. Her reference to the actual despatch of the queen by six designated assassins was oblique but when taken in conjunction with Babington's letter of the 6th became quite clear. A frisson of excitement ran through her written words as she contemplated her release.

> The affairs being thus prepared and forces in readiness both without and within the realm, then shall it be time to set the six gentlemen to work taking order, upon the accomplishing of their design, I may be suddenly transported out of this place, and that all your forces in the same time be on the field to meet me in tarrying for the arrival of the foreign aid, which then must be hastened with all diligence.[24]

Mary entered enthusiastically into the enterprise by suggesting three possible ways in which she might be 'snatched'.

Everyone in any way privy to these negotiations was now in a high state of nervousness – and that included Walsingham. There was so much at stake, as he confided to Leicester on 9 July:

> I have acquainted this gentleman with the secret to the end he may impart the same unto your lordship. I dare make none of my servants here privy thereunto. My only fear is, that her majesty will not use the matter with that secrecy that appertaineth, though it import it as greatly as ever anything did sithence she came to this crown, and surely, if the matter be well handled, it will break the neck of all dangerous practices during her majesty's reign. I pray your lordship make this letter an heretic after you have read the same [ie burn it]. I mean, when the matter is grown to a full ripeness, to send some confidential person unto you, to acquaint you fully with the matter.[25]

For Walsingham this was the big one and he was anxious not to let it slip off the hook.

One problem was holding Babington to the sticking place. The young man might have decided where his prime loyalty lay but he was still jittery, capable of aborting the exercise or, worse still, going into hiding. Walsingham had to decide the right moment to bring him and his accomplices in. The longer they were at large, the more incriminating evidence his surveillance team could gather. But also the greater was the risk that they would become suspicious and that some of them might make their escape. Indeed, there were so many agents and double agents involved that it is remarkable that matters were brought to what Walsingham considered a satisfactory conclusion. It was not until the early days of August that he gave the orders for the conspirators to be rounded up. Then began the work of extracting confessions and information, mostly under torture. The trials took place on the 13, 14 and 15 September. Execution by hanging, drawing and quartering followed a few days later.

Even while these events were taking place, Walsingham moved decisively against Mary. He had her transferred, without warning, from Chartley to another nearby location and held there for two weeks while her quarters were thoroughly searched and all her papers parcelled up and taken to London, where he examined them minutely. At the same time all Mary's staff were brought south for interrogation. Early in September the Council met to discuss how to proceed against the ex-queen. There could not really be any doubt about their decision. The evidence against her was overwhelming. She had to be put on trial for her life.

The problem, as ever, was the reaction not of Mary, but of Elizabeth. She responded emotionally to the plot and her advisers knew that it would be very difficult to hold her to a logical course of action. The whole Babington affair had frightened and outraged her. She insisted that the executions of her would-be assassins should be carried out with the maximum cruelty. When hanged, they were to be cut down while still breathing and forced, in their final pain-racked minutes, to watch themselves being disembowelled. Only when officials reported back to her that this barbarity had been counter-productive, drawing sympathetic murmurings from the crowed, did she relent and order the next batch of executions to be carried out more humanely (ie the victims were hanged until dead). The queen's ferocity extended also to her rival. She sent word to Paulet to remove all Mary's money and servants, deny her any privileges and subject her to virtual solitary confinement. There was, doubtless, an element of calculation in this. It would have suited Elizabeth's book for Mary to die of natural causes, thus lifting the burden of responsibility from herself. It might be that subjecting the prisoner to the utmost privations would hasten her end. From Walsingham's point of view this would have been the worst possible outcome. Mary's devotees would immediately have proclaimed her a martyr. There had to be a trial, so that her crimes could be publicly demonstrated and no doubt cast upon the justice of her subsequent punishment.

The councillors' anxieties were hinted at in Burghley's report to Leicester of 1 October:

For the greatest matter here in hand, we find the cause so manifest against the party [Mary], the party so dangerous to our queen, our country, and, [what] is of most importance, to the whole cause of God's church throughout Christendom, as without a direct and speedy

proceeding it had been less danger to have concealed [rather] than
revealed this great conspiracy. I hope that God, which hath given us
the light to discover it, will also give assistance to punish it, for it was
intended not only against her majesty's person, and yours and mine,
but utterly to have overthrown the glory of Christ's church, and to
have erected the synagogue of Antichrist.[26]

For Burghley and his colleagues the obvious way forward was an
official trial, leading to a sentence and execution, all ratified by a
specially summoned parliament. Elizabeth, for her part, was all too
aware of the constitutional consequences of such a process. Parliament
to endorse the judicial murder of an anointed sovereign? Where
might that lead? As the issues were argued out at Windsor where the
court was in these weeks, Elizabeth was finally brought round, though
she refused to have Mary detained in the Tower – too close for
comfort. Finally Fotheringhay Castle in Northamptonshire was fixed
upon for Mary's detention and trial. It was almost equidistant from
London and her former place of confinement and was very secure,
being currently in use as a prison. Mary was installed there at the end
of September and most of the forty-two commissioners appointed to
hear her case arrived on 11 October.

Walsingham and Leicester, the two leading hawks, had not been
present at the earlier deliberations. Mr Secretary was, once again, laid
aside by illness. The earl was still in the Netherlands but he made his
position on Mary's trial quite clear in letters to Walsingham, Burghley
and the queen:

> if you shall defer it, either for a parliament or a great session, you will
> hazard her majesty more than ever, for time to be given is [what] the
> traitors and enemies to her will desire . . . I do assure myself of a new,
> more desperate attempt if you shall fall to such temporising solemnities
> and her majesty cannot but mislike you all for it. For who can [keep]
> these villains from her if that person live . . . God forbid! And be you
> all stout and resolute in this speedy execution, or be condemned of all
> the world forever . . . if you will have her majesty safe, it must be
> done, for justice doth crave it besides policy.[27]

Walsingham finally arrived at Fotheringhay on 13–14 October. One can imagine that, whatever the state of his health, this was an engagement he would not have missed for worlds. Thus it was that the two great enemies met for the first – and last – time. The prosecution was led by the state's lawyers and Walsingham played no major part in it. However, there was one moment of high drama which did turn the spotlight on him and which raised the kind of questions which must always be raised concerning the ethics of covert activities. His trump card was Mary's letter to Babington of 17 July. The defendant had no idea that this had fallen into the government's hands. She assumed that Babington had burned it, as instructed. When it was read out in court she was shattered. But, of course, it was *not* her dictated letter that was being offered in evidence. It was a copy – doubtless a very proficient one – of the transcript made by Phelippes of the coded original. When Mary had recovered herself she turned and faced Walsingham and denounced the document as a forgery. It was now his turn to assume an air of wounded innocence: 'I call God as witness that as a private person I have done nothing unbeseeming an honest man, nor, as I bear the place of a public man, have I done anything unworthy of my place. I confess that being very careful for the safety of the Queen and the realm, I have curiously searched out all the practices against the same.'[28]

His answer was no answer (though Mary graciously accepted it). It was the politician's ploy of using a high principle to vault over an accusation of base conduct. 'Careful for the safety of the Queen and the realm' was no more than a formula for suggesting that ends justified means. There is no reason to doubt that the documents presented to the court accurately represented what Mary and her correspondents had written but some were only copies and could easily have been doctored. Mary was not allowed to examine them and her secretaries were not brought forward to face cross-examination. Justice was undoubtedly done – but in a very roundabout way.

The commissioners completed their examination on 15 October and were scheduled to deliver their verdict immediately. All was poised for Mary's condemnation, which would pave the way for the cutting out of the political cancer that had, for so long, debilitated

Elizabeth's government. Then came one of those heart-stopping messages from the queen to which all her councillors had become accustomed. The trial was to be adjourned for ten days. The commissioners were to reconvene at Westminster.

It was in these tense days that personal tragedy struck the Walsingham household. In early May Sir Henry Sidney, his daughter's father-in-law, died at the age of fifty-six. When the news reached Philip Sidney in the Netherlands he immediately applied to Elizabeth for compassionate leave, so that he could return and attend to family affairs. She refused. Sir Henry's widow (Leicester's sister) moved in with the Walsinghams. Hers had been a hard life, made worse by the queen's hostility. Once a great royal favourite, Mary Sidney had in 1562 nursed Elizabeth through smallpox. As a result she had become hideously disfigured, a disaster which had left her as much mentally as physically scarred. In subsequent years she had experienced long periods of loneliness while her husband served in Ireland. Now she was a semi-invalid widow in her mid-fifties and her eldest son, fighting in a foreign land, was denied his wish to come to comfort her. She could, however, derive some consolation from her infant granddaughter, Elizabeth. On 9 August Lady Sidney died. Philip Sidney had lost both parents within the space of a few months. Still he was not permitted to return home.

In June Francis and Ursula Walsingham had to say goodbye to Frances, who went out to Flushing to be with her husband. Though heavily pregnant with her second child, she soon had to do the work of a nurse, for Sidney took a musket ball in the thigh at the siege of Zutphen on 22 September. For three-and-a-half weeks he suffered the ministrations of field surgeons. News of Sidney's condition reaching London in these weeks varied. Some reports spoke of improvement. Others were less sanguine. Anxiety about his daughter and son-in-law nagged at Walsingham as he laboured to bring the business of the Scottish queen to a satisfactory conclusion. It was on the very day that the commissioners reconvened (25 October) that, in distant Utrecht, the Earl of Leicester sat down to write to his friend:

> Sir, the grief I have taken for the loss of my dear son and yours would not suffer me to write sooner of those ill news unto you, specially

being in good hope, so very little time before, of his good recovery; but he is with the Lord and his will must be done . . . For my own part, I have lost, beside the comfort of my life, a most principal stay and help in my service here and, if I may say it, I think none of all hath a greater loss than the queen's majesty herself. Your sorrowful daughter and mine is here with me at Utrecht, till she may recover some strength, for she is wonderfully overthrown through her long care since the beginning of her husband's hurt and I am the more careful that she should be in some strength before she take her journey into England.[29]

Shortly after this Frances returned to England with her husband's body. Within days she was delivered of a stillborn child.

In addition to the personal agony inflicted on Walsingham by these events he now had to face financial hardship. The deaths in quick succession of Philip Sidney and his parents had left the Sidney affairs in a state of confusion. Walsingham, named as one of the executors of Philip's will, took it upon himself to sort out the estate. It transpired that the hero of Zutphen had left debts of at least £6,000. Walsingham assumed responsibility for satisfying the creditors. He turned to Leicester for help.

I have caused Sir Philip Sidney's will to be considered by certain learned in the laws and I find the same imperfect touching the sale of his land for the satisfying of his poor creditors, which I do assure your Lordship doth greatly afflict me, [that] a gentleman that hath lived so unspotted [in] reputation and had so great care to see all men satisfied, should be so [exposed] to the outcry of his creditors. His goods will not suffice to answer a third part of his debts already known. This hard estate of this noble gentleman maketh me to stay to take order for his burial until your Lordship's return. I do not see how the same can be performed with that solemnity that appertaineth without the utter undoing of his creditors, which is to be weighed in conscience.[30]

But the earl had problems of his own and could not help. Walsingham appealed to the queen. Burghley added his voice to the secretary's entreaty, pointing out how indebted the Crown was to this faithful servant, not least for his uncovering of the Babington plot. Elizabeth turned a deaf ear to their pleas. In utter despair Walsingham quit the court. He shared his pain, grief and sense of injustice with Burghley on 16 December:

> I humbly beseech your Lordship to pardon me in that I did not take my leave of you before my departure from the court. Her Majesty's unkind dealing towards me hath so wounded me as I could take no comfort to stay there. And yet if I saw any hope that my continuance there might either breed any good to the church or furtherance to the service of her Majesty or of the realm, the regard of my particular should not cause me to withdraw myself. But seeing the declining state we are running into, and that men of best desert are least esteemed, I hold them happiest in this government that may be rather lookers on than actors.[31]

How may we explain the queen's appalling ingratitude? She certainly found it difficult to sympathize with other people's domestic trials and tribulations because she had never had a family life of her own. Her tyrannical father had ordered the death of her mother whom she scarcely remembered. For whatever reason she had elected the single life and she resented it when those close to her entered into marriage. Very possibly she had never fully reconciled herself to the union of Philip and Frances, even though she had consented to be godmother to their daughter. But, in the autumn of 1586, there were other reasons for her alienation from Walsingham. Nor was he alone in being out of favour. Elizabeth had never felt herself so isolated as she did at this time. Most of her advisers, including Leicester, who returned at the end of November, were advising her to continue a war which was draining the treasury and wreaking havoc on her careful finances without yielding any military or diplomatic return. The international peace she had worked so hard to preserve was on the point of being shattered: Philip II was known to be mustering his fleet for an invasion of England and in the forthcoming conflict England would have to face the might of Spain unaided.

But the issue which dominated all the queen's thoughts and

emotions was the fate of Mary Stuart. In September the commissioners had pronounced that the Scottish ex-queen was guilty and should die. Elizabeth had accepted the verdict. She had had to submit to the unwelcome necessity of recalling parliament to ratify the death sentence. Everyone now waited for her to issue the necessary warrant. Diplomats representing Catholic Europe and James of Scotland urged her to draw back from the fatal deed. As she tried to resist the tide of the inevitable, no one stood beside her or sympathized with her predicament. As she wrestled with her doubts, fears and moral dilemmas and possibly came close to a breakdown, Elizabeth had advisers in plenty – preachers reminding her of her duty; parliamentarians urging her to be revenged on her enemies; councillors steeling her arm for battle – but there was no one who understood her or realized that the policy she was being urged to pursue represented for her a deep personal failure. She lingered at Richmond, refusing to come to Westminster, 'being loath to hear so many foul and grievous matters revealed and ripped up' by parliament. Eventually parliament came to her. On 24 November she received a delegation at Richmond. Her response was a rambling speech which revealed her own inner turmoil. She spoke of her 'woman to woman' concern for Mary, her desire to bring the miscreant to repentance, her lack of personal animosity. Having skirted the problem, she offered the parliamentarians an 'answer answerless':

> You have laid a hard and heavy burden upon me in this case, for now all is to be done by the direction of the queen – a course not common in like cases. But for answer unto you, you shall understand the case is rare and of great weight, wherefore I must take such advice as the gravity thereof doth require . . . To your petition I must pause and take respite before I give answer. Princes, you know, stand upon stages so that their actions are viewed and beheld of all men; and I am sure my doings will come to the scanning of many fine wits, not only within the realm, but in foreign countries. And we must look to persons as well abroad as at home. But this be you assured of: I will be most careful to consider and to do that which shall be best for the safety of my people and most for the good of the realm.[32]

Perhaps it is not surprising that Elizabeth could spare no sympathy for Walsingham's financial problems, particularly as he was prominent among those constantly nagging her about Mary. He had even written for her a long memorandum on the dangers of delaying Mary's execution. Eventually, the queen accepted the inevitable and on 3 December issued a proclamation announcing the death sentence.

In her speech of 24 November Elizabeth had made reference to a group of conspirators 'who within fourteen days have undertaken to take away my life'.[33] The air was thick with rumours of plots. How many were real and how many imagined we cannot know. It may also be the case that some were contrived in order to stir Elizabeth to action. Re-enter William Stafford and Michael Moody. In the last weeks of 1586 these two men put their heads together to concoct one of the most bizarre assassination plots of the reign. Moody, who was currently being held in Newgate in connection with Sir Edward Stafford's debts, was to be released, gain access to the court, lay a gunpowder trail to Elizabeth's bedchamber and blow her to pieces. How he could have hoped to engineer this in the crowded court is not clear and, unsurprisingly, the explosive option was abandoned for an alternative involving poison or the knife. William Stafford drew into the plot the French ambassador, Châteauneuf, and his secretary Leonard des Trappes. He then reported the whole affair to Walsingham. All this sounds suspiciously like a rerun of the Parry plot, an *agent provocateur*'s attempt to win favour. But was Stafford acting unilaterally or was he set on by Walsingham? Much depends on the timing. If this is the plot Elizabeth referred to in her speech then it was already under investigation before Walsingham's departure from court and he could have been an instigator. However, no action was taken against the conspirators until January, by which time Walsingham had taken himself off to Barn Elms to be a 'looker-on rather than an actor'.

The official story was that Stafford made his confession to Walsingham early in the new year. He and des Trappes were then arrested and confined in the Tower and Châteauneuf was placed under house arrest. Subsequently he was examined by a committee of the Council (not including Walsingham). The ambassador confirmed that Stafford had come to him with a hair-brained scheme and that he had totally rejected it. He could not, however, avoid the charge of having concealed knowledge of a conspiracy. The outcome of all the brouhaha was that Moody went back to jail for another three years, des Trappes and Stafford spent a few months in the Tower before being quietly released, and Châteauneuf was kept under close surveillance for a month and forbidden to communicate with his superiors. By May the whole incident was forgotten and Elizabeth joked with the ambassador that it had all been an unfortunate misunderstanding. On balance, it seems more likely that Walsingham was among those who were duped rather than being the originator of the plot. He was ill most of the winter, as well as being alienated from the court. The fact that Châteauneuf was rendered *hors de combat* until after Mary's execution suggests the object of the exercise may have been the closure of diplomatic channels during the tense days leading up to the tragic final scene in the drama of the two queens. Elizabeth or Burghley are more likely to have been the principal actors in this non-conspiracy.

The story of the last traumatic days leading up to Mary's death is well known. The details do not greatly concern us because Walsingham, who had striven hard to bring about the Queen of Scots' ruin, was very little involved. His physical disorders exacerbated by mental stress had brought him very low. The unfortunate official who deputized for him was William Davison, appointed as his assistant in December. On 1 February Elizabeth summoned Davison to her and signed the death warrant. As she did so she made a grim joke. 'Go and tell Walsingham,' she said, 'the grief would grow near to kill him outright.' It now required the great seal, which was appended by Lord Chancellor Hatton the same day. At the same time Elizabeth instructed Davison to bid Walsingham write a letter to Paulet hinting that he might save everyone a great deal of trouble by despatching his prisoner himself. Mr Secretary, though still unwell, had now moved to Seething Lane in order to be more accessible. He did as instructed, knowing full well that Paulet would reject so dishonourable a suggestion. It was Burghley who took over arrangements for the performance of the deed. He called together the available councillors and they planned to see the warrant executed without the queen's foreknowledge. The authorizing document was endorsed by all and brought to Walsingham's sick bed for his signature. On 3 February Robert Beale was despatched to find the Earls of Shrewsbury and Kent, who had been selected to oversee the execution. In later years he would hint angrily that Walsingham had pleaded illness in order to assign this risky task to a deputy. By the 7th the earls were at Fotheringhay. So was the executioner, a man personally recommended by Walsingham for the job. At eight o'clock on the morning of 8 February it was all over. All over, that is, for Mary Stuart. For the others involved in the tragedy the fallout would be catastrophic and there would be important work for Walsingham still to do for queen and country.

Chapter 9

NO TOMB

1587–90

Walsingham must have been relieved not to have been in the direct firing line of the queen's wrath in the immediate aftermath of Mary's execution but his absence from court may well have also been welcome to Elizabeth and there is the possibility that it was engineered. As usual the queen had expected to have her cake and eat it. She had wanted Mary out of the way but she had not wanted to shoulder the responsibility for her execution. So when the Queen of Scots was beheaded on her direct order, signed with her hand and endorsed with her great seal, she had to find some way of convincing foreign courts that she had not intended her warrant to be acted on; that one of her minions had exceeded his orders. Had Walsingham been at his post in those crucial February days he would have been the obvious fall guy but Elizabeth would not have wanted to dismiss and utterly disgrace such a valuable servant. So it was highly convenient that William Davison, a comparative nobody, was standing in for the secretary when the death warrant was signed, despatched and acted on.

This raises the question of whether Walsingham's merely marginal involvement in the final act of Mary Stuart's life was all it seemed. Was he really as ill as he claimed? Was he assiduously keeping out of trouble? Or were others implicit in his absence? Did he deliberately allow Davison to take the rap for him? Or was he innocent of his friend's humiliation? The Davison of whom we are allowed shifting glimpses through the mists of time looks like one of nature's victims. Despite having rendered valuable service in missions to Scotland and the Netherlands for twenty years, he seems never to have learned pragmatism. He was a zealous Puritan and, perhaps, remained rather naïve. He enjoyed the friendship of Leicester and Walsingham, who shared his opinions but not his forthright expression of them. It was Davison on whom Mr Secretary urged caution in 1578: 'it were very dangerous that every private man's zeal should carry sufficient authority of reforming things amiss.' A careful understanding of political realities, Mr Secretary suggested, would persuade Davison to 'deal warily in this time when policy carrieth more sway than zeal'.[1]

Davison was with Leicester in the Low Countries in 1585–6 and it was he whom the earl despatched to Elizabeth to explain why he had disobeyed orders in assuming the governorship of the rebel state. Stoically the emissary bore the brunt of the queen's fury, though at one point he, like others before him, contemplated resignation. What he found harder to stomach was Leicester's reaction. The disgraced favourite tried to put the blame for his actions on Davison's shoulders. 'You did chiefly persuade me to take this charge upon me,' without waiting for the queen's approval, he asserted.[2] It was probably quite true that Davison, in his enthusiasm for the Protestant cause had urged Leicester to be bold but that does not excuse Leicester's cowardly behaviour in trying to shelter behind an underling. Walsingham obviously thought the same, though he expressed himself more tactfully in a letter to Dudley: 'The gentleman is very much grieved with the dislike he understandeth your lordship hath of him. For my own part, I do not find but that he hath dealt well, both for the cause and towards your lordship, whose good opinion and favour he doth greatly desire.'[3]

In the following September Davison was appointed to assist Walsingham, in view of the secretary's fluctuating health. He was thus thrust into the centre of government at a time of great crisis. While other councillors, including Walsingham, were busy at Fotheringhay and Westminster, he was attendant on the queen at Windsor, then Richmond, taking every opportunity to urge on her the necessity for Mary's execution. Then, in December, when the Council came together again, Walsingham absented himself from court and Davison was once more left exposed. Everyone at this stage was walking on eggshells. They knew how difficult it was going to be to obtain Elizabeth's irreversible decision and they also had a sense that it was now or never. Davison was very aware of his situation and refused to present the warrant for Elizabeth's signature until she requested it via a senior Council member (in this case Charles Howard, Lord Admiral).

Once the warrant was signed there followed a succession of hurried secret meetings. No one wanted to be held personally responsible. Davison reported to Burghley, Walsingham, Leicester, Bromley, Hatton and Robert Beale. He told them of his anxiety that the queen would change her mind. When the next day (2 February), she instructed him to delay having the great seal attached, the councillors' worst fears were confirmed. The sealing had already been done but the warrant's despatch could still be halted. Walsingham was not present at the Council meeting on the 3rd when eleven of his colleagues decided to arrange for the execution. Both queen and Council made sure that Walsingham was kept fully informed of developments. The letter authorizing the warrant's despatch to Fotheringhay was rushed from Greenwich to Seething Lane for his signature and, as we have seen, Burghley and Walsingham communicated over the choreography of the execution. Davison and Robert Beale also maintained contact with their chief. When Beale was selected as the courier to ride post haste into North-amptonshire with the Council's covert instructions, it was in his interests as well as his colleague's to ensure that Walsingham knew what they were doing. They had no intention of being ground between the upper and nether millstones of queen and Council. They knew perfectly well that there would be unpleasantness ahead.

The storm burst on 10 February. Elizabeth ordered Council members to her private chambers for a dressing down. Walsingham was not present. Nor was Burghley, who was, apparently, suffering from a riding accident. Absence did not save the Lord Treasurer from the royal fury. He was banned the court for more than a month and even then he had not heard the end of the matter. On 15 March he complained to Hatton of 'the late sharp and most heavy speech of her

Majesty to myself in the hearing of my Lord of Leicester and Mr Secretary Walsingham.'[4] We know, therefore, that Walsingham was by then back at court. He had, in fact, returned on the 14th of the previous month – ie as soon as the immediate furore was over. Of all the major players in the events of February, he seems to have been the one who came through relatively unscathed. Elizabeth had already decided to throw the book at Davison. She even enquired of her lawyers whether she might use her prerogative powers to send the unfortunate man to the block. Walsingham did his best for his friend. As soon as he heard of Davison's incarceration he wrote to Burghley expressing his genuine shock and urging the treasurer to intervene. He wasted no time in doing so, pointing out to the queen that to despatch a councillor to the Tower, except on a charge of treason, was quite unprecedented and would raise eyebrows in foreign courts. Walsingham had the prisoner set down his own version of events and, on 11 March, he sent a mutual friend, Thomas Randolph, to discuss the situation with him. As well as being a wise senior diplomat, well versed in Scottish affairs, Randolph was Walsingham's brother-in-law (husband of his sister, Anne). Randolph discovered a depressed but unrepentant Davison who rejected the charge that he had disobeyed the queen by failing to keep the signed warrant a secret (and thus enabling the Council to go behind her back in authorizing the execution). His perfectly reasonable defence was that he had only shared the information with leading members of the Council who were in the queen's confidence. Over the next few days Davison was visited by other councillors. By the time the poor man's *in camera* trial took place in the Star Chamber on 28 March, his story had changed. He now accepted full responsibility on the basis that he must have misunderstood the queen's intentions. He meekly received his sentence – an open-ended prison term and an enormous fine he could not possibly pay. He doubtless knew that there was never any intention that the fine should be paid. After nineteen months of probably not very onerous confinement he was quietly released, on the authority of Burghley and Walsingham. Although he never returned to his job he continued to draw his pay and, in 1594, Elizabeth made him a generous grant of lands.

A distinct odour of fish hangs over the whole of these proceedings. A deal had been struck. Davison allowed himself to be used to protect the reputations of his seniors and particularly the queen. The only way the Council majority's determination to get rid of Mary could be squared with Elizabeth's determination to keep her hands clean was to put the blame on someone else. The obvious candidate was the intermediary between queen and Council, the secretary. In normal circumstances that would have been Walsingham. It is inconceivable that Elizabeth would have put him on trial, shut him up in the Tower and, in effect, sacked him from his job. Walsingham was an internationally known and respected figure. Even foreign diplomats and courtiers who loathed his religion acknowledged his honesty and intellectual stature. His disgrace would have been a huge scandal which would have reflected on the queen. Another reason for keeping Walsingham out of the firing line was that Elizabeth needed him – now more than ever. She had to have help in disseminating through diplomatic channels the official account of Mary's execution. She had to know how that account was being received in foreign courts. More important still, it became daily more vital to have intelligence about Philip II's invasion plans. If someone had to be thrown to the wolves it could not be Francis Walsingham.

The only question which remains is, how complicit was Walsingham, himself, in these shabby dealings? Robert Beale, who was highly indignant at the treatment meted out to himself and his colleague, exonerated his brother-in-law from blame. Describing the events of February 1587 years later he claimed, 'Mr Secretary Walsingham was thought too stout, and would utter all. Therefore, Mr Davison must bear the burden.' The word 'stout' carried, at that time, a range of meanings, viz: 'proud', 'stubborn', 'unyielding', 'defiant', 'uncompromising', 'honest'. What Beale was saying was that Walsingham was too straightforward to be a party to the underhand dealings of either the Council or the queen. We may recall the advice Beale gave in 1592 regarding the conduct of the principal secretary and which had Walsingham's example very much in mind:

Bear reproofs, false reports and such like crosses, if they be private and
touch you not deeply, with silence or a modest answer. But if it be in
company or touch your allegiance, honour or honesty, mine advice is
that you answer more roundly, lest your silence cause standers-by to
think ill of you and to retain it in memory and thereupon to work your
farther indignation and discredit.[5]

Walsingham was too honest to condone by his silence Elizabeth's
subterfuge and too canny to shoulder the blame for her actions.

What I believe happened was something like this: the previous
December there had been a falling-out between the queen and her
secretary which had resulted in the latter leaving the court. He had
subsequently been taken ill and was completely incapacitated
throughout most of January. By the end of the month he was
sufficiently recovered to return to his house in the City and to
conduct business from his sickbed. It now suited Elizabeth to keep
him away from the centre of the action, even though vitally important
matters of state were cropping up thick and fast. The business of the
warrant would never have worked if Walsingham had been the
courier. Therefore, she deliberately delayed his recall until mid-
February. If anyone contrived Walsingham's absence during the
crucial days covering the end of the Mary Stuart affair it was the
queen.

If Elizabeth had any doubts whatsoever about the priceless value of
Walsingham's service she had only to peruse the letter he wrote to
John Maitland, his opposite number in Scotland, within days of his
return to court. Reactions to Elizabeth's execution of a foreign royal
personage had been predictably harsh. Her brother monarchs in
France and Spain were genuinely shocked and outraged by the deed,
as were many of their Catholic subjects. Reports poured into
Walsingham's office of formal diplomatic protests and popular de-
mands for revenge. On the quayside at Rouen mobs attacked English
ships and their crews. From Paris Stafford sent so many accounts of
French outrage that Walsingham abruptly told him to stop providing
information that was upsetting their mistress. But the country most
closely affected by Mary's death was, of course, Scotland. On 14

February, Elizabeth had sent Sir Robert Carey to Edinburgh with instructions to give James the official version of his mother's death. In a personal note she wrote of 'the extreme dolour that overwhelms my mind for that miserable *accident*' (my emphasis). She proclaimed her innocence and assured the king: 'I am not so base-minded that fear of any living creature or prince should make me afraid to do that were just or, done, to deny the same . . . as I know this [the execution] was deserved, yet if I had meant it I would never lay it on other's shoulders.'[6] Well might we conclude, 'The lady doth protest too much!' The letter was not delivered. Carey arrived at the border to find it closed and all communication between the two nations at a standstill.

The execution of Mary had been a severe affront to Scottish national pride and popular demonstrations demanded reprisals. At court James' nobles were urging him not to submit, in cowardly fashion, to this blow against his dignity. One courtier appeared before the king in full armour, claiming that this was the only suitable mourning to wear for the ex-queen mother. More seriously, the French ambassador pounced upon the death at Fotheringhay as a means of turning James' affections away from England and back to the 'auld alliance'. It was to stiffen the young king's resistance to any such blandishments that Walsingham wrote his long letter, fully intending it to be brought to James' attention. Could he succeed where the queen had failed?

Walsingham wasted no ink justifying what had been done. His letter was couched purely in terms of *realpolitik*, with a large element of bluff. He advised the king not to allow himself to be drawn into a warlike alliance against England, a nation which was 'so prepared . . . to defend itself, both otherwise and by the conjunction of Holland and Zeeland's forces by sea' that it 'need not fear what all the potentates of Europe, being banded together against us can do'. Walsingham preyed upon James' known dislike of violence by suggesting that any war might result in the king being taken prisoner or slain. France, he warned, was only interested in restoring Catholicism in Scotland. And let not James, Walsingham lectured, delude himself into thinking that he could ride the tiger of Spanish militarism and avoid the inevitable consequences. Philip would be no more disposed than Henry III to permit the union of England and Scotland, nor would he allow James to exercise his own religion.

Should he seek to placate the powerful continental monarchs by voluntarily converting to Catholicism, this would not save him. He should contemplate the fate of Dom Antonio, a devout Catholic prince despoiled of his inheritance by his voracious neighbour. Finally, Walsingham pointed out that espousing the Roman faith would not win him support south of the border. English Catholics, he averred (presumably with tongue in cheek) were all united in their loyalty to the Crown. English people would not welcome him: 'the Protestants because he had renounced the religion wherein he was with great care brought up, the papists because they could not be assured in short space he was truly turned to their faith. Yea, all men should have reason to forsake him who had thus dissembled and forsaken his God.'[7]

This letter certainly struck the right note insofar as James VI was very carefully weighing his options. If he bided his time and meekly took his pension then the chances were that the ripe fruit of the English Crown would eventually fall into his lap. On the other hand, with foreign help he might harvest that Crown much sooner. Walsingham tried to persuade Elizabeth formally to acknowledge James as her heir but she was as immovable as ever on that subject. However, James was, very slowly, brought to regard discretion as the better part of valour and to resist the sabre-rattling of his more belligerent nobles.

Scotland was only one of Walsingham's worries. He was still busy keeping the Low Countries war going and trying to persuade Elizabeth to succour the Huguenot cause. He was even trying to persuade the Ottoman sultan to renew anti-Spanish hostilities in the Mediterranean. As he confessed to a friend: 'I had never more business lying on my hands sithence I entered this charge, than at present.'[8]

But the great challenge was preparation for Philip's Armada. Walsingham forced his ailing body to keep going long enough to cope with that crisis he had always known as inevitable. The coming together of Catholic forces against England which he had feared was now a reality. Everyone knew that Spain's long-mooted invasion was imminent. But there was no agreement as to what Philip's strategy was, how large his fleet would be, when or at what precise target it would be launched. Never was intelligence work more important than in these nail-biting months and Walsingham's expenditure on his network increased dramatically. Accurate figures are impossible to achieve but we shall not be far out if we reckon that in 1587–8 Walsingham spent half as much again as in the previous year. He reorganized the system. A 'Plot for intelligence out of Spain', drawn up in spring 1587, made provision for the setting up of a clearing house in Rouen to handle information gathered by agents in France's Atlantic ports and for staff in other agencies to be increased. One reason for this reconstruction was that in 1585 Philip had closed all Spanish ports to English merchants. Intriguingly, Italy was the most vital intelligence nerve centre for keeping up to date on Spanish activities. All the independent states in the peninsula maintained their own embassies in Spain and were often the first to discern significant movements of ships and men. They were usually quite obliging about selling on information to England. Walsingham's couriers were constantly toing and froing along the roads between Italy and the Channel coast.

A glut of information can be just as dangerous as a dearth. The true art lies in properly evaluating it. Throughout the summer his staff tried to decipher and co-ordinate reports that simply could not be squared. In July, fifty-seven ships and 10,000 troops were supposedly assembled in Lisbon and only waiting to link up with the convoy vessels from the silver fleet. But another report gave the numbers as a hundred ships and 15,000 soldiers. By mid-September the Armada had, reputedly, set sail – en route for a landing in Scotland. These alarmist messages were all false. Any estimate of Spain's preparedness for the Enterprise of England was complicated by many factors. Philip kept changing his plans. He received conflicting advice from Parma and from his chief naval adviser, the Marquis of Santa Cruz. Negotiations with Sixtus V went unsatisfactorily because the pope was reluctant to make the degree of financial commitment the king looked for. When Philip did begin to assemble his fleet annoying attacks by Francis Drake obliged him to modify his plans. Another

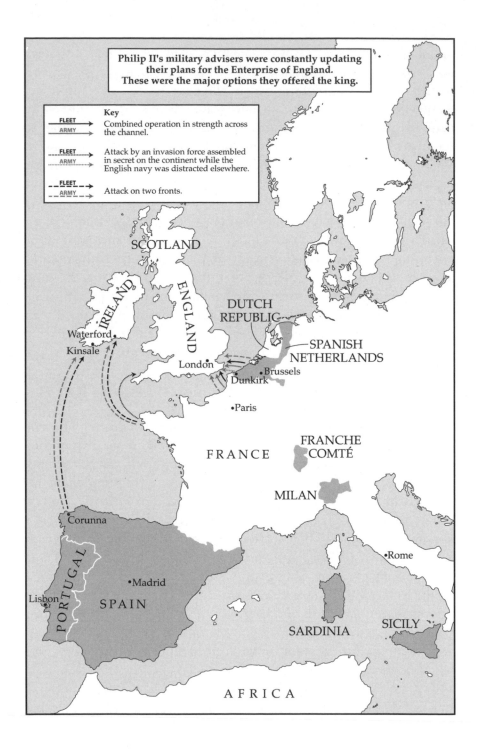

Philip II's military advisers were constantly updating their plans for the Enterprise of England. These were the major options they offered the king.

Key

Combined operation in strength across the channel.

Attack by an invasion force assembled in secret on the continent while the English navy was distracted elsewhere.

Attack on two fronts.

problem Walsingham had to contend with was the deliberate mis-information coming from Stafford in Paris. The ambassador fed the English government with stories provided by Mendoza: Philip's intentions were entirely pacific; Elizabeth had more to fear from France than from Spain. He even tried to make the queen believe, in January 1588, that Philip had disbanded his fleet. This was a parti-cularly reckless ploy to try, flying as it did in the face of all the evidence Walsingham had to the contrary. It also created family tensions. The brother of Stafford's wife was Lord Admiral Howard, the man whose secrets Stafford was betraying. Howard's embarrass-ment was acute, as he told Walsingham: 'I cannot tell what to think of my brother [-in-law] Stafford's advertisement; for if it be true that the King of Spain's forces be dissolved, I would not wish the Queen's Majesty to be at this charge that she is at; but if it be a device, knowing that a little thing makes us too careless, then I know not what may come of it.'[9]

There was a certain subtlety to Stafford's 'device' because it told the queen what she wanted to hear. Keeping ships and men in readiness to face invasion was an expensive business. Throughout 1587 Ho-ward, backed by Walsingham and the other hawks, had to fight for every penny the navy needed. At the same time the doves, headed by Sir James Croft, were in communication with Parma about the possibility of English withdrawal from the Low Countries. Philip's governor was only stringing England's envoys along but Elizabeth persisted in believing that all-out war with Spain could be avoided.

To hold the queen to a firm stance Walsingham needed every scrap of reliable intelligence he could lay hands on. Fortunately the net-work he had painstakingly built up over the years was equal to the challenge. His best placed agent was another of those adventurous Catholic exiles for whom personal survival counted more than religious zeal. Anthony Standen had been a member of Mary Stuart's household before 1568. After Mary's escape from Scotland, Standen, who was currently in France, considered himself an agent for his former mistress, while also establishing contact with Walsingham. After sundry adventures he fetched up in the household of the Medici Duke of Tuscany. Standen cultivated many Spanish contacts but his most useful were the Tuscan ambassador to Spain who passed on information from Philip's court and a certain Fleming who was a close attendant on the Marquis of Santa Cruz, the Spanish Grand Admiral. Thanks to Standen, Walsingham received intermittent reports of the extent and disposition of Philip's ships and men and the evolution of the king's plans. He was able to conclude that the Armada would not sail in 1587 but that all efforts were being directed towards an invasion in the following year. The political plan, as it emerged after the death of Mary Stuart, was that Philip's daughter, Isabella, would be proclaimed queen after she had been suitably married off to one of her Habsburg cousins. The interim government would be placed in the hands of none other than Dr William Allen who would oversee the restoration of Catholicism and the confiscation of every acre of church land seized by Henry VIII half a century earlier. It is as well for the modern reader to be aware of the chaos and inevitable bloodshed which would have resulted from a successful invasion in 1588. Standen, who rapidly proved his value, was generously pensioned by Elizabeth in 1588, when he travelled to Madrid and reported directly from the enemy camp.

From various sources Walsingham learned of the impact of Francis Drake's raid on Cadiz. This was an enterprise either conceived or encouraged by Walsingham and Leicester. As soon as Walsingham was back at court, and while Burghley remained under a cloud, Elizabeth was persuaded to authorize a strike which might inhibit Philip's preparations. A purely private scheme originated by some London merchants to make a piratical attack on Spanish vessels to recoup losses they had sustained as a result of Philip's trade embargo was taken over by the government. Seven naval vessels were added to the fleet and Drake was put in charge of the operation. This was in mid-March. Now preparations had to be completed at speed before the queen experienced one of her changes of mind. Drake and his ships got away from Plymouth on 2 April. A week later a fast pinnace was despatched severely restricting Drake's orders. The queen demanded that he should only apprehend enemy vessels on the high seas and not enter any of Philip's harbours. 'Unfortunately' the pursuing ship encountered contrary winds and was obliged to turn back, the message undelivered. The result was the celebrated 'singeing of the King of Spain's beard', the devastation of Cadiz harbour, the destruction of some two dozen ships and the capture of four vessels which Drake loaded with loot, including supplies which had been intended for the Enterprise of England. In terms of military advantage the Cadiz raid achieved little. The loss of a few ships was unlikely to deter Philip from his grand project. But the audacious attack did further unhinge Philip's plans. It deterred several captains, en route from the Mediterranean to rendezvous with the Armada, from venturing into the Atlantic and it demonstrated the vulnerability of galleys to English vessels with superior fire power. Santa Cruz's plan had relied heavily on the use of galleys to move well inshore and take on board many of the troops Parma was to assemble on the Channel coast. This scheme was now drastically revised.

Another tactical coup which may, to some extent, be attributed to Walsingham, took place in France. There a vicious, three-cornered conflict was in progress. Henry, duc de Guise and the Catholic League were confronting, not only the Huguenot forces of Henry of Navarre but also Henry III, the ineffectual monarch who did not want to hand the Crown on to a Protestant successor but who also feared the power of the Guises. Walsingham, as ever, vigorously urged his queen to support the Huguenot cause, both to succour England's religious allies and also to prevent the Guises and their Spanish paymasters gaining the upper hand in France at a time when control of the Channel ports might be a vital element in the coming conflict. By the late summer of 1587 the 'War of the Three Henries' was in full spate. Constant nagging from Elizabeth's hawks had persuaded her to subsidize an incursion of German mercenaries, headed by John Casimir of the Palatinate. His intervention proved fairly ineffectual but it did have the effect of obliging Guise to lift the siege of Boulogne, a deep-water port Philip was relying on as a potential rendezvous point for his seaborne and land forces.

The situation in the Netherlands was not dissimilar. In June, Elizabeth, again after being harangued by Walsingham and Leicester, allowed Dudley to return. This time he was there less than five months – five militarily disastrous months. Largely as a result of squabbles with his allies, Leicester failed to prevent the loss of Sluys, the important foreport of Bruges. In November the English commander washed his hands of the United Provinces and returned home, having had a medal struck for his supporters, bearing the legend, 'I reluctantly leave, not the flock, but the ungrateful ones.'

But what English intervention had achieved was tying up Parma's forces and slowing his advance. By the time the Armada arrived in the Narrows, the barges needed to carry his soldiers were pinned down by Dutch blockades in Nieuport and Dunkirk. He had not gained control of the ports of Holland and Zeeland and he had not neutralized the United Provinces' navy. In order for Philip II's complex battle plan to succeed all the pieces had to lock securely into place. The Spanish fleet had to arrive in good order off the Flanders coast and maintain naval supremacy long enough for a smooth junction with Parma's contingent. It was always going to be a tall order. Philip's noble Enterprise of England really fell apart in February 1588 when Santa Cruz, his extremely able and experienced admiral, died of a fever. The Duke of Medina-Sidonia who replaced him was an administrator who had never led men in battle. He lacked the flair and flexibility so vital at times of military crisis. A skilled commander just might have found answers to the unseasonable weather, the harrying tactics of Lord Howard's navy, the unavailability of a safe haven on the Channel coast and Parma's unwillingness to risk running the blockade. Beset by all these difficulties, the Spanish Armada failed in its purpose and the defeat which was, in fact, only one episode in a European war that continued to the end of Elizabeth's reign and beyond, took its place among the heroic national legends of England.

Intelligence-gathering and foreign affairs were not the only matters that Walsingham had to oversee at this time of mounting crisis. The whole of England had to be mobilized in case any enemy forces did manage to come ashore. Putting the country on a war footing was an unprecedented task and one for which there was no existing organization. For a dozen years or so a system of 'trained bands' had been developed which provided basic instruction in arms and drill but such periodic assemblies took place on a very ad hoc basis and depended on the enthusiasm of local authorities. Now, as a real threat loomed, the government took steps to put this home guard on a more regular footing. A special commission organized recruitment and training and established a chain of muster points around the southern coasts from Yarmouth to Anglesea. It was all very last minute and there were complaints from several localities about the costs involved. Elizabeth, too, was, as ever, concerned about the drain on her treasury and her councillors had to argue the case for almost every defence need. Walsingham was, of course, impatient. His grumbles to Leicester had become, by now, almost routine: 'The manner of our cold and careless proceeding here in this time of peril and danger maketh me to take no comfort of my recovery of health, for that I see apparently, unless it shall please God in mercy and miraculously to preserve us, we cannot long stand.'[10] So he wrote on 12 November on returning to his desk after another six weeks of illness.

In addition to the local militias, a 'guard' of between 30,000 and 45,000 foot and mounted troops was assembled in the summer of 1588 for the protection of London and the queen. Of these the bulk was stationed near the capital with a reserve force of some 16,500 under Leicester's command at Tilbury. For all Walsingham's espionage endeavours the government did not know exactly where Parma proposed to make his landfall. It might have been anywhere on the coast of Kent or Essex. The defence strategy adopted allowed for the initial attack to be countered by forces either side of the estuary and slowed down until the bulk of the English army could converge to meet it.

Walsingham himself contributed readily to the English land force. He raised a troop of sixty mounted men and 200 infantry to form part of the royal bodyguard. He even, in some haste, ordered a suit of armour from Amsterdam. The thought of the semi-invalid, fifty-eight-year-old councillor in breastplate and helmet riding out in the queen's train to Tilbury on 9 August 1588 to be present at the most famous PR exercise of the reign borders on the bizarre. And yet, if he was so accoutred for that semi-theatrical event, there would have been an appropriateness about his appearance. As Elizabeth expressed her 'foul scorn' for Parma and his master she was figureheading that defiance Walsingham had always expressed of the massive Catholic conspiracy he had seen over the years gathering its powers to strike at Protestant England. Vice-Admiral Henry Seymour spoke no more than the truth when he told Walsingham, 'you have fought more with your pen than many have in our English navy fought with their enemies'. By then the Spanish fleet was retreating into the grey North Sea and towards the perilous coasts of Scotland and Ireland. The war was far from over but the immediate crisis was. And the long-term crisis also. For the failure of the Catholic invasion and the legends which were built up around it formed the coping stone of the English Reformation. There could be no doubt that, after this event, England would identify itself, once and for all, as an independent, Protestant nation which had earned its right to stand alone and which was emerging as a maritime power pursuing its own colonial ambitions.

It is a cliché but, nevertheless, true to say that the Armada year was the turning point of Elizabeth's reign. In the 1590s members of her court and government had two new preoccupations: creating a myth and preparing for the next reign. It was by now evident that Elizabeth was the last of her line. Her chastity, therefore, had to be made into her highest virtue. So was born the cult of the Virgin Queen. Her people hoped that they would not have long to wait before 'normal hereditary service' would be resumed and they would have a 'proper' king and royal heirs in perpetuity. Courtiers and ministers with an eye to the future developed their contacts with the monarch-in-waiting over the border. But Elizabeth lived on . . . and on. Inevitably, the era of the aged, childless queen became something of a twilight zone. Her very longevity dulled the edge of old controversies, notably the religious one. People got used to the church by law established. There were still Catholics and there were still Puritans but more and more of them com-promised and conformed. New phenomena gave the last years of the reign a different character. London pulpits had fresh rivals – the playhouses – the Theatre, the Curtain, the Rose, the Swan, the Hope, the Fortune, all located in the nearer suburbs. In 1590 Shakespeare's first play was performed. Popular imagination was also widened by tales of strange places to be seen and fresh opportunities for commerce and even settlement in the New World. Horizons were widening.

But in the narrow confines of the court it was the change of personnel which made the real difference. Infirmity and death removed many of the queen's old friends and servants. She found herself increasingly surrounded by younger men – a matriarchal figure rather than a woman to be wooed. In the immediate aftermath of Philip's failed invasion Robert Dudley, Earl of Leicester, died. This was a profound shock. The queen went into purdah and was for several days inconsolable. Within months she also lost Francis Walsingham. His bouts of illness had become longer and more debilitating. Every winter laid him by the heels. He was confined to bed in January and February 1587, from November 1587 to March 1588 and from February to June 1589. When his health permitted he tried to work with his habitual industry and devotion but he was aware of his failing powers and his need to rely increasingly on members of his staff.

Though he made his will in December 1589, he apparently did not even contemplate resigning until the end of March 1590, and by then death was only days away. As well as state business he had his own affairs to attend to. He worked assiduously to clear his personal debts and those of Philip Sidney's that he had shouldered. He did not die in poverty, as has sometimes been claimed, but he was keenly aware that he left his wife in a 'mean state'. According to Robert Beale, there was on his book account with the queen a deficit of £42,000 arising from official expenditure for which he had not obtained privy seal warrants. In material terms this civil servant-cum-statesman-cum-courtier cannot be said to have been fairly compensated for his services to queen and country. At a time when conspicuous consumption marked the lives of most great Elizabethans; when Leicester created his fairytale castle at Kenilworth and William Cecil built impressive mansions at Burghley House and Theobalds, Walsingham lived modestly.

Sir Francis Walsingham died in his house in Seething Lane on 6 April, 1590. In accordance with his will he was buried in St Paul's Cathedral 'without any such extraordinary ceremonies as usually appertain to a man serving in my place'. As if to underline his humility, even in death Walsingham was shouldered aside by another Elizabethan celebrity. His coffin was interred beside that of Sir Philip Sidney on the north side of the choir. The following year Sir Christopher Hatton was laid to rest nearby. A sumptuous monument erected to his memory took up so much space that a contemporary versifier observed:

> Philip and Francis have no Tomb
> For great Christopher takes all the room.

Death may not always be the great leveller but time is. The Great Fire of 1666 destroyed alike the memorials of pompous churchmen, self-important aristocrats and hard-working, self-effacing royal servants. Walsingham's last resting place was consigned to obscurity.

But not his reputation. Burghley's testimony to one of Walsingham's friends was no mere formal eulogy: 'the Queen's Majesty and her realm and I and others his particular friends have had a great loss, both for the public use of his good and painful long services and for the private comfort I had by his mutual friendship'.[11] And there was much more than that to Sir Francis Walsingham. The very nature of the surviving evidence and his obvious importance in affairs of state mean that the historical focus tends to be on his political and diplomatic activities. It is scarcely surprising that Elizabeth found him irreplaceable. For six years she appointed no successor, preferring to load yet more work on to Burghley's shoulders until it became obvious that that venerable servant could no longer bear the burden. But Edmund Spenser, in *The Faerie Queen*, called Walsingham

> The great Maecenas of this age
> As well to all that civil arts profess
> As those that are inspired with martial rage.

The label 'Puritan' should not impose on us a false interpretation of the man as a narrow philistine. His deep religious conviction caused him to avoid ostentation and to attend to his duties with sober industry but his years abroad had made him a cosmopolitan who well understood the rich culture of Renaissance Europe. He was a fluent linguist, a scholar as well versed in the classics as he was in the Bible and the theology of Calvin. His wide international network of friends and acquaintances embraced scholars and poets as well as diplomats and the denizens of the espionage underworld. He even had an interest in the new study of horticulture. The list of men who gained or confidently sought his patronage extended to poets, classicists, architects, writers on navigation and foreign travel, poor students at university and even the queen's fool, Richard Tarlton.

Walsingham was one of the foremost backers of maritime enterprise. As well as investing in Francis Drake's more adventurous voyages, he put his capital and influence to use in the Muscovy Company, the Levant Company and the Merchant Adventurers. Walsingham was passionately interested in overseas trade and exploration. The most enduring legacy to this was his patronage of Richard Hakluyt, the greatest geographer of the age. One of the last projects Sir Francis supported was Hakluyt's *Principal Navigations, Voyages and Discoveries of the English Nation made by sea or land to the most remote and farthest distant quarters of the earth* (1589). This seminal work, dedicated to Walsingham, was symbolic of an expansionist vision which the author shared with his patron and the boldest spirits of the age. It is in the context of this group of advanced thinkers that we really need to see Francis Walsingham. His Protestantism, his advocacy of overseas expansion, his reading of contemporary events (particularly the cosmic clash between evangelicalism and the Roman Antichrist) and his turbulent relationship with Queen Elizabeth stemmed from a world vision to which he was intensely committed. This was why he served a monarch for over twenty years with whom he was often at loggerheads and endeavoured to steer her into courses which were to him both obvious and holy.

A vigorous state censorship operated in Elizabethan England. As early as May 1559 a royal proclamation had prohibited the performance of plays dealing with religion and governments and affirmed that such subjects were 'no meet matters to be written or treated upon but by men of authority, learning and wisdom'. Preachers and parliament men claimed higher authority in defying such a ban but they did so at their peril. We have only to remind ourselves of the fate of Edmund Grindal, Peter Wentworth, John Stubbe and Thomas Norton to see how Elizabeth frequently moved to silence critics of the regime. Her passionate dislike of Puritans sprang from their insistence on airing their views on the succession, on the treatment of Catholics and, especially, on the need to deal drastically with Mary Stuart. Venturing on matters which were none of their business, in her opinion, smacked of disrespect and even of incipient republicanism.

But if the queen felt deeply about marriage, the nature of divine kingship, the duty of subjects and religious uniformity, so did most of her people and especially those who belonged to the Protestant intelligentsia. At the summit of this group stood the Earl of Leicester's circle which embraced Edmund Spenser, Philip Sidney, Thomas Digges, John Dee, Thomas Norton and a variety of scholars, poets, dramatists and preachers who set the course for the Elizabethan literary Renaissance. (Shakespeare was only ten years younger than Sir Philip Sidney.) This creative coterie might almost be thought of as a cult, committed to a philosophy which drew upon history, the Bible, Platonism, alchemy, astrology and the arts of navigation to evolve an elaborate mission statement for the queen and her nation. (Elizabeth and even the level-headed Burghley encouraged Dee and his assistant, Edward Kelly, in their quest for the philosopher's stone. The secret of turning base metals into gold had a distinct appeal to the cash-strapped English queen.)

The immense pressures of political and religious isolation produced a diamond seam of Protestant nationalism, a defiant vision of a new Albion embarked on a divine crusade. It was stated most clearly in a book by the polymath, Dr John Dee, published in 1577. *The General and Rare Memorials Pertaining to the Perfect Arts of Navigation* was much more than a manifesto for overseas exploration. Dee presented Elizabeth as the direct descendant of the heroes of classical Rome and of the legendary King Arthur. She was called upon to fulfil an inescapable destiny, to carry the standard of reformed religion into Europe and, through the development of the navy, the discovery of new lands and sea routes (such as the North-West Passage and the North-East Passage) and energetic mercantile endeavour, to the ends of the earth. This was a vision for a time of crisis, for a nation hemmed in by foes and opposed by enemies determined to undermine the politico-religious foundations. It was a morale-boosting philosophy for a people who seemed to have their backs to the wall. Such, at least, was the view of the international situation held by committed Protestants like Francis Walsingham.

Their frustration arose from the fact that Elizabeth showed no enthusiasm for donning the heroic mantle. She had no dream of a greater England. She was not proactive. Her political philosophy, such as it was, was based on survival – of herself, first of all, and then of the Crown. That being the case, poets, playwrights and preachers could not avoid offering criticism. Court entertainments were important vehicles for making political points. As well as the entertainments offered to Elizabeth as she progressed around the mansions of her wealthier subjects, members of the inns of court regularly performed plays and masques before the queen. Leading courtiers and councillors were closely involved in these dramatic presentations and assiduously oversaw their scripting. Flattery was de rigueur and any proffering of advice or reproof had to be wrapped up in heavy allegory but, throughout the reign, political dissatisfaction was a recurring leitmotif in court entertainment. To understand this is to see more clearly the reverse face of the Gloriana mythology. The radiant Virgin Queen dazzles us from the head side of the coin but the design on the tail side is much darker.

Two works which had their origins in the Leicester circle were *Gorboduc* and *Arcadia*. *Gorboduc* was performed at the Inner Temple in 1561 and subsequently at court. In 1570 it was published for a wider audience. Its authors were Thomas Norton and his companion at the inn, Thomas Sackville (later Lord Buckhurst and Cecil's successor as treasurer). Gorboduc, the ruler of a mythical golden-age Britain, spurns the advice of his wise councillors and hands over his realm to his two sons. As a result of their rivalry the country descends into civil war, anarchy and foreign invasion. The moral is that only weak rulers abandon their responsibilities, foremost among which is careful provision for the succession.

Arcadia was not published until thirty years after *Gorboduc* but its underlying theme is little changed. Its author, Philip Sidney, wrote what was, on the face of it, a pastoral idyll, a poem about shepherds and princes set in an idealized world. The work went through several changes under Sidney's hand and appeared in variant forms after his death, as the *Old Arcadia* and the *New Arcadia*. The work had its genesis at a time when Sidney was frustrated and angry at having received, in his estimation, scant reward for his diplomatic services and no promotion. He was also strongly opposed to the Anjou match and in 1579 wrote *A Letter to Queen Elizabeth touching her Marriage with Monsieur*. The letter circulated in manuscript at the same time that John Stubbe's *Discovery of a Gaping Gulf* was published and certainly did not improve his relationship with the queen.

The political sub-text of *Arcadia* concerns the bad decisions of the ruler, Basilius, who declines to accept the good counsel of Philanax (possibly meant to represent Walsingham). Like Gorboduc, King Basilius retires from his regal position to seek sylvan seclusion. This provides the opportunity for Cecropia, former heiress to Arcadia but debarred by Basilius' late marriage and begetting of children, to launch a bid for power. Amidst the confusion and disarray which follow Basilius mistakenly takes a sleeping draught and appears to the other characters to be dead. Sidney presents Basilius as a tyrant, not because he is cruel or vindictive – no one could be more amiable than this ageing monarch – but because he is governed by his own will rather than by reason or law. It was the same message that Walsingham had delivered to the young James VI: when monarchs regard themselves as absolute 'they leave to be kings and become tyrants'.[12] The parallels with the state of England are obvious: the threat of a rival queen, the rejection of sound advice, the inability to make decisions. (Elizabeth's dithering suggests that she might as well, like Basilius, be drugged.) Sidney even makes a more direct comparison between Elizabeth and his fictional monarch, for, when Basilius is crossed by his advisers, he tends to fly into petulant rages.

It is ironic that Sidney, who came to be regarded as a paragon courtier/poet/warrior, in reality held the Elizabethan court in contempt. He despised its flattery and factionalism. He resented the queen's ingratitude, especially as demonstrated towards his own family, and also that poverty which prevented him from taking what he conceived to be his proper place at the centre of affairs. Together with other members of Leicester's circle he was profoundly anxious about the disastrous future towards which England seemed to be drifting. Walsingham, from his own perspective as councillor rather than courtier, reached almost identical conclusions. We might remind ourselves of the long letter he wrote to the queen in 1581 from the depths of his concern over the Anjou match:

> I cannot deny but I have been infinitely grieved to see the desire I have had to do your Majesty some acceptable service (in the present charge committed unto me) so greatly crossed. But I will leave to touch my particular though I have as great cause as any man that ever served in the place I now unworthily supply, being at home subject to sundry strange jealousies and in foreign service to displeasure, though I dare make the greatest enemy I have the censurer of mine actions and proceedings in such foreign actions as have been committed unto me. If either ambition or riches were the end of my strife my grief would be the less. But now to the public, wherein if any thing shall escape my pen that may breed offence, I most heartily beseech your Majesty to ascribe it to love, which can never bring forth evil effects, though sometimes it may be subject to sharp censures.

Having reflected unfavourably on the queen's decisions on major policy issues he concluded:

> If this sparing and unprovident course be held still, the mischiefs approaching being so apparent as they are, I conclude therefore, having spoken in heat of duty, without offence to your Majesty, that no one that serveth in place of a Councillor, that either weigheth his own credit, or carryeth that sound affection to your Majesty as he ought to do, that would not wish himself in the farthest part of Ethiopia rather than enjoy the fairest palace in England.[13]

As we have repeatedly seen, the queen and her councillors were frequently at loggerheads. Elizabeth used and abused her advisers by failing to give a clear lead, by thrusting them into impossible situations, by blaming them for policy failures and by going over their heads in diplomatic negotiations. They responded by ganging up on her, by going behind her back and sometimes by simply staying away. Having read so many complaints by Walsingham, Burghley and various of their colleagues, we may wonder why they soldiered on. Of course, the queen was the fount of patronage and there were perks to be had. But so often the servants of this niggardly sovereign found themselves out of pocket, having been obliged to fund government expenditure from their own resources. Certainly in Walsingham's case when we examine the balance sheet of his 'business' with Elizabeth we have to conclude that she was his debtor many times over. What he gained from his exhausting endeavours over two decades in no way reflected his value to the regime. It is trying to understand this tense and troubled relationship that really takes us to the heart of political and, indeed, national life in the last decades of the sixteenth century.

We can, I am sure, take it as read that Walsingham, Cecil, Dudley and Elizabeth's other close advisers were devoted patriots. They were as one in acknowledging that 'there was never so dangerous a time as this' and they had a duty to support the Crown in such dark days. They stayed at their posts because their sovereign was a woman who could not be expected to govern unaided, because she was manifestly in need of the wisest counsel the nation could provide and because the very survival of the Protestant state was at stake. Thomas Norton told the Commons in 1571, 'her Majesty was and is the only pillar and stay of all safety, as well for our politic quiet as for the state of religion . . . therefore that for preservation of her estate, our care, prayer and chief endeavours must be.'[14] But we need to set our plough to dig deeper if we would know what other convictions motivated councillors and why it was that they felt constrained to save the queen – often from herself.

Although they were her subjects, there was also a sense in which she belonged to them. It was the same Thomas Norton who, in one of his treatises, having in mind Elizabeth's unwillingness to deal, once and for all, with Mary Stuart, pointed out that 'princes who expose their persons to perils' are 'liberal of that which is not their own to give . . . the prince is not a private but a public person'.[15] Lawyers like Norton and Walsingham were fully aware of the current debate in legal circles about the rights and responsibilities of monarchy and the relationship between prince and people. These were complex issues whose importance was greatly magnified by the succession crisis. Elizabeth insisted that she and she alone would decide whom she would pass the Crown to. The legal fraternity disagreed. Henry VIII had made a will excluding the Stuart line of succession. Edward VI had also tried to prevent either of his sisters taking the crown. This royal 'right' was disputed by many lawyers, who insisted that kings could not by mere will (in all senses of that word) take decisions which would profoundly affect the commonwealth. In an attempt to define the relationship between monarch and state, legal experts had come up with the concept of the queen's 'two bodies':

> for the purposes of law it was found necessary by 1561 to endow the Queen with two bodies: a *body natural* and a *body politic* . . . the body politic was supposed to be *contained within the natural body of the Queen*. When lawyers spoke of this body politic they referred to a specific quality: the essence of *corporate perpetuity*. The Queen's natural body was subject to infancy, infirmity, error and old age; her body politic, created out of a combination of faith, ingenuity and practical expediency, was held to be unerring and immortal.[16]

What may seem to us a piece of sophistical word play was, in fact, an attempt to deal with an urgent constitutional problem for the centralized state created by the Tudors. No one, not even the most dedicated Calvinistic admirer of the Geneva system, would have contemplated any other kind of government than a divinely anointed monarchy, but the repeated failure of the Tudor dynasty to perpetuate itself forced politicians and legists to consider how the Crown might be passed on without the kind of conflict which had made the previous century so bloody. The framers of the Bond of Association had devised a Council which should be the custodian of Elizabeth's body politic, defending her from harm and, in the event of her sudden death, transferring that mystical entity to a successor. It is not surprising that the queen, though professing gratitude to all the signatories of the Bond, distanced herself as far as possible from its underlying philosophy. It implied some limitation of royal absolutism and that she would never concede. In 1582 Walsingham wrote a letter on his mistress' behalf to the Earl of Shrewsbury, because his prisoner, Mary Stuart, had communicated directly with the Council:

> Of which [misconception] of the said Queen and misunderstanding of the absoluteness of her Majesty's government, she thinketh meet she should by your Lordship be better informed: For although her Highness doth carry as great regard unto her Council as any of her progenitors have done, and hath just cause so to do in respect of their wisdom and fidelity, yet is she [ie Mary] to be [made to] understand that they are Councillors by [royal] choice and not by birth, whose services are no longer to be used in that public function than it shall please her Majesty to dispose of the same.[17]

If councillors, claiming the greater interest of the commonwealth, were allowed to meddle with succession issues, on what other areas of prerogative might they not also encroach, using the same excuse?

The very same problem presented itself to the advisers of the 'impossible' woman who occupied the English throne. Sir Francis Knollys expressed it to the assistant secretary Thomas Wilson in these terms:

> I do know that it is fit for all men to give place to her majesty's will and pleasure, and to her [passions], in all things that touch not the danger of her estate; but I do know also that if her majesty do not suppress and subject her own will and her own [passions] unto sound advice of open counsel in matters touching the preventing of her danger . . . her majesty will be utterly overthrown.[18]

For Walsingham and his Puritan colleagues there was only one basis for 'sound advice'. In 1586 Mr Secretary confided to Leicester, the

queen 'greatly presumeth [on] fortune, which is but a [very] weak
foundation to build upon. I would she did build and depend upon
God, and then all good men should have less cause to fear any change
of her former good hap'.[19] Genuine as was Walsingham's loyalty to
Elizabeth, he had a higher commitment to the cause, and it was this
that emboldened him to speak plainly to the queen. God's truth was
enshrined in Protestantism. It was the onward march of the Gospel
against papist superstition and rank unbelief which was always his
prime concern. The difference between his own motivation and the
queen's was very succinctly stated in that throwaway line in his letter
to Leicester. Elizabeth did, indeed, trust to fortune. She did not
possess and, therefore, could never understand the religious passion
which both powered Walsingham's life and informed his political
philosophy.

Elizabeth would have been furious to know that her close attendants believed she did not trust in God. She was regular in attendance
at her chapel. She often carried a little book which contained her own
hand-written prayers. Part of one reads:

> Create in me, O Lord, a new heart and so renew my spirit within me
> that Thy law may be my study, Thy truth my delight, Thy Church my
> care, Thy people my crown, Thy righteousness my pleasure, Thy
> service my government, Thy fear my honour, Thy grace my strength,
> Thy favour my life, Thy Gospel my kingdom, and Thy salvation my
> bliss and my glory. So shall this my kingdom through Thee be
> established with peace; so shall Thy Church be edified with power;
> so shall Thy Gospel be published with zeal; so shall my reign be
> continued with prosperity; so shall my life be prolonged with happi-
> ness; and so shall myself at Thy good pleasure be translated into
> immortality.[20]

Yet however Elizabeth may have regarded her own piety, to her
Puritan advisers (who, after all, knew her very well) she was not their
kind of Christian. 'Popish dregs' adorned her chapel. She employed
Catholic musicians to perform the divine office. She favoured celibate
clergy. She was lukewarm (at best) in her support of persecuted

Protestants abroad and in her prosecution of Catholics at home. She was more concerned with outward uniformity than the building of a holy nation. Above all, she had no love of a preaching ministry, the principal tool, as the Puritans saw it, for winning the hearts and minds of the people.

Historians have debated whether Elizabeth was indifferent to religion or even atheistical. The truth is more subtle and revolves around two fixed points. The first was her conviction that the royal authority achieved in both state *and* church by her father must be safeguarded at all costs. The second was her own religious upbringing. Like most people, Elizabeth's basic attitudes were formed by the time she reached her mid-teens. In Catherine Parr's entourage she had been influenced by what might be labelled 'humanistic Lutheranism'. When English Protestantism moved on in the decade after 1547 Elizabeth did not move with it. Therefore she could do nothing but oppose, both temperamentally and intellectually, the Calvinistic and Zwinglian trends of the progressives. Sensing herself to be at odds with her most trusted advisers, she could not commit herself to a clearly thought out religious policy. This was Walsingham's understanding of the situation. In a memorandum of 1578 he identified the three major ills which plagued the nation:

First, discontentment in the subjects for that her Majesty seeketh neither by marriage nor establishing of succession to provide for the continuance of the happy quiet they enjoy under her blessed government.

The second, the disunion of the subjects minds in respect of the diversity of religion.

The third, the falling away in devotion of the subjects of this realm unto the competitor [Mary Stuart] in respect of religion and the expectation she hath of this crown.[21]

We cannot open a window into Elizabeth's soul but, as far as the outworking of her beliefs in policy is concerned, Walsingham was right, she did 'presume on fortune' rather than God. That is, she was reactive, waiting on events, rather than being motivated by any politico-religious philosophy.

So it was that, throughout the crisis years of the reign, England found itself in the extraordinary position of being governed by an executive whose two principal components were engaged in an intermittent tug o' war. There was a conflict between a monarch determined to maintain her own freedom of action, ring-fenced by prerogative, and a body of advisers who had a responsibility for the wellbeing of the nation. That basic clash of interests manifested itself over and again in the queen's outbursts of rage, in her banishing outspoken councillors from court and in councillors taking themselves into voluntary exile. We have seen over and again how Walsingham incurred royal displeasure for speaking his mind and we have read some of the many grumbles he, Burghley, Leicester and others exchanged about Elizabeth's behaviour.

We would be just as wrong automatically to take such complaints at face value as we would to accept uncritically the queen's frequent assertions of her commitment to the wellbeing of her subjects. My belief is that we come closer to the truth by grappling with the clash of ideas, ideals and beliefs that marked the relationship between the last Tudor and her closest advisers. Elizabeth's outlook on life had been shaped by her earlier experiences. If she was determined to be her own woman it was because for the first twenty-five years of her life her destiny, and even her continued existence, had been decided by others. If she was parsimonious it was because her father had squandered an immense fortune and thus put the Crown in pawn to parliament. If she was sceptical of religious enthusiasm it was because she had seen England batted to and fro by Catholic and Protestant partisans. She had learned the arts of survival by not allowing herself to be enslaved by principles. Under Edward VI she had been a Protestant. During Mary's reign she had attended mass.

Walsingham, by contrast, had never deviated from the convictions he had espoused in his family circle and at university. Rather than being content to survive during Mary Tudor's reign he had taken himself abroad, deepened his radical beliefs and seen at first hand the bitter cosmic struggle between the rival versions of Christianity. He understood in a way that Elizabeth never could the irreconcilability of Rome and Geneva. Everything he experienced in subsequent years served to underscore his convictions – Elizabeth's excommunication, the St Bartholomew's Massacre, the French wars of religion, the suppression of Protestantism in the Netherlands, the state-sponsored terrorism of Madrid and Rome, the treason and near-treason of Catholic infiltrators. Elizabeth believed a *via media* could be pursued which would satisfy the bulk of her subjects. Time proved her right. She believed that an imposed ritual uniformity could make all Englishmen her kind of Protestant. Time proved her wrong. Walsingham was convinced that an extensive preaching ministry would reach hearts and minds and produce a godly commonwealth. Thanks to Elizabeth and Whitgift that theory was never put to the test. The England that emerged from the crisis years 1570–90 was, in large measure, the result of these diverse viewpoints.

The Tudor Age is one which has for us an undying fascination. The members of the ruling dynasty were remarkable people. England began its movement towards a dominant position in world affairs. Unprecedented ideological conflict touched the lives of every individual. Native and immigrant artists and writers have left us impressions of England's version of the Renaissance. Yet one of the most notable features of the nation's political life is the roll call of gifted royal servants, from Thomas Wolsey to Robert Cecil, who maintained the machinery of government and were creative forces in the fashioning of a new national identity. In *As You Like It*, which Shakespeare wrote within a decade of Walsingham's death, the shepherd Silvius expatiates on the meaning of 'love':

> It is to be all made of faith and service
> . . . All made of passion, all made of wishes;
> All adoration, duty and observance,
> All humbleness, all patience, and impatience,
> All purity, all trial, all obedience.

Transfer those words from the romantic context to that of affection for queen and country and you have a fair portrait of Francis Walsingham.

NOTES

Preface

1 W.T. MacCaffrey, ed., *William Camden – The History of the most renowned and victorious Princess Elizabeth, late queen of England*, Chicago, 1970, pp.5–6
2 H.M. Margdiouth, ed., *Poems and Letters of Andrew Marvell*, 1952, 1, p.195

Chapter 1 Background and Beginnings, 1532–53 pp. 3–18

1 D. MacCullough, *Reformation*, 2003, p.199
2 H.C. Porter, *Reformation and Reaction in Tudor Cambridge*, Cambridge, 1958, p.68
3 *Ibid.*, p.54
4 J. Fortescue, *A Learned Commendation of the Politique Lawes of England*, trs R. Mulcaster, 1567, fol. 114v–115
5 J. Bruce, ed., *Correspondence of Robert Dudley, Earl of Leycester during his Government of the Low Countries*, Camden Society, 1844, p.192

Chapter 2 Travel and Travail, 1553–8 pp. 19–32

1 J.G. Nichols, ed., *Chronicles of Queen Jane and of Four Years of Queen Mary*, Camden Soc., Old Series, XLVIII (1890), 2. xi, p.272
2 *Ibid.*, p.11
3 L. Serrano, ed., *Correspondencia diplomatica entre España y la Santa Sede*, Madrid 1914, I, p.316. Quoted in P. Pierson, *Philip II of Spain*, 1975, p.167
4 J. Milton, *Paradise Lost*, Bk 1

5 See W. Haller, *Foxe's Book of Martyrs and the Elect Nation*, 1963, p.64
6 *Ibid.*, p.75
7 H. Höpfl, *The Christian Polity of John Calvin*, 1982, pp.162–3
8 D. Laing, ed., *The Works of John Knox*, Woodrow Soc. (1846–64), IV, p.373
9 *Ibid.*

Chapter 3 'The Malice of This Present Time', 1558–69 pp. 33–59

1 H. Robinson, ed., *The Zurich Letters*, 1st series, 1842, pp.4–5
2 *Ibid.*, 2nd ser., 1845, p.1
3 *Ibid.*, 1st ser., p.4
4 *Ibid.*, 2nd ser., p.9
5 *Ibid.*, 2nd ser., p.37
6 *Ibid.*, lst ser., p.8
7 *Ibid.*, 2nd ser., pp.12–14
8 *Ibid.*, 2nd ser., p.5
9 See P.W. Hasler, *The House of Commons 1558–1603*, III, p.572
10 *Ibid.*, III., p.573
11 Surrey Record Office, Loseley Correspondence, 3/56
12 State Papers Domestic, Elizabeth, XLVIII, 61
13 R.B. Wenham, *Before the Armada: The growth of English Foreign Policy, 1485–1588*, 1971, p.239
14 H. Robinson, *op.cit.*, 2nd ser., p.250
15 See M.P. Holt, *The French Wars of Religion, 1562–1629*, Cambridge, 1995, p.44
16 *Ibid.*, p.62
17 H. Robinson, *op.cit.*, 1st ser., p.252
18 *Ibid.*, 1st ser., pp.149–150
19 *Ibid.*, 2nd ser., p.168
20 *Ibid*, 1st ser., pp.208–210
21 See Conyers Read, *Mr Secretary Walsingham and the policy of Queen Elizabeth*, 1925, I, p.57
22 Calendar of the Manuscripts of the Most Honourable the Marquess of Bath preserved at Longleat, Wiltshire, HMC, V, Talbot, Dudley and Devereux Papers, 1533–1659, 1980 (Hereafter referred to as 'Cal. Bath MSS'), p.184
23 *Ibid.*

Chapter 4 'In Truth a Very Wise Person', 1569–73 pp. 61–84

1 It is printed in full in Conyers Read, *op.cit.*, I, pp.68f

2 *Ibid.*, p.79
3 See P. Collinson, *The Elizabethan Puritan Movement*, 1967, p.82
4 H. Robinson, *op.cit.*, 1st ser., pp.214–5
5 See Conyers Read, *op.cit.*, p.66
6 *Ibid.*, p.67
7 C.T. Martin, ed., *Journal of Sir Francis Walsingham*, Camden Miscellany VI, 1870, p.2
8 See Conyers Read, *op.cit.*, I, p.68
9 See G. Parker, *The Grand Strategy of Philip II*, New Haven, 1998, p.162
10 John Strype, *The Life and Acts of Matthew Parker*, 1711, I, p.298
11 Cal. S.P. For. 1569–71, 1632
12 J. Guy, *Tudor England*, 1988, p.279
13 See G. Parker, *op.cit.*, p.101
14 See C. Read, *Lord Burghley and Queen Elizabeth*, 1965, p.91
15 See A. Stewart, *Philip Sidney – A Double Life*, 2000, p.88
16 See C. Read, *Walsingham*, I, p.228
17 *Ibid.*, p.247
18 BL. Cotton MS Vespasian Fvi, fol.261
19 Cal. Bath MSS, p.184

Chapter 5 'To Govern that Noble Ship', England, 1574–80 pp. 85–114

1 Walsingham & Leicester, 23 May 1586, J. Brace, ed., *Correspondence of Robert Dudley, Earl of Leycester . . .*, Camden Soc., 1844, p.279
2 C. Read, *Walsingham*, I, p.322
3 Cal. S.P. Span. I.468
4 H. Robinson, *op.cit.*, 2nd ser. p.286–7
5 See S. Budiansky, *Her Majesty's Spymaster*, 2005, pp.109–110 (No source cited)
6 L.S. Marcus, J. Mueller and M.B. Rose, eds., *Elizabeth I – Collected Works*, Chicago, 2000, pp.105–6
7 Cal Bath MSS, Dudley Papers, p.185
8 See, C. Read, *Walsingham*, I, pp.423ff for all citations from Beale's treatise
9 P. Collinson, *Elizabethans*, 2003, p.42
10 Huntingdon Library, MSS HA 13067
11 D. Digges, ed., *The compleat ambassador*, 1655, p.424
12 See A. Hogg, *God's Secret Agents*, 2006, p.71
13 H. Robinson, *op.cit.*, 1st ser. p.314
14 *Ibid.*, 1st ser., pp.256–9
15 Cal. S.P. For. 1575–7, pp.468–9
16 P.W. Hasler, *The House of Commons 1558–1603*, 333, 1981, p.599
17 See P. Collinson, *Archbishop Grindal 1519–1583: The Struggle for a Reformed Church*, 1979, p.242

18 *Ibid.*, p.244
19 *Ibid.*, p.245
20 State Papers 12/113/17
21 See C. Read, *Walsingham*, II, pp.264–5
22 B.L. Cotton MS Caligula C iii, fol.217

Chapter 6 'God Open Her Majesty's Eyes': Foreign Affairs, 1578–80 pp. 115–146

1 H. Robinson, *Op.cit.*, 1st ser., p.325
2 See P. Collinson, *Godly People: Essays on English Protestantism and Puritanism*, 1983, p.380
3 See C. Read, *Walsingham*, I, pp.377f
4 *Ibid.*, II, p.170
5 *Ibid.*, II, p.186
6 L.S. Marcus, J. Mueller and M.B. Rose, eds., *op.cit.*, p.169
7 See C. Read, *Walsingham*, I, p.310
8 *Ibid.*, p.334
9 See P. Collinson, *Archbishop Grindal*, p.262
10 See J.H. Pollen, *The English Catholics in the Reign of Queen Elizabeth*, 1920, p.257
11 See P.W. Hasler, *op.cit.*, III, p.460
12 H. Robinson, ed., *op.cit.*, I, p.332
13 *Ibid.*, II, pp.287–8
14 Cal. S.P. Dom. XIV, 27
15 See C. Read, *Walsingham*, I, pp.393–4
16 *Ibid.*, I, p.416
17 *Ibid.*, II, p.16
18 Cal. S.P. Dom. Addenda, XVII, 31
19 J.B.M.C.K. de Lettenhove, *Relations Politiques des Pays Bas et de l'Angleterre*, (1882–1900) X, p.678
20 Cal. S.P. For. 1579, 80, 112
21 BL. Harley MSS 540, fol.102
22 See C. Read, *Walsingham*, II, p.57

Chapter 7 'She Seemeth to be Very Ernestly Bent to Proceed', 1581–4 pp. 147–178

1 L.S. Marcus, J. Mueller and M.B. Rose, *op.cit.*, pp.249–250
2 D. Digges, *op.cit.*, 408
3 Cal. S.P. Span. III. 226
4 See J.E. Neale, *Elizabeth and Her Parliaments, 1559–1581*, 1953, pp.383–4

5 *Ibid.*, pp.384–5
6 BL., Add. MS 48023, fol. 48v; Graves 203
7 J.E. Neale, *op.cit.*, p.402
8 See P.W. Hasler, *op.cit.*, III, p.573
9 *Talbot Papers*, Bath MSS., V, pp.33–4
10 Cal. S.P. For. 1583–4, 102
11 *Ibid.*, 1583–4, 286
12 Cal. S.P. For. 1583–4, p.459
13 Cal. S.P. Dom. 1583–4, p.84
14 See C. Read, *Walsingham*, II, p.218
15 *Ibid.* II, p.341
16 Cal. S.P. For. 1583–4, pp.652–3
17 See P. Collinson, *Elizabethans*, 2003, p.74n
18 See C. Read, *Walsingham*, II, p.382
19 Cal. S.P. Dom. 1583–4, p.584

Chapter 8 'Be You All Stout and Resolute', 1584–8 pp. 179–222

1 Cal. S.P. For. 1583–4, pp.387–8
2 Hatfield MSS, III, p.45
3 See P.W. Hasler, *op.cit.*, III, p.181
4 Letter to the Lord Mayor of London quoted in G. Adland, *Amye Robert and the Earl of Leicester*, 1870, pp.56–7
5 See Read, *Walsingham*, II, p.415
6 *Ibid.*, II, p.419
7 W. Shakespeare, *Midsummer Night's Dream*, V.1.21
8 W. Camden, *History of the most renowned and victorious Princess Elizabeth*, ed. W.T. MacCaffrey, Chicago, 1970, p.178
9 See P. Collinson, *Elizabethans*, p.50
10 P.W. Hasler, *op.cit.* II, p.37
11 J. Ayre, ed., *The Works of John Whitgift, DD*, Parker Society, Cambridge, 1852, II, pp.263–4
12 L.S. Marcus, J. Mueller and M.B. Rose, *op.cit.*, pp.178–9
13 See C. Read, *Walsingham*, III, p.52
14 See J. Corbet, ed., *Papers Relating to the Navy during the Spanish War* 1585–1587, Navy Records Society, 1987, pp.41–2
15 J. Bruce, ed., *Correspondence of Robert Dudley, Earl of Leycester . . .*, Camden Soc., 1844, p.4
16 *Ibid.*, pp.22–24
17 L.S. Marcus, J. Mueller and M.B. Rose, *op.cit.*, p.273
18 See C. Read, *Walsingham*, II, p.139
19 Cal. S.P. For. 1584–5, p.266

20 See C. Read, *Walsingham*, III, p.60
21 *Ibid.*, II, p.143
22 *Ibid.*, III, p.148
23 See J.H. Pollen, 'Mary Queen of Scots and the Babington Plot', in *Scottish History Society*, 3rd ser., 3 (1922), p.126
24 J.H. Pollen, *op.cit.*, pp.38–46
25 J. Bruce, *op.cit.*, pp.341–2
26 *Ibid.*, pp.420–21
27 *Ibid.*, p.431
28 C. Read, *Walsingham*, III, p.53
29 J. Bruce, *op.cit.*, pp.445–6
30 C. Read, *Walsingham*, III, p.168
31 *Ibid.*, III, p.169
32 L.S. Marcus, J. Mueller and M.B. Rose, *op.cit.*, p.189
33 *Ibid.*

Chapter 9 No Tomb, 1587–90 pp. 223–252

1 See C. Read, *Walsingham*, II, p.265
2 J. Bruce, *op.cit.*, p.169
3 *Ibid.*, p.343
4 See C. Read, *Lord Burghley and Queen Elizabeth*, p.374
5 See C. Read, *Walsingham*, I, p.441
6 L.S. Marcus, J. Mueller and M.B. Rose, *op.cit.*, p.296
7 See C. Read, *Walsingham*, III, pp.182–6
8 See G. Parker, *The Grand Strategy of Philip II*, New Haven, 1998, p.226
9 M. Leimon and G. Parker, 'Treason and plot in Elizabethan England: the "fame of Sir Edward Stafford" reconsidered', in *English Historical Review*, CU (1996), p.1154
10 See C. Read, *Walsingham*, III, p.296
11 *Ibid.*, III p.448
12 *Ibid.*, II, p.218
13 *Ibid.*, II, pp.87–8
14 P.W. Hasler, *op.cit.*, III, p.146
15 T.E. Hartley, ed., *Proceedings in the Parliament of Elizabeth I 1558–1581*, Leicester, 1981, p.203
16 M. Axton, *The Queen's Two Bodies: Drama and the Elizabethan Succession*, 1977, p.12
17 See E. Lodge, *Illustrations of British History*, 1791, II, pp.276–7
18 See T. Wright, ed., *Queen Elizabeth and her Times*, 1838, II, p.75
19 J. Bruce, *op.cit.*, p.276
20 L.S. Marcus, J. Mueller and M.B. Rose, *op.cit.*, p.321
21 See C. Read, *Walsingham*, II, p.14

BIBLIOGRAPHY

Anyone wishing to explore the life and times of Francis Walsingham in more detail will, as a starter, need to track down a copy of Conyers Read, *Mr Secretary Walsingham and the Policy of Queen Elizabeth*, 3 vols, 1925. A reprint by Archon Books, Hamden, Connecticut, was produced in 1967. Read included a comprehensive survey of all the relevant archival sources available at that time and it is still relevant. The most easily accessible source material is to be found in printed calendars and collections of contemporary documents. The basic relevant volumes for Walsingham are:

Calendar of State Papers Domestic of the Reign of Queen Elizabeth, 1856–72
Calendar of State Papers Foreign of the Reign of Queen Elizabeth, 1863–1950
  (Most of these are available on DVD)
Calendar of Letters . . . in the Archives of Simancas . . . 1892–99
Calendar of State Papers relating to Scotland and Mary, Queen of Scots, 1898–1952
Calendar of State Papers relating to Ireland, 1860–1905
Calendar of State Papers, Venetian, 1864–98
Historical Manuscript Commission (HMC) Calendar of Manuscripts of Marquis of Bath at Longleat, 1904–80
HMC Calendar of Manuscripts of Marquis of Salisbury at Hatfield House, 1883–1923
Journal of Sir Francis Walsingham (ed. C.T. Martin), Camden Miscellany VI, 1870
Correspondence of Robert Dudley, Earl of Leycester during his government of the Low Countries (ed. J. Bruce) Camden Soc. Ser 1. 27, 1844
Zurich Letters, 1558–1579 (ed. H. Robinson) Parker Soc. 2 vols, 1842–5
The compleat ambassador, or, Two treatises of the intended marriage of Queen Elizabeth, comprised in letters of negotiation of Sir F. Walsingham . . . (ed. D. Digges), 1655
Original Letters Illustrative of English History (ed. H. Ellis), 1st ser., 3 vols. 1842

Relations politiques des Pays-Bas et de l'Angleterre sous la regne de Philippe II (ed. J.M.B.C. Kervyn de Lettenhove and L. Galliodts-van Severen), 11 vols, 1882–1900

Hamilton Papers . . . illustrating the political relations of England and Scotland . . . (ed. J. Bain), 1890–92

Collection of State Papers, relating to affairs in the reign of Queen Elizabeth . . . (ed. W. Murdin), 1759

Elizabeth I Collected Works (ed. Leah S. Marcus, Janel Mueller and Mary Beth Rose), University of Chicago Press, 2000

The more important publicly available archive collections are:

British Library: Add. MSS 5752–5754, 30156, 33531, 33594, 35841; Egerton MSS 1693–1694, Cotton MSS, corresp. and papers, Harley MSS, corresp. and papers, expense account kept as ambassador to the Low Countries, M 488, letters to William Ashby, Egerton MS 2598, letters to Edward Wotton, Add. MS 32657, Yelverton MSS

Walsingham letter-book, Hatfield House, Hertfordshire, letters and papers

Lincolnshire Archive Office, Correspondence with Lord Willoughby

National Archive, State Papers 12, 15, 46, 52, 70, PROB 11/75 PCC 33 DRURY

National Library of Scotland, correspondence relating to Mary, Queen of Scots

Sheffield Archive Office – Wentworth Woodhouse MSS

The following list of classic books and articles and more recent scholarship cannot possibly be exhaustive but does cover most valuable contributions on specific issues or Elizabethan background.

Adams, S.L., 'Eliza Enthroned? The Court and its Politics', in Haigh (ed.), *Reign of Elizabeth I*, pp.55–77

Allen, J.W., *A History of Political Thought in the Sixteenth Century* (1964)

Andrews, K.R., *Elizabethan Privateering: English Privateering during the Spanish War, 1585–1603* (Cambridge, 1964)

Archer, J.M., *Sovereignty and Intelligence: Spying and Court Culture in the English Renaissance* (Stanford, California: Stanford University Press, 1993)

Aveling, J.C.H., *The Handle and the Axe: The Catholic Recusants in England from Reformation to Emancipation* (1976)

Axton, M., *The Queens' Two Bodies: Drama and the Elizabethan Succession* (1977)

Bartlett, K.R., 'The English Exile Community in Italy and the Political Opposition to Queen Mary I', *Albion*, 13 (1981)

Bartlett, K.R., 'The Role of the Marian Exiles', in P.W. Hasler (ed.), *The House of Commons, 1558–1603*, I, app. xi

Basing, P., 'Robert Beale and the Queen of Scots', *British Library Journal*, 20 (1994), 65–82

Baumgartner, F.J., *Radical Reactionaries: The Political Thought of the French Catholic League* (Geneva, 1975)

Bellamy, J., *The Tudor Law of Treason* (Toronto, 1979)

Berry, L.E., (ed,), *John Stubbs' Gaping Gulf, Folger Documents Series* (Virginia, 1968)

Bossy J., *Under the Molehill: an Elizabethan Spy Story* (2001)

Bossy, J., *Giordano Bruno and the Embassy Affair* (1991)

Camden, W., *The History of the Most Renowned and Victorious Princess Elizabeth, Late Queen of England* (ed. W.T. MacCaffrey, Chicago, 1970)

Caraman, P., *The Other Face, Catholic Life under Elizabeth I* (1960)

Clegg, C.B., *Press Censorship in Elizabethan England* (1997)

Cliffe, J.T., *The Puritan Gentry* (1984)

Cole, M.H., *The Portable Queen: Elizabeth I and the Politics of Ceremony* (Amherst, Mass., 1999)

Collinson, P., 'De republica Anglorum, or, History with the politics put back', in P. Collinson, *Elizabethan Essays* (1994)

Collinson, P., 'The Elizabethan Church and the New Religion', in Haigh (ed.), *Reign of Elizabeth I*, pp.169–94

Collinson, P., 'The monarchical republic of Queen Elizabeth I', *The Tudor monarchy*, ed. J.A. Guy (1997), 110–34

Collinson, P., *Archbishop Grindal, 1519–1583: The Struggle for a Reformed Church* (1980)

Collinson, P., *Elizabethan Essays* (1994)

Collinson, P., *Elizabethans* (2003)

Collinson, P., *Godly People* (1983)

Collinson, P., *Godly Rule: Essays on English Protestantism and Puritanism* (1983)

Collinson, P., *The Elizabethan Puritan Movement* (1967)

Collinson, P., *The English Captivity of Mary, Queen of Scots* (Sheffield, 1987)

Collinson, P., *The Religion of Protestants: The Church in English Society, 1559–1625* (Oxford, 1982)

Davies, C.S.L., *Peace, Print and Protestantism: 1450–1558* (1977)

Donaldson, G., *All the Queen's Men: Power and Politics in Mary Stewart's Scotland* (1983)

Donaldson, G., *The Scottish Reformation* (Cambridge, 1960)

Doran, S., 'Revenge her Foul and most Unnatural Murder? The Impact of Mary Stewart's Execution on Anglo-Scottish Relations', *Historical Association*, 85, 2000

Doran, S., *Monarchy and Matrimony: the Courtships of Elizabeth I* (1996)

Edwards, E., *Robert Persons: The Biography of an Elizabethan Jesuit* (St Louis, 1995)

Elton, G.R., *England under the Tudors*, (1974)

Elton, G.R., *Studies in Tudor and Stuart Politics and Government* (3 vols, Cambridge, 1974–83)

Elton, G.R., *The Parliament of England 1559–1581* (Cambridge, 1986)

Elton, G.R., *The Parliament of England, 1559–1581* (Cambridge, 1986)

Elton, G.R., *The Tudor Constitution* (Cambridge 1960, 2nd edn 1982)

Elton, G.R., *The Tudor Constitution: Documents and Commentary* (Cambridge, 1965)

Evans, F.M.G., *The Principal Secretary of State: A survey of the Office from 1558 to 1680* (1923)

Foxe, J., *The Acts and Monuments of John Foxe*, ed. G. Townsend (8 vols, 1843–9)

Garrett, C.H., *The Marian Exiles: A study in the Origins of Elizabethan Puritanism* (1938)

Gee, H., and Hardy, W.J., (eds.), *Documents Illustrative of English Church History* (1910)

Graves, M., 'Thomas Norton, the Parliament Man: An Elizabethan MP', *Historical Journal*, 23, 1, 1980

Graves, M., *Thomas Norton, The Parliament Man* (Oxford, 1994)

Grell, O., *Calvinist Exiles in Tudor and Stuart England* (Aldershot, 1996)

Guy, J., *My Heart is my Own: The Life of Mary Queen of Scots* (2004)

Guy, J., *Tudor England* (Oxford, 1990)

Haigh, C., (ed.), *The Reign of Elizabeth I* (1984)

Haller, W., (ed.), *Foxe's Book of Martyrs and the Elect Nation* (1963)

Haugaard, W.P., *Elizabeth and the English Reformation: The Struggle for a Stable Settlement of Religion* (Cambridge, 1970)

Haynes, A., *The Elizabethan Secret Services* (Stroud, 2000)

Hoak, D., (ed.), *Tudor Political Culture* (Cambridge, 1995)

Holmes, P.J., *Resistance and Compromise: The Political Thought of the Elizabethan Catholics* (Cambridge, 1982)

Holt, M., *The Duke of Anjou and the Politique Struggle During the Wars of Religion* (1986)

Holt, M.P., *The French Wars of Religion, 1562–1629* (Cambridge, 1995)

Israel, J.I., *The Dutch Republic – its Rise, Greatness and Fall, 1477–1806* (Oxford, 1995)

James, M., *Society, Politics and Culture: Studies in Early Modern England* (Cambridge, 1986)

Jensen, D., *Diplomacy and Dogmatism: Bernardino de Mendoza and the French Catholic League* (1964)

Johnson, P., *Elizabeth I: A Study in Power and Intellect* (1974)

Kingdon, R., *Myths About the St Bartholomew's Day Massacres 1572–76* (Cambridge, Mass., 1988)

Lake, P.G., 'Calvinism and the English Church, 1570–1635', *Past and Present*, no.114 (1987)

Lake, P.G., *Moderate Puritans and the Elizabethan Church* (Cambridge, 1982)

Leimon, M. and Parker, G., 'Treason and Plot in Elizabethan diplomacy: the "Fame of Sir Edward Stafford" Reconsidered'. *EngHR*, 111 (1996)

Loades, D.M., *England's Maritime Empire – Seapower, Commerce and Policy 1490–1690* (2000)

Loades, D.M., *Politics and the Nation, 1450–1660* (1974)

Loades, D.M., *The Reign of Mary Tudor: Politics, Government, and Religion in England 1553–1558* (1979)

Loades, D.M., *The Tudor Court* (1986)

MacCaffrey, W.T., *Elizabeth I: War and Politics, 1588–1603* (1992)

MacCaffrey, W.T., *Queen Elizabeth and the Making of Policy, 1572–1588* (Princeton, NJ, 1981)

MacCaffrey, W.T., *The Shaping of the Elizabethan Regime: Elizabethan Politics, 1558–1572* (1968)

Manning, R.B., 'The Crisis of Episcopal Authority during the Reign of Elizabeth I', *Journal of British Studies*, 11 (1971)

McCullough, D.E., *Sermons at Court: Politics and Religion in Elizabethan and Jacobean Preaching* (Cambridge, 1998)

McDermott, J., *England and the Spanish Armada: The Necessary Quarrel* (New Haven, 2005)

McGrath, P., *Papists and Puritans under Elizabeth I* (1967)

Neale, J.E., *Elizabeth I and her Parliaments* (2 vols, 1969)

Neale, J.E., *The Elizabethan House of Commons* (1963)

Nolan, J.S., *Sir John Norreys and the Elizabethan Military World* (Exeter, 1997)

Parker, G., 'The Place of Tudor England in the Messianic Vision of Philip II of Spain', *Transaction of the Royal Historical Society* 2002

Parker, G., *Spain and the Netherlands, 1559–1659* (1979)

Parker, G., *The Dutch Revolt* (1977)

Parmalee, L.F., *Good Newes from Fraunce: French Anti-League Propaganda in late Elizabethan England* (Rochester 1996)

Parry, J.H., *The Spanish Seaborne Empire* (1966)

Pulman, M.B., *The Elizabethan Privy Council in the 1570s* (Berkeley, Ca; 1971)

Read, C., *Lord Burghley and Queen Elizabeth* (1960)

Read, C., *Mr Secretary Cecil and Queen Elizabeth* (1955)

Seaver, P.S., *The Puritan Lectureships: The Politics of Religious Dissent, 1560–1662* (Stanford, Ca., 1970)

Simon, J., *Education and Society in Tudor England* (Cambridge, 1966)

Smith, A.G.R., *The Government of Elizabethan England* (1967)

Smith, L.B., *Treason in Tudor England: Politics and Paranoia* (1986)

Soman, A., (ed.), *The Massacre of St Bartholomew's: Reappraisals and Documents* (The Hague, 1974)

Somerset, A., *Elizabeth I* (1991)

Stewart, Alan, *Philip Sidney: A Double Life* (2000)

Stow, J., *A Survey of London* (ed. C.L. Kingsford), 2 vols (Oxford, 1908)

Sutherland, N.M., 'The Marian Exiles and the Establishment of the Elizabethan Regime', *Archiv für Reformationgeschichte*, 78, 1987

Trimble, W.R., *The Catholic Laity in Elizabethan England* (1964)

Wernham, R.B., *Before the Armada: The Emergence of the English Nation, 1485–1588* (New York, 1972)

Wernham, R.B., *The Making of English Foreign Policy, 1558–1603* (Berkley, Ca, 1980)

Wilson, C., *Queen Elizabeth I and the Revolt of the Netherlands* (1970)

Wilson, D., *Sweet Robin: A Biography of Robert Dudley, Earl of Leicester 1553–1588* (1997)

Wilson, D., *Uncrowned Kings of England: The Black Legend of the Dudleys* (2005)

Worden, B., *The Sound of Virtue: Philip Sidney's Arcadia and Elizabethan Politics* (1996)

Yates, F., *Astraea: The Imperial Theme in the Sixteenth Century* (1975)

Yates, F., *The Occult Philosophy in the Elizabethan Age* (1979)

INDEX

*A Discourse touching the pretended
Match between the Duke of
Norfolk and the Queen of
Scots* 61, 62–3, 65–6
*A Letter to Queen Elizabeth touching
her Marriage with
Monsieur* 244
'A Plot for intelligence out of
Spain' 231
Act of Uniformity 104
Admonition to the Parliament 64
Albigensian Crusade 21
Allen, William 105, 130, 132, 183,
184, 208, 234
Alva, Duke of (Fernando Alvarez de
Toledo) 55–6, 68, 71–2, 80,
82, 124
Anderson, Edmund 160
Angus, Earl of 166
Anjou *see* Francis, duc d'Anjou;
Henri, duc d'Anjou *and* Henry
III of France
*Answer to a little book that was
published against the marriage of
the Duke of Norfolk and the
Scottish Queen* 63–5
Arcadia 243–4
Arran, Earl of 170, 206–7
Arundel, Charles 185, 186–7
Arundel, Earl of 61, 74, 175,
184, 208

Ascham, Roger 11
Aylmer, John (Bishop of
London) 133

Babington, Anthony 209–12 *see
also* conspiracies
Bacon, Sir Nicholas 128, 178
Bailley, Charles 71
Bale, John (Bishop of Ossory) 25,
26–7
Ballard, John 208, 210, 222
Barker, Christopher (printer) 109
Barlow, William (Bishop of
Chichester) 34
Bartlett, John 64
Battle of Alcazar 123
Bawde, John 7
Beale, Robert 95–102, 159, 164,
170, 225, 227, 239
Beaton, James 164
Bible 112
  English translation of 11
Bill, Dr William 34
Boleyn, Anne 7, 8–9, 10, 11
Boleyn, Mary 8–9
Boleyn, Sir Thomas 8–9
Bond of Association 189–91,
247–8
*Book of Martyrs (Acts and Monuments
of the Christian Religion)* 26,
49, 64, 110

Bothwell, Earl of (James Hepburn)
    52 *see also* Mary Queen of
    Scots/Mary Stuart
Bowes, Robert   166, 167
Bright, Timothy   80
Bromley, Sir Thomas   159, 176
Bruno, Giordano   168–9, 176
Bryan, Sir Francis   8, 9, 13
Bucer, Martin   15, 32
Buckhurst, Lord   204
Bullinger, Heinrich   25, 33, 53, 106
Burghley, Baron *see* Cecil, William
Butts, William (royal physician to
    Henry VIII)   12

Cadiz raid   234–5 *see also*
    Drake, Francis
Calais   48
Calvin, John   17, 25, 30, 109,
    153, 241
Calvinism/Calvinists   28, 42, 46,
    49, 50, 52, 53, 54, 63, 73, 75,
    90, 108, 109, 247
Campion, Edmund   141, 159–60,
    163, 184
Cambridge   12, 13–16
Carey, Sir John   8, 9, 10
Carey, Sir Robert   229
Carisbrooke Castle.   40–1 *see also*
    Horsey, Edward
Carleill, Christopher   198
Cartwright, Thomas   192
Cashel, Archbishop of   122
Casimir, John   235
Castelnau   175, 176, 185, 206, 209
Catherine of Aragon   8, 10
Catholic League   116, 118, 163,
    189, 209
Catholicism   ix, xi, xii, 3, 34, 49,
    62, 66, 67, 79, 100, 103–7,
    115, 120, 122, 129–30, 152–7,
    161, 163, 172, 179–80, 183,
    184, 188, 195, 206–7, 211,
    228, 230, 233, 238, 249–50
Cecil, Robert   252

Cecil, William   15, 24, 33, 34,
    35–9, 41–2, 52, 57–9, 61–3,
    68–72, 74–5, 78, 89, 90, 92,
    93, 94, 100, 113, 125, 126,
    132, 44, 145, 166, 170, 180,
    183, 185, 189, 191, 193,
    194, 196, 198, 199–201, 204,
    213–14, 217–18, 221, 225,
    226, 239, 243, 246, 251
Champagny, Sieur de   86–7
Charles, Archduke of Austria   63
Charles V of France   42
Charles V of Spain   21–2
Charles IX of France   46, 77, 78–9,
    82, 83, 103, 117, 124, 125
Châteauneuf   220–1
Cheke, John   15, 25, 31
Christopherson, Bishop (of
    Chichester)   34
church in England   102–3, 106,
    153, 192–3 *see also*
    Protestantism
    reform of   157–8, 192–5
Cobham, Lord   204
Coligny   77, 79
Collinson, Professor   93, 97
*Commonplaces of Christian
    Religion*   73
conspiracies   58, 62, 66–7, 69–70,
    142–3, 172–5, 180–81, 183,
    186, 188–9, 192, 199, 203,
    208–9, 220–1, 238 *see also*
    Ridolfi, Roberto
    Babington plot   179, 207, 209–
    12, 213
    'Enterprise of England'   68, 71–
    3, 76, 104, 117, 122, 124, 169,
    176, 203, 227, 236
    Throckmorton plot   172–5, 177,
    186, 209
Consularius of the English
    Nation   31
Cooke, Sir Anthony   33, 36
Cooke, William   24
Council, the   92, 95–8, 100, 104,

120–1, 126, 128, 149, 155–6,
175, 176, 190–1, 194, 196,
225, 226, 248
Council of the North 97
Council of Trent ix, 44, 45, 80
Counter-Reformation 17–18, 76,
85, 105
Court of Augmentations 13
Courtenay, Edward (Earl of
Devon) 30
Cox, Bishop of Ely 106–7
Cox, Richard 25, 28
Cranmer, Thomas (Archbishop of
Canterbury) 10, 11, 14–15,
21, 25, 28, 66
Cranmerian liturgy 36
Crichton, William 163, 165, 180,
181, 182–3, 184
Croft, Sir James 199, 204,
206, 233
Cromwell, Thomas 7, 10, 11, 92
Crowley, Robert 64–5

d'Aubigny *see* Esmé Stuart, Seigneur
d'Aubigny
Darnley, Lord (Henry Stuart)
51–2, 57, 87
Davison, William 114, 167, 171,
221, 223–7
Day, John 24, 66
de Castlenau, Michel 168–9
de Feckenham, John 132
de Guise, Charles (Cardinal of
Lorraine) 49
de Guise, duc 79, 175, 187
de l'Aubespine, Claude 209
de Medici, Catherine 46–7, 48, 50,
75, 77, 78–9, 82, 103, 117–18,
125, 126, 148–9, 209
de Medici, Francis, duc
d'Alençon 75 *see also* Francis,
duc d'Anjou
de Medici, Henri, duc d'Anjou 75,
76, 98, 100, 117 *see also* Henri
III of France

de Mendoza, Bernardino 126
de Silva, Guzman (Spanish
ambassador) 88
de Spes, Guerau 68, 69, 72, 73,
74, 78, 122
de Valois, Margaret 79
Denny, Anthony 8–9, 11–12,
13–14
Denny, Sir Edmund 8
Denny family 7–9, 24–5
des Trappes, Leonard 220–1
Desmond Rebellions 122, 123,
153
Diet of Worms 9
Digges, Thomas 191, 242
Discovery of a Gaping Gulf 130–1,
141, 244
Dom Antonio of Avis 149–50,
230
Don John of Austria 117, 122,
123, 127, 118–19, 134, 137–8
Drake, Francis x, 85, 117, 143–5,
149–50, 163, 197, 231–2, 234–
5, 241
Dudley, Ambrose (Earl of
Warwick) 48–9, 65, 90
Dudley, John (Earl of
Warwick) 12, 13
Dudley, Robert (Earl of
Leicester) 40, 48, 51, 59, 63,
65, 68–9, 84, 90, 92–4, 100,
108, 128, 133, 135–6, 140,
148, 149, 151, 159, 161, 166,
171, 178, 183, 185–6, 189,
194, 199–201, 204–5, 211, 212,
214, 216–17, 224, 225, 226,
234, 235–6, 237, 239, 245,
246, 248–9, 251
Dudley, Sir Henry 23

Earl Grey de Wilton 123
Edward IV 88
Edward VI 13, 18, 19, 29, 33, 247
Elizabeth I (and) ix–x, xii, 3, 10,
12, 19, 29–30, 35–7, 39, 43,

47–8, 59, 66–7, 68, 74, 85–
100, 104–5, 106, 108, 110–16,
120, 123–8, 130–1, 143–53,
155–7, 160, 163–5, 169–70,
176–7, 180, 183–4, 186, 188–
92, 193–8, 201, 204–5, 213–14,
218–30, 233, 235, 237–9,
242–3, 246–52
criticism 99, 110–11
Drake's circumnavigation
  voyage 145
free speech 91
Grindal 112–13
lack of heir 50, 75, 190–1, 230,
  247
marriage negotiations/Anjou
  match 75–6, 82, 98, 118, 121,
  125, 130–1, 134–5, 137, 139–
  41, 147–51, 154, 160, 242,
  244, 245
Mary Stuart 213–14, 219–29,
  242, 247
money to Anjou for
  Netherlands 150, 162
piety of 249–50
Protestantism 33–4
Robert Dudley 51, 92–4,
  135–6, 235, 239
secret peace talks 205
Spain 56–7
supremacy bill 37
self-preservation 87
Pope Gregory XIII 105
principle of divine right 90
seizure of Spanish gold 56, 61
the church 92, 108, 128–9,
  194–5
Emerson, Ralph 184–5
English New Testament 9
English Reformation *see*
  Reformation, the
English seminaries abroad 105–6,
  116, 129–30, 132, 142, 161,
  163–4, 208
Esmé Stuart, Seigneur

d'Aubigny 94, 141, 162, 163,
  166–8, 120–1, 162, 181, 206
evangelicals 3, 11, 12, 13, 17–18,
  89, 127, 241
exiles 103

Farnese, Allesandro (Alexander),
  Duke of Parma 119, 141,
  151, 162, 172, 176, 197, 198,
  204, 208, 231, 233, 237
Fénélon, La Mothe 167
Ferrabosco, Alfonso 138
Field, John 64, 73
Field of the Cloth of Gold 6
*First Blast of the Trump Against the
  Monstrous Regiment of Women,
  The* 29
Fisher, Bishop John 7
Fitzmaurice Fitzgerald, James 122–3
Flodden, battle of 6
Forster, Sir John 165
Fortescue, Sir John 16
Fowler, William 168–9
Foxe, John 26, 27, 49, 66, 73, 110
France ix, 2, 46, 47–9, 50, 57, 73,
  77–8, 90, 114, 116, 122, 124,
  132, 157, 168, 188, 203, 209,
  228, 229, 252
Francis, duc d'Anjou 117–19,
  125–6, 130, 134–5, 136, 139,
  141, 147–51, 154, 160, 161–2,
  164, 197
Francis I of France 42
Francis II of France 46, 50

Galpin, George 178
Gardiner, Stephen (Bishop of
  Winchester) 15–16, 20, 30
Gates, Geoffrey 13
Gates, Sir John 12, 13
*General and Rare Memorials Pertaining
  to the Perfect Arts of Navigation,
  The* 242
Geneva 92, 109, 131, 247, 251
Geneva Bible 109–110

George, Duke of Clarence 88
Gerard, Balthazar 179–80
Gifford, Gilbert 208–10
Gloriana myth 85–6, 243
Golden Hind 143, 145
Gorboduc 153, 243
Gowrie, Earl of 167–8
Great Fire of London 3, 240
Gray, Patrick 206–7
Grey, Catherine 87–8
Grey, Lady Jane 19
Grindal, Edmund (Archbishop of
    Canterbury) 26, 56, 99, 108–
    9, 112, 128, 192, 242
Gualter, Rudolph 35, 36–7, 44
    and letters to Elizabeth
    Tudor 36–7
Guises, the 46–7, 58, 60, 65, 75,
    77, 79, 118, 162, 163, 166,
    167, 176, 184, 186, 203, 206,
    208, 209, 235

Hakluyt, Richard 241
Hall, Hugh 172
Hapsburg Empire 21
    and war with France 23
Harrison, Thomas 138
Hasler, P.W. (historian of
    parliament) 39
Hastings, Henry (Earl of
    Huntingdon) 88
Hatton, Sir Christopher 144, 158–
    9, 177, 181, 194, 196, 198,
    204, 221, 225, 240
Hawkins, John 71
Henri, duc d'Anjou 75, 76, 98,
    100, 117
Henry, Lord Cobham 136
Henry II of France 46
Henry III of France 117–18, 124–6,
    145, 148–9, 161, 162, 167,
    176, 197, 203, 209, 230, 235
Henry VII 50
Henry VIII ix, xi, 6, 8–12, 13, 27,
    29, 42, 44, 87, 92

Henry of Navarre 79, 118, 125–6,
    209, 235
Henry Tudor, Earl of Richmond 4
heresy 9, 103–4, 130
*History of the most renowned and
    victorious Princess Elizabeth* x
Hooker, Richard 103
Horsey, Edward 40–1, 48
    as adventurer-pirate 41
    as patron of Calvinist clergy 41
    and Dudley plot 40
Howard, Catherine 7
Howard, Henry 169, 177–8
Howard, Lord Admiral
    Charles 225, 233, 236
Howard, Thomas 22, 66, 68, 71
Huguenot(s) 41, 42, 47, 54, 79–83,
    118, 124, 125–6, 163, 230, 235
    and Edict of Saint-Germain
    46–7
Hullier, John 31
Humphrey, Dr Laurence 115

*Institution of the Christian
    Religion* 17, 153
Ireland 100, 120, 122–3, 134,
    145, 152
Islam 54, 78, 106
Isle of Wight, importance of 40

James, Earl of Moray 59, 120
James V of Scotland 50
James VI of Scotland 53, 120–1,
    162, 165–8, 170, 191, 206–7,
    219, 229–30
James Douglas (Earl of
    Morton) 120–1
Jesuits 49, 105, 116, 143, 152–3,
    158–60, 163, 181, 184,
    192, 208
Jewel, John (Bishop of
    Salisbury) 25, 36, 52

Kelly, Edward 242
Kent, Earl of 222

King's College, Cambridge   13–14
Kingston, Sir William   6
Knollys, Francis   38, 39, 248
Knox, John   25, 28, 29, 30, 32, 41,
     50–1

Latimer, Hugh (Bishop of
     Worcester)   14
Laws of Ecclesiastical Polity   103
Leclerc, Nicolas (Sieur de
     Courcelles)   169
Leicester's Commonwealth   183–4,
     185, 187
London, Bishop of   64
Lords of the Congregation *see*
     Calvinism/Calvinists
Lorraine, Cardinal of   50
Low Countries   76, 80, 90, 115,
     118, 126, 132, 134–5, 145,
     178, 200–1, 230, 233 *see also*
     Netherlands
Lussault, Mathurin   1
Luther, Martin   9, 14
Lutheranism   17

Maitland, John   228
Man, John   73–4
Manucci, Jacomo   125
Manwood, Sir Roger   129
Margaret of Austria   55
Marian appointees   34
Marian exiles and persecution   28,
     31, 108
Marian statute   131
Marvell, Andrew   x
Mary of Guise   29, 50
Mary Queen of Scots/Mary
     Stuart   ix, xi, 48, 54, 58, 61–2,
     65–7, 70, 78–9, 85, 90, 93,
     116, 120, 124, 141, 162–5,
     169–70, 175–6, 177, 179–82,
     184, 191, 203, 206–7, 209,
     211–13, 227, 228, 34, 247, 248
  as claimant to English
     throne   50–1

  as hope of Catholics   57
  Bothwell   52–3
  Casket Letters   59–60
  death of   219–29
  imprisonment of   53, 67
  marriage plans for   66, 69, 87
Mary Tudor   xii, 19–24, 29, 30,
     31–2, 33, 34, 40, 66, 73, 75
Mayne, Cuthbert   129, 130, 132,
     157
Medina-Sidonia, Duke of   236
Mendoza, Bernardino de   127, 143,
     149, 151, 163, 164–5, 169,
     172–7, 187, 208, 233
Merchant Venturers   114, 178, 241
Mildmay, Sir Walter   12–13, 90,
     152–3, 158
Milton, John   27
Monson, Robert   131
Moody, Michae   202–3, 220–1
Mont, Christopher   53
More, Sir Thomas   7, 10
Morgan, Thomas   180, 184, 187,
     209
Morton, Earl of   134, 162
*Mr Secretary Walsingham and the Policy
     of Queen Elizabeth*   xi
Murray (Scottish regent)   65
Musculus, Wolfgang   73

Netherlands   100, 124, 128, 136,
     138, 128, 149–51, 196, 197,
     203–4, 211, 235–6, 252
Neville, Edmund   181
New Testament translation
     (Laurence Tomson)   109
Newhaven Venture   48–9
Norfolk, Duke of   61–2, 66–7, 70,
     177
Norreys, Sir John   199
Norris, Sir Henry   75, 95
Northern Rebellion   67, 69, 124,
     177
Northumberland, Duke of   20, 62,
     67–8, 175

Norton, Thomas 66, 153–4, 156–7, 159, 160–1, 174–5, 242, 243, 246–7

Oxford, Earl of 186

Pacification of Ghent (1577) 119
Padua 25, 30–1
Paget, Charles 184, 187, 208
Paget, Lord 175
papacy, the ix, 44–6
  Pope Gregory XIII (Ugo Boncompagni) 78, 80, 105, 116–17, 122, 124, 175, 180
  Pope Pius IV 44
  Pope Pius V (Antonio Ghislieri, Grand Inquisitor) ix, 45, 49, 104, 122
  Pope Sixtus V 231
papal bulls/directives 45–6, 129
  Regnans in Excelsis 45, 69, 104, 154
Paris 2, 43, 46–8, 77–80, 118, 149, 164, 167, 170, 186, 196, 209, 228
  and St Bartholomew's Massacre 79–83
Parker, Matthew (Archbishop of Canterbury) 73, 108
Parliament 35–7, 39, 111, 151, 155, 156, 191
  House of Commons 12, 39, 91, 112, 156, 157–8, 194, 246
  and policies of concern 39
  Protestant representation in 35–7
Parry, William 180, 182–3, 191–2
Paulet, Sir Amias 182, 206, 213, 221
Percy, Henry (Earl of Northumberland) 177–8
Persons, Robert 141, 163, 184, 186
Phelippes, Thomas 210
Philip II of Spain ix–x, 21–3, 47,
  34–5, 51–6, 71, 74, 78, 86, 105, 116–17, 119, 122, 124, 126–7, 131, 138, 143, 145, 149–50, 162–3, 166, 175–7, 179–81, 197–9, 203, 205, 218, 230–3, 236
Pilgrimage of Grace (1536–7) 67, 110
Pole, Reginald 30
Poley, Robert 210–11
Politique Discourses 138
Posset, John (Bishop of Winchester) 25
prayer book 104, 193
  Edwardian (1552) 28, 56
  Elizabeth's 64
  English 14
  Puritan version of 110, 114
Prayer Book Rebellion (1549) 110
Principal Navigations, Voyages and Discoveries of the English Nation 241
prophesyings, suppression of 110–13, 131
Protestant league 98
Protestant refugees 23–8, 33–4
Protestantism ix, xii, 3, 18, 33–5, 46, 50, 62, 90, 92, 98, 103–104, 115, 116, 120, 188, 206, 208, 209, 224, 230, 241, 249, 250, 252
Puritans/Puritanism xii, 28, 41, 63, 66, 89, 95, 99, 106–7, 109, 129, 130, 132, 130, 149, 152, 155, 156, 157–8, 189, 193, 194–5, 211, 224, 240, 242, 248–9, 250

Radcliffe, Egrement 138
Randolph, Thomas 226
Read, Conyer xi
Recusancy Act 155–6
recusants/recusancy 106, 155, 158–9, 185, 208–9
Reformation 11–12, 13, 14, 18,

19, 21, 28, 50, 77, 106, 107, 122, 238
Revelation, Book of   27
Ridley, Nicholas   14, 15–16, 21, 31
Ridolfi, Roberto   68–73, 76, 104, 122, 124 *see also* conspiracies
Rizzio, David   52
Rogers, Thomas aka Nicolas Berden   188
Rome   43–5, 69, 92, 116, 122, 131, 132, 143, 180, 251
Ross, Bishop of   70, 71
Russell, Francis (Earl of Bedford)   30, 34–5

St Bartholomew's Massacre   2, 79–83, 85, 90, 95, 103, 118, 124, 252
St Giles, Cripplegate   41, 64–5
St Mary Aldermanbury   3, 41
St Paul's Cathedral   3, 239
Sackville, Thomas   243
Sandys, Edwin (Bishop of Winchester)   33, 34
Santa Cruz, Marquis of   231, 234, 236
Savage, John   208, 210
Scambler, Edmund (Bishop of Peterborough)   92–3
Scotland   6, 43, 50, 52, 57, 61–2, 120, 121–2, 141, 162–4, 168, 169–71, 183, 206–7, 228–30
Scriptorum Illustrium Maioris Britanniae Catalogus   26
Sebastian, King of Portugal   117, 123
Seymour, Edward (Duke of Somerset)   12, 13
Seymour, Henry (Vice-Admiral)   238
Seymour, Thomas   12
Shakespeare   18, 238, 252
Sharington, William   13
Shelley, William   175
Shephard's Calendar, The   141

Shrewsbury, Earl of   72, 162, 182, 209, 222, 248
Sidney, Philip   138, 171, 183, 216–17, 239, 240, 242, 244–5
Singleton, Hugh   141
Sledd, Charles   142–3, 160
Smith, Sir Thomas   48, 78, 89
Somerville/Somerfield, John   172
Spain   ix, 53–7, 61, 68, 74, 76–7, 86, 100, 114, 121–2, 138, 145, 149–50, 153, 157, 168, 178, 197, 228, 229–31
Spanish Armada   x, 85, 179, 183, 230–1, 235–6
Spanish Inquisition   22, 103, 194
Spenser, Edmund   xi, 240, 242
Stafford, Sir Edward   166, 180, 185–7, 196, 201, 220
Stafford, William   203, 220–1, 228, 233
Standen, Anthony   233–4
state censorship   241–2
States General /United Netherlands   197–9, 204, 236
Stewart, Robert (messenger)   42
Stubbe, John   130–1, 140–1, 148, 156, 160, 242, 244
Stukeley, Thomas   122–3, 124, 134, 138
Sturmius, John   89, 131–2
Sussex, Earl of   100, 138, 144

Tamworth, John   25
Tankerville, Alice   7
Throckmorton, Francis   169, 172–5, 177 *see also* conspiracies
Throckmorton, Sir Nicholas   19–20, 41–2, 47–9, 169
Tower of London   6–7, 10, 16, 20, 31, 111, 138, 143, 157, 160–1, 173–5, 177, 181, 226
treason, penalties for   155
Treason Act (1351)   160
treaties of Nonsuch   198
Treaty of Berwick   207

Treaty of Blois 78, 82
Treaty of Cateau-Cambrésis 47–8,
54
Tregian, Francis 129
Tuscany, Duke of 233
Tyndale, William 9

Venice 30
Vermigli, Peter Martyr 25

Walsingham, James 4, 6
Walsingham, Mary 12–13
Walsingham, Sir Edmund 6–7, 12
Walsingham, Sir Francis (and)
  accusation of
    Presbyterianism 108
  advice from Beale 97–8, 99–
    100, 101–2
  alliance of England and France
    against Spain 78–9
  Anglo-Scottish relations 121
  as ambassador in France 59, 71,
    72–3
  as Bible-based Protestant 107
  as English ambassador in
    France 1–2
  as MP for Bossiney,
    Cornwall 35–6
  as parliamentary member for
    Surrey 156
  as Puritan 204
  as trusted intermediary 41–3
  as venture capitalist 149–50
  at Fotheringhay 215
  at King's College,
    Cambridge 13–16
  audience with Charles of
    France 81
  banishment from court 141
  belief in Reformation 107
  birth of 8, 10
  Catholic detention centres 132–
    3, 155
  Catholic plots against
    Elizabeth 58

Catholic resurgence, fear of 132–4
Cecil (Lord Burghley) 41–3, 57–
  8, 84, 166, 196
  chancellor of the Order of the
    Garter 127
  coups and crisis
    management 235–7
  dangers facing England 123–4
  daughter's marriage to Sir Philip
    Sidney 171
  death and interment of 239–40
  demand from Elizabeth for closure
    of seminaries 164
  dilemmas of 99–101
  diplomatic mission to
    France 70–1
  Dorset constituency 39
  Dutch rebels 125
  financial hardship 217–18
  early years of 10–11
  English–French amity 82–3
  espionage 57–8, 163, 202–4
  evangelical beliefs, origins of 13
  evangelicalism of 88, 127
  exile years of 24–32
  expenditure on secret
    service 187–8
  falling-out with Elizabeth 228
  family and family
    responsibilities 4–8, 12–13,
    24–5
  foreign policy 145
  foreign travel 17
  Francis Drake 143–5, 149–50
  genealogical tree of 4–5
  grasp of international affairs 93
  hatred of Catholicism 2
  ill-health of 98, 124, 128, 178,
    196, 204, 221–2, 237, 239
  in Padua 24–5, 30–1
  in Scotland 169–72
  information sources 100–1
  ingratitude of Elizabeth 218
  intelligence service of 93–5,
    100–2, 151, 180–87, 236

intelligence-gathering 142
interrogation of Ridolfi 68–70
interrogation of Thomas
    Franchiotto 58, 59
kidnapping of James VI 121,
    167, 168
knighthood 127
letter from Dr Thomas
    Wilson 115
letter to John Sturmius 131–2
letters to Elizabeth 98–9, 245
letter to William Davison on
    Prayer Book 114
letters of 88–9, 108–9, 137
letters to/from Cecil 41–3, 59,
    68–9, 80, 83, 113, 125, 139,
    196–7, 218
Magdalen College, Oxford 108
marriage to Anne Carleill 38
marriage to Ursula Worsley 40
Mary Stuart 162–7, 181–2, 206–
    16, 221–5, 227
merchant venturing 38, 241
memo (1578) on ills plaguing
    nation 250
memorial and remains of 3
Mendoza 176–7
mission to Henry III of
    France 146
motivation of xii
naval treaty 178
negotiations for Elizabeth's
    marriage 76
opposition to Anjou
    marriage 135
other Council members 99–100
patronage of 107–8
payments for espionage 142
personal tragedy 216–17
Privy Seal 101
property and estates of 38, 39,
    40, 41, 95
Puritan zeal of 90, 95, 108
re-education of Catholics 154
reputation of 240–1

responsibilities in France 75–6
Robert Dudley 108, 166, 199–201
royal marriage fracas 139–40
St Bartholomew's massacre 1–2,
    80, 81–3
St Giles, Cripplegate 41, 64–5
Scotland 120, 206–7
sequestering of archbishop
    Grindal 113–14
Sir Edward Stafford 185–6
spies in French embassy 168–9
strong convictions of 98
study at inns of court/Gray's
    Inn 16, 17–18, 20
support for English intervention in
    France 49
sympathy with Calvinism 28–30
Thomas Norton 160–1, 174–5
Throckmorton plot 173–5
war with Spain 231, 233–5
William Davison 223–7
zeal of 59
Walsingham, William 7–8
Walsingham family 12
Watson, Thomas 132
Wentworth, Paul 99, 152
Wentworth, Peter 13, 111–12, 242
Westmorland, Earl of 62, 67–8, 138
Whitgift, John 192–4, 196, 204,
    252
Whittingham, William 26, 41
Wiburn, Percival 92–3
Wilkes, Thomas 125, 175
William the Silent, Prince of
    Orange 55, 78, 119, 125–7,
    136, 178, 179–81
Wilson, Dr Thomas 115, 158, 248
Winchester, Bishop of 49–50
Wolsey, Thomas 252
Wotton, Sir Edward 95
Wray, Sir Christopher 160
Wren, Christopher 3
Wyatt, Sir Thomas 23–4

York, Archbishop of 131